The New Complete
BLOODHOUND

Ch. Curate of Giralda, owned by Edd and
Pearl Armstrong.

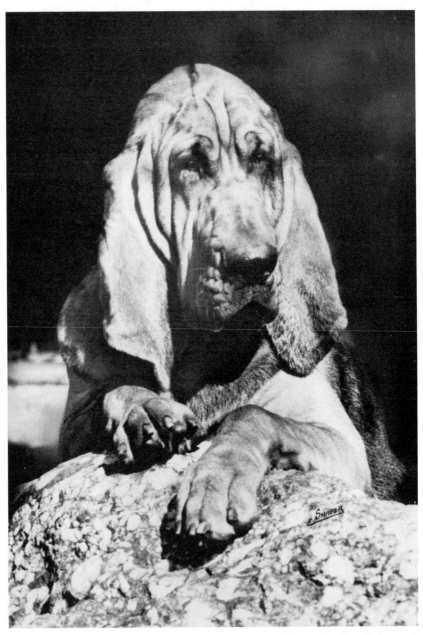

"The expression is noble and dignified, and characterized by solemnity, wisdom and power." The words of the breed Standard are well translated by the memorable Ch. Giralda's King Cole. *Shafer*

The New Complete
BLOODHOUND

Catherine F. Brey & Lena F. Reed

New York

Maxwell Macmillan Canada
Toronto

Maxwell Macmillan International
New York   Oxford   Singapore   Sydney

Howell Book House
Macmillan Publishing Company
866 Third Avenue
New York, NY 10022

Maxwell Macmillan Canada, Inc.
1200 Eglinton Avenue East, Suite 200
Don Mills, Ontario M3C 3N1

Macmillan Publishing Company is part of the Maxwell Communication Group of Companies.

Library of Congress Cataloging-in-Publication Data
Brey, Catherine F.
    The new complete bloodhound / Catherine F. Brey and Lena F. Reed.
        p. cm.
    Updated ed. of: The complete bloodhound. 1st. Ed. 1978
    ISBN 0-87605-077-1
    1. Bloodhounds.   I. Reed, Lena F.   II. Brey, Catherine F.
    Complete bloodhound.   III. Title.
    SF429.B6B73   1991
    636.7'53—dc20   91-23201

Macmillan books are available at special discounts for bulk purchases for sales promotions, premiums, fund-raising, or educational use. For details, contact:

                    Special Sales Director
                    Macmillan Publishing Company
                    866 Third Avenue
                    New York, NY 10022

10 9 8 7 6 5 4 3 2 1

Printed in the United States of America

Contents

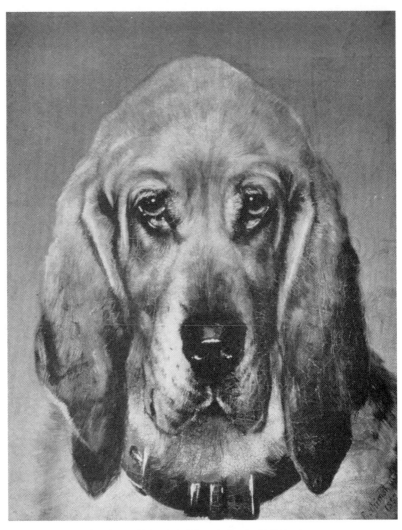

Bloodhound Head (1852), painting by E. Grimstone.

About the Authors

CATHERINE F. BREY, owner with her husband, Vincent, of Dakota Bloodhound Kennels, in Grand Forks, North Dakota, grew up on a farm where show horses and cattle were raised. Her spirit for competition was encouraged early. At the age of sixteen she transferred her interest to the dog shows, her first show dog being a Bullmastiff.

Mrs. Brey bought her first Bloodhound in 1960 and fell in love with the breed. Prior to that time she had been interested in obedience training, but with ownership of a Bloodhound came mantrailing. Since then the Breys have worked not only with their local police but throughout the state of North Dakota. Their record has included the first Bloodhound testimony in a North Dakota court.

In the years since that first Bloodhound the Dakota Kennel has produced over fifty champions, in spite of restricting breeding to no more than two litters a year. One of these is Ch. Pooh Bear of South Dakota, who matched the record of Ch. Fancy Bombardier and Ch. Buccaneer of Idol Ours II by six Best in Show wins. Cathy Brey strongly recommends that careless breeding and overbreeding should be discouraged, and that those litters bred should be raised with individual attention.

In addition to the Bloodhounds, members of the Brey family have owned and shown Pointers, Bassets and Whippets.

Catherine and Vincent Brey have long been active in the Grand Forks Kennel Club, of which she is a past president, and in 1972 they founded the Humane Society of Grand Forks, of which she is now a director. She is a past president of the American Bloodhound Club and wrote the breed column for

Popular Dogs for two years. For several years she has worked with a veterinarian, and there is usually at least one foster child in the Brey home.

In 1974 Mrs. Brey entered the show ring as a judge, and she now judges Bloodhounds, Bassets and Beagles.

The Brey family displays a considerable collection of trophies won in the show ring, but Cathy Brey says her favorite exhibit is the certificate with the big gold seal, signed by the governor of the state of Tennessee. It names Catherine F. Brey as an honorary citizen of that state.

LENA F. REED grew up on a northern Wisconsin farm, moving to Chicago to enter high school. Years later, with husband Clyde and a young family, she returned to rural life in the Puget Sound area of western Washington. For several years she was a 4–H Club leader.

When the children grew up and left home she decided that she would not be one of the "empty nest" mailbox watchers. She decided instead to try an old dream. She joined a creative writing class and experimented with writing short stories and articles. After she began making sales, her dreams advanced to writing a book.

The Reeds became interested in Bloodhounds through their daughter, whose husband was stationed at Grand Forks AFB. Bobbi worked for the only veterinarian in the county, where she met the Breys and the Bloodhounds. She told her parents stories of the mantrailing exploits of the Dakota Bloodhounds, planting the seed for their future ownership of the breed. When a child was lost in the junglelike western Washington rain forests, they wondered why a Bloodhound was not used in the search. This led to their purchase of the puppy who was to become Ch. Boomerang of Dakota. Since then, two bitches have been added to the team.

Boomerang's performance as a mantrailer convinced many of the local skeptics and encouraged others in the area to buy and train Bloodhounds. This led to the formation, in 1973, of Northwest Bloodhounds Search and Rescue, with Lena Reed as secretary. Two of Boomerang's sons have proven themselves as mantrailers, as have others in the area. Many owners outside the region have been encouraged and assisted in training and using their Bloodhounds.

At an after-the-show discussion between judge Cathy Brey and the exhibitors, there was general mourning over the fact that there was not a comprehensive, recent book on the breed, that so little could be found in libraries. Cathy Brey suggested that she and Lena Reed combine her knowledge of Bloodhounds with Mrs. Reed's writing skills and produce such a book. The result is *The Complete Bloodhound*.

While the book is written in the first person for smoothness, the "I" is sometimes Cathy Brey and sometimes Lena Reed. Both of us, however, sincerely thank the many Bloodhound owners who so generously contributed the use of their photographs. Many of these are irreplaceable treasures, and many were furnished at much inconvenience and expense by their donors.

Foreword

(It is a tremendous honor for the authors and for the publisher to have this Foreword by the renowned commentator Roger A. Caras for The Complete Bloodhound. *Mr. Caras is widely known for his Pets and Wildlife broadcasts on WCBS radio and for his numerous efforts on behalf of all animals. His knowledge of all phases of his subject and his eloquent manner have benefited animals everywhere. His is also a Bloodhound family as will be seen in chapter 6. The extent of his regard for the breed can be seen by what follows.)*

THE BLOODHOUND is not a dog that one simply owns or belongs to; it is a breed that totally envelops everyone who even casually becomes involved. There are no Bloodhound owners but lots of Bloodhound people.

What distingushes Bloodhound people from other dog folk? Well, at least once in their lives they have involved themselves in a mutual ownership pact with a representative of the breed. They probably wear a Bloodhound buckle or pendant or other decoration and may have slogans adorning their cars—things like I LOVE BLOODHOUNDS. They are quite silly about it, generally.

There are other things, too. They probably have a drawerful of yellowing newspaper clippings about Bloodhounds catching bad guys and finding lost kids. Even when they don't know the crooks, the kids or the hounds, they cheer. (When two bitches ''nailed'' James Earl Ray a cheer went up from Bloodhound people all across the country.)

Many Bloodhound people seem to have one arm that is a little longer than the other (walking on a lead is not always this breed's crowning achievement in deportment), and one other thing—all Bloodhound people haunt the vendor stands at all dog shows hoping upon hope that someone has published a complete

Bloodhound book. There have been few; they are *not* complete; they are old and sell for appalling prices.

Now, Howell Book House has done it—there is, at last, a book called *The Complete Bloodhound* and after examining the advance text it is a complete joy.

If *The Complete Bloodhound* does nothing else, it has told the truth about the breed and who should become involved with it. All true Bloodhound people shudder at the thought of the breed ever becoming a fad as did the St. Bernard, the Old English Sheepdog and some others that patently suffered from too much breeding by too many who didn't know what they were doing.

As *The Complete Bloodhound* is published, the breed it is devoted to ranks about fifty-fifth in popularity. We all pray it never rises above that and if any non-Bloodhound people happen upon this book, it is to be hoped that they carefully heed the warnings. Because it is such a large breed, because it needs an enormous amount of exercise to retain health and condition (and appearance), because it is such a highly sensitive breed (and such a devoted one), it demands much of the owner and even more of the breeder. It is a terrible first breed and is enough to put a new, inexperienced owner off all dogs for life. Consider these things:

A Bloodhound that may weigh as much as 150 pounds should—a lot of experienced breeders, owners and handlers feel—be fed several times a day in order to avoid bloat or gastric torsion. Diet should be very carefully controlled and Bloodhounds do not tolerate "table scraps" and junk foods as well as other breeds.

Bloodhounds have absolutely no road sense. A wandering Bloodhound is a dead dog.

Bloodhounds need miles of exercise, not short walks. They need that exercise daily. Because they are such heavy animals their feet will "break down" unless much of that exercise is on soft ground—beach sand is perfect. City streets and sidewalks are murder on a large dog's feet and legs.

Bloodhounds not only drool, they slobber "gloop" all over the room, as this book so well points out. All Bloodhound people have enormous cleaning bills for their clothing and their drapes and their slipcovers.

Bloodhounds eat a lot.

Bloodhounds hate to have their nails cut and they need to have their nails cut, often. If not, if that ritual is skipped, their feet will not knuckle up and they will look awful.

Bloodhounds are expensive; at least they should be. "Cheap" examples of the breed are highly suspect and are to be avoided. It is nothing at all to spend between $500 and $1000 on a good example.

All good Bloodhound breeders are pests. They will sell you a dog for a fortune and then haunt you for the rest of your life to be sure you are taking proper care of their baby. You adopt their dog and they adopt you. The contract may not read that way but that is what happens.

All Bloodhound people are snoops. Everyone in the country will know what you are doing, saying and thinking. The underground information network is terrifying.

Now that you realize all that, it is to be hoped that if you are to become a new dog owner you will decide on another breed. Other dogs cost less, require less food, exercise and care. They don't drool and spit and spray and spume the way Bloodhounds do. Of course, they don't interact with people the way Bloodhounds do; they don't do the lovely warm things to your heart that these great mantrailers do; they probably aren't as reliable with kids, in many cases; and they aren't as absolutely delightful in action and repose as the great *slobber-jowls* are. Unless you are a totally devoted, totally responsible and madly determined dog person you may just have to miss out on some wonderful Bloodhound things.

The Complete Bloodhound has been long awaited. Anyone coming across it, whether they are a Bloodhound person or not, is urged to read it very carefully. If they are devoted to this breed they should come to know everything that is in this book. If they are not yet converted they will require every word of advice and information herein contained in order to make intelligent decisions. I hope that when you have read this book from cover to cover you too will find yourself worthy. If you are not, I am sorry for you, but there are over 120 lesser breeds to choose from. If you are a worthy, congratulations! You are about to become a slave.

Brought to Bay (1898), by Maud Earl, was commissioned by Edwin Brough and shows his Chs. Barbarossa, Babbo and Benedicta. This magnificent painting is now in the possession of the Kennel Club (England).

The Bloodhound has been the faithful ally of man for many centuries. Many sporting and hound breeds of more recent vintage are the result of crossings with other breeds to incorporate the fabled talents of the "King of Trailing Hounds."

Courtesy, Mrs. Robert V. Lindsay

1

Origin and History

$\mathbf{A}$ WELL-KNOWN COSMETICS firm recently added to its
"collectible bottle" line an item in the shape of a pipe with a Bloodhound head
as the container. This dramatically illustrates the degree of recognition the breed
has achieved just since 1970, when my husband took our hound on the search
for a missing child, and was greeted by the mother with the exclamation, "My,
but that's the biggest Basset I've ever seen!" Or the young man who turned pale,
and rushed his girlfriend in the opposite direction as my husband led the leashed
hound across the beach. "Stay away from him!" the stranger warned her. "Those
dogs will tear you to pieces!"

Even in the more canine-wise world of dog shows, the appearance of a
lone Bloodhound at a benched show would guarantee a traffic jam, with widely
varied opinions as to whether he was ugly, comical, a picture of wisdom or a
hanging judge. Times have changed since he was recognized as a fit gift for
royalty and the lawbreaker he trailed was as good as convicted. Few are aware
of his long and respected history.

I recall the newspaper reporter who wound his way among the exhibitors
at a benched show, questioning the owners as to the origin of their breeds. He
seemed sincerely interested, and of course, impressed by the Bloodhounds.
"Well," we thought, "this time we should get an intelligent news story."

The next day we drove five miles to a stand that carried out-of-town
newspapers, so we could add this discerning young man's report to our canine
souvenirs. The sports page greeted us with the headline THE WORLD'S BIGGEST
SANDBOX. Below was a flippant article describing the writer's "discovery" that
owners of almost every breed in the show claimed their pet's ancestry was
rumored to go back to ancient Egypt, as dogs resembling them were pictured in

the tombs of the pharaohs. If Egypt served as home of that many canine families, the reporter facetiously concluded, it must have been one giant sandbox.

I shall deny this rumor as far as Bloodhounds are concerned by introducing a rumor of my own. Bloodhounds originated in the area of Asia Minor between the rivers Tigris and Euphrates, known to historians as the Fertile Crescent. This favored land acquired the fertility which made it the cradle of Western civilization as a result of the large numbers of Bloodhounds which roamed it in ancient days. Anyone who has ever operated a pooper scooper behind a litter of Bloodhound puppies will find this theory (which I hasten to remind you is a rumor of my own fabrication) highly feasible.

THE ANCIENT HOUNDS

Recorded history does, however, lend credence to the above theory. A terra-cotta plaque found in ancient Babylon, dating to between 2000 and 1000 B.C., shows a picture of a hound which strongly resembles a Bloodhound with a very "gay" (curled over the back) tail. These hounds were bred in ancient Mesopotamia (now known as Iraq) and were frequently used as war dogs. According to the ancient historian Herodotus, they were so important that the kings used the taxes from four cities to support them. Unfortunately we are not told the sizes of these cities, but even the taxes of one small, modern American city would support a sizable pack of Bloodhounds.

Another illustration of pendulous-eared hounds which may have been the ancestors of both Bloodhounds and Mastiffs is the carving on a stone slab, five feet high, which was found in the palace of the king at Nineveh, dating to the seventh century B.C. These were powerful-looking animals, and judging by the illustration, were used for hunting. Since hunting was vital to ancient man, both in securing food and in eliminating predators, their hounds were most highly regarded.

This book is intended as a record of the Bloodhound in America and its use as a mantrailer, and a guide for the American breeder or pet owner. However, it would be incomplete without some history of the breed and acknowledgment of those who devoted much time and expense to its improvement and survival.

Whatever their origin, large, long-eared hounds of notable scenting ability were found and written about in most of the Mediterranean countries before the Christian era. Whether they developed naturally across a wide range or were distributed through trade is subject to speculation. One story claims that descendants of the Trojans, who had escaped the fall of Troy, took hounds with them to what is now France. Later they occupied England, again taking their hounds along.

The Romans recorded that they found hounds and Mastiffs in Britain when they arrived in 55 B.C. These hounds were of such superb quality that they were repeatedly mentioned in the histories of the Romans. They were described as being unmatched in their scenting abilities, and of the greatest perseverance in

ASSYRIAN HUNTING DOGS

The king of Nineveh mantained a pack of dogs that were used for hunting game and in combat. It is believed that these dogs may have been early ancestors of the Bloodhound and the Mastiff.

finding their quarry. These distinguishing characteristics have remained with the Bloodhound through the centuries.

Hounds are the group of dogs distinguished as hunters of fur-bearing game. They are further divided into the sight hounds (gazehounds) such as the Greyhound, which hunt by sight and depend upon their amazing speed to capture their prey; and the scent hounds, which are slower but possess the greater olfactory development, and hunt by following a trail. The oldest of the scent hounds, and the one having the keenest sense of smell of any dog, is the Bloodhound.

THE ST. HUBERT HOUND

The name "Bloodhound" was not derived from any sanguine connection, as some have assumed, but from the expression "blooded hound," meaning a hound of pure breeding. Thanks to the selective breeding practices of church officials and noblemen who maintained sporting packs, the Bloodhound developed distinctive strains early in his history as a breed. The most famous of these were the St. Hubert hounds, established in the seventh century A.D. in Ardennes, France. They were named after the monk Francois Hubert, who later became bishop, and was subsequently canonized as St. Hubert, the patron saint of hunters. He had been born to the nobility and was an ardent hunter. After his wife's death he entered a monastery, where he continued breeding a hunting pack of Bloodhounds. It was believed he originally obtained his stock from southern France. This breeding was carried on after his death by the abbots who succeeded him.

At first the St. Hubert hounds were black, but later they developed small tan markings, which gradually increased in size. There were also some white hounds, which were a larger strain, kept separately; but these were not as popular as the black and tan line. They were noted for their courage and endurance.

Crusaders added to the Bloodhound line by bringing back new strains from their pilgrimages to the Holy Land. In England, hounds of a greyish red later appeared, which were called Dun hounds, and in the sixteenth century a chocolate-colored sort appeared.

When William the Conquerer invaded England in 1066 he brought St. Hubert hounds with him; and his son, William Rufus, continued breeding them. Bloodhounds at that time were used for hunting deer, a favorite sport of the wealthy. The high regard in which the hounds were held is indicated by the fact that they were frequently given as gifts among royalty and the nobility, and large packs were maintained by many of the English and French kings and bishops. Each year for almost seven hundred years, the St. Hubert Monastery sent three pairs of St. Hubert black and tan Bloodhounds to the King of France. St. Hubert hounds were sent to Queen Elizabeth I by the King of France, who recorded the fact that the Earl of Essex maintained eight hundred of these hounds. He does not record how many cities paid taxes to support this mighty pack.

The St. Hubert Hound was a celebrated strain of Bloodhound type. Originally the St. Hubert Hound was solid black, but eventually tan markings appeared as a result of introducing new strains. This fact is mentioned in the *The Noble Art of Venerie, or Hunting*, London, 1576. *Courtesy, British Museum*

White hounds of various strains were well known to the nobililty of medieval and renaissance France. The most famous of these white hounds, the Talbot, was one of the ancestors of the modern Bloodhound. *The Noble Art of Venerie, or Hunting*, London, 1576.
Courtesy, British Museum

The true St. Hubert strain survived until the nineteenth century. St. Hubert's Day is still celebrated in France, Belgium and Ireland on November third, and it includes a blessing of the hounds.

THE TALBOT HOUND

It was believed that the white St. Huberts were crossed with other white French hounds, and that from these came the early Talbot hounds. These were also introduced to England in 1066 by William the Conquerer and the Talbot family, which came from Normandy. The Talbot hounds died out in Continental Europe in the sixteenth century, but continued in England until about the beginning of the nineteenth century. Along with the black and tan St. Huberts, the Talbot hounds were ancestors of our modern Bloodhounds and many other breeds of sporting dogs.

THE BLOODHOUND'S ROLE IN EARLY SOCIETY

Bloodhounds have also been known as Limier, Lyme-ho, and Lymer, because they were led on a line (lyam) when nearing the quarry. They were called Sleuth or Slot hounds, meaning tracking hounds. They were much used by medieval night watchmen to protect themselves against the ever-present danger of criminal violence. It was not until about the sixteenth century that the Bloodhound was used extensively to hunt man, especially poachers and sheep thieves on the Scottish border. So highly was their testimony regarded that they were given the legal right to follow a trail anywhere, including into homes. A man refusing to allow a trailing Bloodhound to enter his house was assumed to be involved in the crime. They were considered a great deterrent to crime, as lawbreakers naturally had a greater fear of being trailed to their homes in the morning than they did of being caught on the scene by watchmen in the dark of night.

As the large estates and forests were reduced in size and the deer population declined, the nobility and other gentlemen of leisure changed their sport from deer hunting to fox hunting. This required a faster hound, and to fill the need the Foxhound was developed through a cross of the Talbot hound and the Greyhound. This new breed was followed by Harriers, Beagles and others, which gained their keen noses from a Bloodhound cross.

It was at this time that the unexcelled nose of the Bloodhound was turned to use in mantrailing. The breed's amazing ability at trailing has given it a place in history and fiction. It is unfortunate that unrealistic portrayals have misled people into the belief that Bloodhounds are savage, dangerous beasts. There are many stories in England and America on the use of these hounds in solving criminal cases. Some of these will be told in the following chapters.

Gradually, however, the breed dwindled. By the early 1800s there were comparatively few Bloodhounds left. Most of these were kept in packs, except for the few used by law officers and gamekeepers.

The first picture of an English dog show, from the *Illustrated London News,* February 8, 1851.

Here is graphic proof that the Bloodhound of today varies but little from his ancient ancestor. Giralda's Eliza, Adam of Giralda and Amanda of Giralda mirror the timelessness of their kind in this painting by Ward Binks.   *Juley & Son*

THE BEGINNING OF DOG SHOWS

The breed was saved from almost certain extinction by the introduction of dog shows in 1859. The first dog show, held in Newcastle, England, had an entry of sixty Pointers and setters. Later that year in Birmingham there was a show for sporting dogs only; and in 1860 the first all-breed show was held in the same city. Bloodhounds were among the entries. As dog showing rapidly became a fashionable recreation, Bloodhound breeding continued. According to some of the old records, many of the hounds of that day lacked the temperament we like to see, being either excessively shy and nervous or overly aggressive and unmanageable.

Dog shows resulted in the breeding of more companionable Bloodhounds. They were raised by Baron Rothschild and Lord Faversham, among others, and it was from hounds of their lines that Mr. T. A. Jennings bred the famous Bloodhound Druid, the breed's first champion. Together with another, Welcome, he later sold Druid to Prince Napoleon for breeding for what at that time was considered an outstanding price. His neighbors, Major Cowen and Mr. J. W. Pease, apparently were encouraged by Mr. Jennings's success to enter into Bloodhound breeding on their own. Until 1868 hounds owned by these three gentlemen monopolized the prizes at the shows, except for two specimens named Rufus, one owned by a Mr. Broom and one by Mr. Edwin Brough, who was the author, together with Dr. Sidney Turner, of the first Standard for the breed. These two hounds were also basically of the Rothschild and Faversham bloodlines.

In 1869 another famous Bloodhound appeared. This was Regent, owned by a Mr. Holford, and he, again, was of the same background. No new bloodlines were added to the first-prize winners until 1870, when Dr. Reynolds Ray introduced his Roswell. This dog held first place at the shows almost without exception until he died in 1877. He was the sire of Ch. Rollo.

If you visit the Kennel Club in London, one of the first sights to catch your eye will be the Champion Rollo Silver Challenge Shield. This huge shield of solid silver, with its magnificent bronze head study of Ch. Rollo, is on display over the reception desk in the main office.

The Edwin Brough Records give the following information on Rollo.

Champion Rollo, whelped in July 1873, was a lovely black and tan hound bred by Dr. Reynolds Ray. Rollo was sired by Roswell ex Peeress.

He made his first appearance on the show bench at the Kennel Club summer show, held at the Crystal Palace in June 1875, when little more than a puppy. He was highly commended in a strong class of 16 entries, with first prize falling to Baron (his brother from a former litter) and Brutis being placed second. He was next exhibited at Nottingham, where he was awarded first prize; and from this date till the time he was withdrawn from competition he secured a place in the ribbons (never lower than second) every time he was exhibited. As a show dog Rollo was very nearly perfect, but not quite, his faults being a slight weakness of loin and hind legs, with his ears, although good in length, a trifle thick in substance, at times preventing that complete curl which admirers of the breed prize so much. On the other hand, Rollo's head was marvellously good in shape and quality, combin-

The first champion in the breed was Mr. T. A. Jennings's Druid, the model for this bronze by J. B. Gelibert. Druid was subsequently sold to Prince Napoleon III.

ing, as it did, the two essentials so greatly valued (and which breeders know too well the difficulty of obtaining): The deep heavy wrinkle on the lean, long head.

There was one flaw, however, in Rollo's morality—he had somewhat cloudy ideas about the Eighth Commandment. Rollo was a bit of a thief, and the ruling passion was strong even in death. A few days before he died, and he was past feeding, he crawled about with a stolen biscuit in his mouth.

Rollo was ten years old at the time of death.

Mr. J. H. Walsh, one of the judges at that first dog show, who wrote under the name Stonehenge, describes the Bloodhound in his book *Dogs of the British Isles*, which evolved from articles he began writing about 1865 for the magazine *The Field*, and was updated several times during the next many years. One of his goals was the setting of a Standard for breeds, which would certainly be of assistance to both breeders and judges. In writing of the Bloodhound, he admires its majestic head, which attracted the attention of writers and artists, Sir Edwin Landseer being prominent among them. It was Sir Edwin who selected for Queen Victoria the Bloodhounds which she owned and showed. A study of Landseer's paintings shows a hound without the heavy wrinkle or obvious haw.

Mr. Brough, writing in 1892, discusses color in Bloodhounds and states that while the most admired color of his time was the black and tan, Bloodhounds had formerly been known to have white flecks on the back making the animal look as if it had come in out of a snowstorm, a white star on the chest and white on the tip of the stern (tail). A deep red with tan markings was common, but Mr. Brough especially admired a tawny, more or less mixed with black on the back.

The Kennel Club was formed in Britain in 1873, with the Prince of Wales, later King Edward VII, as its first patron. The prince also exhibited Bloodhounds, Mastiffs, Deerhounds and Greyhounds. Succeeding monarchs continued the patronage. At this time 40 breeds or varieties were recognized, a number which grew to 110 by 1967. The royal patron no doubt had much to do with the popularity of both dog showing and Bloodhounds among the ladies and gentlemen of the day. In 1874 the first Stud Book was published, with some of the pedigrees going as far back as 1859.

BLOODHOUND TRIALS IN ENGLAND

In 1886 an experiment was conducted with the object of testing the olfactory ability of the Bloodhound. No conclusion was reached, but in 1898 the Association of Bloodhound Breeders promoted manhunting trials as a sport. The only hounds available at that time were those which had been bred for many years simply for exhibition or as companions. The trials showed that the show ring had not destroyed their natural abilities. The first trials involved a simple type of trailing, as many entries had to be tested in one day. Lines were about a mile long, and hounds were set on them within fifteen minutes after the runner reached the end of the trail.

While no real test of a Bloodhound's ability, these trials served to attract

Dignity and Impudence (1839) is one of Sir Edwin Landseer's most famous and best-loved dog portraits.

public attention, and roused considerable interest in trailing among Bloodhound owners. As a result, these meetings are continued to this day, with the season ending in a competition for a trophy, the Brough Cup. The trail now must be at least six hours old, and the hound must identify the runner from among a group of people, after having followed the trail. Hounds are not worked on lead as in the United States, but turned loose and followed by owners on horseback.

Descriptions of these trials are interesting, especially in view of their difference from the way Bloodhounds are trained and used in the United States in search and rescue or criminal work. The trail would be laid over grassy fields, with no interference other than walls which could be easily jumped. An hour or so before the trial, the runner would be taken to the starting place by car. He would hold a handkerchief in his hands, so that by the time he arrived at the starting point it would be well impregnated with his scent. At the start of the trail he would fasten the handkerchief to a stake and move off across the country.

The hounds would be brought to the starting point, accompanied by the sportsmen on horseback. The hounds, a full pack, would be turned loose, and would cast for the scent, and follow in full cry. This is a contrast to our hounds working silently on lead. At times their speed would force the riders to a full gallop; at other times they might be forced to slow down and puzzle out the line. The trail ended where the hounds caught up with the runner, when they lost interest in him. One report tells of a trail of eight miles, which the pack covered in fifty-five minutes.

The publicity attendant to the early trials induced several constables to use Bloodhounds in law enforcement, and they proved instrumental in bringing many lawbreakers to justice. Mainly, however, mantrailing in England has been considered an inexpensive sport.

During the course of their history, Bloodhounds served in additional capacities. In 1898 they were used as ambulance dogs with the Russian Army Red Cross, in the Russian–Japanese war. From 1911 to 1913 they were used as sentry dogs in expeditions in India. When World War I broke out, they were used as ambulance dogs in Belgium, as well as sentry dogs in France and the Dardanelles.

When the now-famous Crufts all-breed shows originated in England in February 1891, the Bloodhound was the first breed listed in the first catalog.

At various times, a Foxhound cross has been introduced into Bloodhound lines, and in the later nineteenth century some crosses were made with French hounds. After World War II, when Bloodhound stock in Britain was severely depleted, a Foxhound cross was again made by British breeders, with the exception of the Brighton, Abingerwood and Barsheen kennels, which kept their stock pure. White markings on present-day Bloodhounds are said to be the result of these Foxhound crosses, though possibly they are a throwback to the old lines.

AMERICAN HOUNDS AND ENGLISH RECONSTRUCTION

Following the war many excellent Bloodhounds were imported from the United States and Canada, and were used to help renew stock. From a low of

Ch. Barsheen Dolorous, the breed's first champion following the conclusion of World War II. *Pace*

Abingerwood Lime Tree Pendragon, one of the American-bred hounds sent to Great Britain after World War II to help the breed regain some of the ground lost during the years of fighting. *Cumbers*

Wanted

BY ONE OF OUR
AMERICAN COLONIES!!

FOR THE BETTER PROTECTION OF THE
FRONTIER INHABITANTS, AND
MORE EFFECTUAL PURSUIT OF THE
MURDERING INDIANS!

Fifty Couple of true Blood Hounds; as the Indians make their Attacks by Surprize, on single Families; and having murdered Men, Women and Children, escape thro' unknown Ways, and their Track in the Woods is soon lost by the Pursuers: It is tho't, if the Breed of true Blood Hounds could once be obtained there, they would be of great Use in such Pursuits; and by discovering the Enemy in their Retreat, give our People frequent Opportunities of coming up with them, and recovering the Captives and Plunder, and thereby more effectually discourage their Attempts, & induce them to sue for, and more faithfully keep Peace with us; and that during the War, such Hounds, by discovering the Indian Ambuscades, may be a means of saving many Lives of our poor Countrymen.

It is, therefore hoped, that Gentlemen who have Dogs of that kind, which they know to be good, will be kind enough to spare them on this Occasion; it is intended to furnish every scouting Party of the Soldiers, appointed to guard the Frontiers, with some of these Hounds. Two Persons skilled in the Breeding and Management of Blood Hounds, are wanted to go over with them, to whom being well recommended, good Encouragement will be given.

Those who are disposed to sell or give such Hounds for the Service aforesaid, are desired to give notice.

WILLIAMSBURG, VIRGINIA:
THE KING AND QUEEN PRESS
1963

A self-explanatory measure of the Bloodhound's place in society during Colonial times.

14

six pregistrations in 1944, Britain now produces a large number of quality Bloodhound puppies. Many of these are exported to fanciers in far-flung corners of the world.

Americans visiting England with the intention of bringing back a Bloodhound puppy should be aware that it must be registered in Britain with the Kennel Club while still in that country. Otherwise, it will be ineligible for registration either there or in the United States.

Those devoted breeders who imported stock to rebuild British kennels should be properly appreciated. In addition to the considerable expense they incurred in purchase and shipping costs and the lengthy quarantine, one must consider the risks taken when they purchased stock sight-unseen in hopes that the hounds they bought would live up to their expectations.

Especially notable among these imports were Ch. Spotter of Littlebrook, who had been used with considerable success as a mantrailer in the United States; Westsummerland Montgomery of Bre-Mar-Har-Ros; Barsheen Bynda of Huguenot; The Chase's Mimsy of Brighton; Knightcall's Black Cherry; and Abingerwood Lime Tree Pendragon. Numerous progeny of these hounds have returned as imports to America.

Possibly one of the oldest kennels to remain in one family is the Brighton Bloodhound Kennels, founded by Mr. Henry Hylden, great-grandfather of Lilian Hylden Ickeringill, the present owner, with her husband George Ickeringill. Other famous British breeders are Mr. and Mrs. Dennis Piper (Abingerwood), Mr. Douglas Appleton (Appeline) and Yvonne Oldman (Barsheen).

The first Bloodhounds came to America before the Revolution, although the date is unknown. *The American Bloodhound Bulletin*, December 1971, reprinted the advertisement on the following page, which is self-explanatory.

EARLY HISTORY IN THE UNITED STATES

In the United States, purebred Bloodhounds, however, were not extensively used to trail runaway slaves. The dogs used on plantations for this purpose were mongrels with some Bloodhound in their background, mixed with Great Danes, Mastiffs or other large dogs. Many were truly vicious. Nor should the animals sometimes referred to as "Cuban Bloodhounds" or "Spanish Bloodhounds" be confused with the true English Bloodhound. Judging by the information available on them, they were prick-eared, pointed-nosed mongrels, not even resembling a hound, and were vicious animals used as watchdogs.

Uncle Tom's Cabin gave the Bloodhound such a fearsome connotation that to this day many people believe he is a savage and dangerous animal. I remember a dog show I attended with our first Bloodhound. I was explaining to another exhibitor that we intended using him for search and rescue work, and she shuddered. "I couldn't bear to think of those monsters chasing after my baby," she said. And this was a mother presumably contemplating the loss of her child! My veterinarian—a professional in animal care—was no better. "I hate to think of the poor devils with a pack of these vicious brutes baying on their trails,'' he said, as he checked over my newly arrived bundle of puppy love.

"Doc,'' I said, "don't worry about it. They're really silent trackers.'' He had obviously seen too many movies, and I am not sure yet if I convinced him that Bloodhounds trail strictly for love.

The emotional climate of the pre–Civil War days worked toward the Bloodhound's temporary decline in America. Jefferson Davis, president of the Confederacy, was known to have imported a pack for breeding purposes, and Northern troops were given orders to kill on sight every Bloodhound found. It was reported that forty-seven purebred hounds were killed at Mr. Davis's home, victims of literary slander.

AMERICAN RENAISSANCE OF THE BLOODHOUND

It was not until 1888 that Bloodhounds were once more seen publicly in America. In that year the Westminster Kennel Club gave a benched show in New York City, and among the dogs exhibited there were three purebred Bloodhounds brought over by Mr. Edwin Brough, mentioned earlier as author of the first breed Standard.

Mr. J. L. Winchell of Fairhaven, Vermont, saw the hounds there. He was himself a breeder of fancy types, and was impressed with the noble appearance of these hounds. He entered into a partnership with Mr. Brough and imported breeding stock for the first Bloodhound kennel in the country since the Civil War. The first pair of Bloodhounds he received were Belhus and Rosemary. Other prominent breeders who soon followed his lead were Dr. C. A. Lougest of Boston, Dr. J. B. Fulton of Beatrice, Nebraska, and Colonel Roger B. William of Lexington, Kentucky, whose Rookwood Kennel was later sold to Captain Volney G. Mullikin, owner of the renowned Nick Carter.

In an August 1910 magazine article, Mr. J. L. Winchell wrote about the Bloodhound, expressing regret that the breed had not been more highly promoted in this country for mantrailing, as those so used (including his) were giving such an excellent account of themselves. He mentioned their use by the police and detective departments of New York Central and Pennsylvania railroads, and by penitentiaries. Unfortunately, he said, they were a delicate breed to raise, and there were only about two hundred purebred Bloodhounds in this country. Most gentlemen owning them seemed satisfied with keeping them as pets and companions.

At that time hounds imported from England cost from $2,000 to $3,500 with some exceptional cases known of $5,000 prices. The price dropped in later years when the breed became less a status symbol, and by 1955 was down to about $100 to $300, with $500 being a high price.

Ch. Brigadier of Reynalton (Ch. Leo of Reynalton ex Comely of Reynalton), owned by Geraldine R. Dodge and bred by Nina E. Elms. This dog was an important winner during the 1930s. From a painting by Ward Binks.

Ch. Giralda's Kriss, owned by Mrs. Dodge.   *Brown*

Ch. Lucifer of Giralda, owned by Mrs. Dodge.   *Brown*

Ch. Giralda's King Cole, owned by Mrs. Dodge.   *Tauskey*

18

GERALDINE R. DODGE

A most celebrated American breeder and Bloodhound enthusiast was Geraldine Rockefeller Dodge, niece of John D. Rockefeller, Sr. Her Giralda Farm Kennel was registered with the American Kennel Club in 1921, and during the next forty years housed eighty-five different dog breeds. Bloodhounds were included among her interests, and her Chs. Giralda's King Kole and Giralda's Kriss, among others, are behind numerous modern bloodlines.

Mrs. Dodge was famous among dog fanciers as the founder of the Morris & Essex show, held on the polo field of her five-hundred-acre Giralda estate. The first show was held in 1927 with an entry limited to 595 dogs. In later years, the entry was as high as 4,456, to make it the largest one-day dog show in the world.

Morris & Essex was the ultimate in dog shows. A staff of up to eight hundred included veterinarians, nurses, doctors, and law officers to protect the entries and trophies and direct traffic. The judges, averaging about seventy in number, came from all over the country as well as from abroad. The show was held outdoors, in huge tents, with a ring for each breed. The prizes alone were worth $20,000 in cash and $10,000 in sterling-silver trophies.

The show was not held during the years of World War II, but was revived in 1946, and continued until 1957. It was discontinued then, after the death of Ray Patterson, Mrs. Dodge's principal supervisor.

Mrs. Dodge was famous not only as a breeder and judge at dog shows, in this country and abroad, but as a philanthropist who provided generously for animal shelters for injured and abandoned animals. When the Morris & Essex shows came to an end, her concerns turned toward animals less fortunate than the pampered show dogs. The next year she opened St. Hubert's Giralda, a shelter for sick and injured dogs. Her interest in animals remained with her until her death in 1973.

EDD AND PEARL ARMSTRONG

Edd and Pearl Armstrong of Long Beach, California, entered the Bloodhound game in 1937. Edd had been in the police force for twenty years, and appreciated the assistance that a trained mantrailing Bloodhound could be in law enforcement. They had to travel to Denver to find a litter available, where they bought Ch. Home's Jurisprudence, to be called Lady. She became their foundation bitch, and produced the famous Ch. Buccaneer of Idol Ours.

Breeder rivalry led to the Armstrongs' purchase of the stud Ch. Curate of Giralda, whelped in England, and bought by the Armstrongs as a champion from Mrs. Dodge's Giralda Kennels. When they had first approached her on the subject of buying a stud dog she had refused, since cross-country shipping of animals was hazardous at that time. Later, she called them to say she would sell them Curate on the condition that they immediately show him in a series of some twenty West Coast shows.

The Armstrongs had never been to a dog show, and had their qualms, but agreed, to get the animal they wanted. Mrs. Armstrong handled him throughout, and Curate immediately won Best of Breed at his first show and many others, and passed on his qualities to his get.

The reason for Mrs. Dodge's change of heart was eventually disclosed; she wanted a dog of her kennel to beat that of a rival on the West Coast. Curate not only satisfied her ambition, but proved to be a good mantrailer as well.

The Armstrongs were in the foreground of West Coast owners in forming the Bloodhound Club of America, which later joined Eastern fanciers in becoming the American Bloodhound Club. At about the same time they decided to show the East Coast that there were good hounds out west, and took their Ch. Buccaneer across the country, including the Westminster show in their circuit. He was Best American-bred in Show at Morris & Essex and at the Los Angeles KC show, and had one other BIS, fifteen GR 1s and out of forty-five shows, was BB forty-four times, always handled by Mrs. Armstrong.

Buccaneer was bred to his litter sister, Black Betty of Idol Ours, to produce Ch. Rumpus of Folsom, who became a trailing hound, as well as dam of the small but outstanding litter of Ch. Buccaneer of Idol Ours II and Ch. Fancy Bombardier, both multiple BIS winners. Their sire was Dr. Leon Whitney's Trooper of White Isle. Buccaneer II was shown seventy-one times, with seventy BBs, twenty-seven GR 1s, six BIS. He took his first five-point major at his second show by being BIS at the Silver Bay KC show at the age of fourteen months.

The Armstrong hounds were not just another pretty face in the show ring; they were trained and used as mantrailers in the tradition of their breed. Edd gives one hint on how to train a hound not to follow a game trail: Catch a rabbit, tie a loosely fastened bag of cayenne pepper to a hind leg, and shortly before the hound comes along the man trail, let the rabbit loose so it crosses the man trail. One experience is all it takes to convince the hound that game trails are too hot to handle.

THOMAS SHEAHAN

In 1954 only 195 new Bloodhound registrations were submitted to the American Kennel Club, and there were probably 1,500 to 2,000 Bloodhounds in the country. It was in this year that Ch. Fancy Bombardier, owned by Thomas Sheahan, of Connecticut, won BIS at the Eastern Dog Club event in Boston. This honor did much to revive interest in the Bloodhound as a show dog, and assisted in his comeback from the "endangered species" list. Mr. Sheahan was an early president of the American Bloodhound Club, and owner of the Fancy Kennels since 1945, when he obtained his first Bloodhound, Fancy of Point o' Forks.

Tom Sheahan's effort added greatly to the organization of Bloodhound breeders and owners, and to the establishment of the Breeders' Bulletin, to aid

Ch. Bucaneer of Idol Ours, owned by Edd and Pearl (handling) Armstrong, was Best Hound and Best American-bred in Show at Morris & Essex in 1941.

Ch. Fancy Bombardier, owned and shown by Thomas Sheahan, was one of the outstanding show dogs of the 1950s. His record includes Group firsts at Westminster and Eastern and a BIS at the latter. *Shafer*

Clarence Fischer with Fischer's Druid at the Ridgefield (Connecticut) State Police Barracks. This photo was taken around 1934. *Courtesy, James Zarifis*

The imported Melody of Brighton meets her new owner and handler, Mrs. Clendenin J Ryan of Panther Ledge and the late Harry Manning.

in the dissemination of information on proper care, feeding, and training as mantrailers. His interest in the breeding of quality hounds is reflected in the fact that the Fancy line is represented in the backgrounds of so many of our modern hounds. Tom Sheahan's death in August 1969 at the age of sixty-five was a loss to all those interested in the breed.

GENEVIEVE AND CORNELIUS BOLAND

Genevieve and Cornelius Boland were another couple whose influence was noteworthy in establishing the breed in America. They were breeders of the Huguenot line, and their Barsheen Bynda of Huguenot and Ch. Black Tommy of Huguenot were especially noted, though many more are shown in the backgrounds of our present-day hounds. The Bolands were active members of the American Bloodhound Club from its early days.

ROBERT AND MARY-LEES NOERR

The early efforts of Robert and Mary-Lees Noerr were instrumental in promoting the breed in this country. The Noerrs' Kennel of the Ring was founded in the early 1940s and produced many outstanding hounds during its period of activity. When fanciers of the breed formed the Eastern Bloodhound Club in 1952, changed in 1953 to the American Bloodhound Club, they immediately took part. Their interest and support continued until their deaths in 1973. Mrs. Noerr was guest of honor and speaker at the 1971 Bloodhound Specialty held in Chicago. Her speech at the dinner brought into focus the dedication it took to bring the breed to its present position.

One bit of wisdom she shared at that meeting is worth repeating. "The greatest downfall of any kennel," she said, "is thinking all your geese are swans."

The Noerrs had kept detailed records of each litter they raised, including weekly weight gain, height, length of ears, muzzle, etc. They also accumulated a treasure of irreplaceable photographs. Since Mr. Noerr had not thought of specifically bequeathing these in his will, his executor refused to allow them to be turned over to another fancier of the breed, where they could have been preserved, but ordered them destroyed.

CLARENCE FISCHER

Another of the early Bloodhound fanciers, noted as a collector of the breed lore, was Mr. Clarence Fischer, whose Renee's Sheba and Sheba's Renee Fischer showed up in the pedigree of Ch. Black Tommy of Huguenot. Mr. Fischer was a member of the American Bloodhound Club since its founding. He had an interest in Bloodhounds from his boyhood, and maintained an extensive correspondence with breeders throughout the ensuing years. Among his friends was the celebrated James Thurber, whose numerous Bloodhound cartoons were no doubt inspired by Mr. Fischer's hounds.

MR. AND MRS. CLENDENIN J. RYAN

Mr. and Mrs. Clendenin J. Ryan, breeders of Panther Ledge Bloodhounds, were also among the founding members of the American Bloodhound Club. The two match shows held by the new club to qualify for the first AKC Specialty Show in 1955 were held at the Panther Ledge Farm, Hackettstown, New Jersey. The Panther Ledge suffix in the background of many a Bloodhound pedigree traces to the winning hounds produced at the Ryans' kennel.

HARRY MANNING

The Ryans' handler was Mr. Harry Manning, who, with his wife, was also an early member of the American Bloodhound Club. As a professional handler of many of the most famous Bloodhounds of his day, he attained perhaps as much fame in the fancy as many of the breeders, and his recommendation of a puppy was highly regarded by those seeking an addition to their kennel.

DR. LEON F. WHITNEY

Dr. Leon F. Whitney, a veterinarian, geneticist and prolific writer, bought his first Bloodhound from Rookwood Kennels in 1921, when it was owned by General Roger Williams. He followed this purchase with several from Barchester Kennels of Mrs. Sadlier in England, together with others. These were the nucleus of his White Isle Kennel in Connecticut.

Dr. Whitney took a keen interest in the training of mantrailers, and many of his breeding served their purpose well on the police forces of surrounding states, including the famous Troop K of the New York State Police. One of his studs, Operator of White Isle, was the sire of Int. Ch. Spotter of Littlebrook, the postwar export to England. Another famous stud from the White Isle Kennels was Trooper of White Isle, whose sons, Ch. Buccaneer of Idol Ours and Ch. Fancy Bombardier, performed so outstandingly for Edd and Pearl Armstrong and Tom Sheahan respectively.

As a geneticist, Dr. Whitney experimented extensively with inbreeding as well as crossbreeding to determine dominant and recessive genes. It must have been a task of monumental proportions merely to maintain the records involved. Yet he found the time to train many famous mantrailers, and answer the calls for their help. His book on training Bloodhounds has been the bible of many a

Ch. Bourbon of Panther Ledge (Ch.
Giralda's Kriss ex Ch. Wuthering Toni of
Brighton), owned and bred by Mr. and
Mrs. Clendenin J. Ryan and handled by
Harry Manning. *Brown*

Ch. Rye of Panther Ledge, a littermate to
Bourbon, also owned by the Ryans. *Shafer*

The celebrated scientist and author Dr. Leon F. Whitney with two of his
accomplished mantrailers.

handler of mantrailers, and articles by or about him have appeared in numerous national magazines and newspapers. Although his theories were sometimes controversial, he was undoubtedly one of the outstanding breeders and promoters of Bloodhounds in his day.

The Bloodhound population in America has now increased to the degree that danger of extinction is well past. Judging by their increased presence at dog shows and the renewed interest in their use as mantrailers, it seems safe to predict the breed is here to stay.

2

The Mantrailers—
The Golden Oldies

THOUGH HIS NUMBERS are small when compared to other breeds, the Bloodhound is widely known because of his celebrated career as a resourceful mantrailer. Part of the breed's fame in this century is attributable to a group of dedicated men, police and civilian, who recognized the Bloodhound's value in their work and, by their example, demonstrated this value to the world. Here then are their stories.

CAPTAIN V. G. MULLIKIN AND NICK CARTER

No book on mantrailing Bloodhounds could be complete without mention of the greatest of them all, Nick Carter. This hound, owned, trained and handled by Captain Volney G. Mullikin of Lexington, Kentucky, has been credited with over 650 finds resulting in criminal convictions. He set a record for following a cold trail that was to stand for more than twenty-five years. He established it by leading Mullikin on the trail of an arsonist, and bringing it to a successful conclusion when the trail was 105 hours old.

In this case, a henhouse had been burned, and the trail led to a house a mile away. A man came to the door and was identified by the hound. "You weren't counting on the hounds when you burned that henhouse, were you?" Captain Mullikin asked, and the startled man replied, "No," thereby admitting his guilt. It was a standard question with Mullikin, and resulted in many quick confessions. These experiences contributed toward making Nick Carter and his owner legends in their own time. As a result, he was frequently handicapped on searches by the crowd of admirers who gathered whenever word spread of his presence on a case.

Captain Mullikin's longest trail was fifty-five miles, during which he had to stop while one of his dogs had puppies. He sent the mother and puppies home, and continued the trail successfully with the male hound.

Mullikin was a young man of twenty when, in Tennessee, he bought a half-interest in some Bloodhounds owned by a veteran detective named John Moore. He served his apprenticeship with Moore, and later he bought the Rookwood Kennels.

Until his death forty years later, Mullikin's life was dedicated to working with Bloodhounds. During those years his hounds were credited with over 2,500 finds resulting in criminal convictions. It was in great part as a result of his activities that several states enacted laws accepting Bloodhound evidence in court cases. More than once his hounds were shot by the criminals they had trailed, and Mullikin himself carried to his grave scars of his encounters. Once, as he was testifying in court, a relative of the captured outlaw shot and severely wounded him through the courthouse window.

Captain Mullikin and his highly trained mantrailers answered the calls of law enforcement officers throughout the southeastern and central states. They were responsible for the capture of several members on both sides of the notorious Hatfield-McCoy feud, described in a once-popular folk ballad.

The record for the shortest trail—ten feet—was one in which Captain Mullikin and his hounds saved the lives of three children. An insane Kentucky woman had tied her children in a chicken coop while she sharpened an ax to use in killing them. Fortunately, someone found them in time; but apparently they were too frightened to accuse their mother. Mullikin's Bloodhound sniffed the ropes with which they had been bound and led ten feet to the mother, who then confessed her plans. She was committed to an institution.

A 1903 newspaper feature in the *Lexington Herald* on Captain Mullikin and his hounds reported that during the previous one-year period Nick Carter, then three years old, had made a record of 126 convictions against a failure rate of 35 during the same period. There was no count kept on the noncriminal cases. In addition to showing an active schedule, this proves out to something better than a 78 percent conviction rate, a record many a human detective would envy.

Frequently there would be breaks in trails, as when culprits had ridden horses or swum rivers, but the hounds were not lost. In one case the search for a desperate murderer led to a cabin, where the man sprang out with a knife and attempted to stab Mullikin's partner, then disappeared into the darkness. To avoid unnecessary risks, the men waited until daylight before putting the hounds on his trail. It led to a hiding place near a railroad track, and then to the tracks, where the trail ended. The men learned which train had passed in the night, and then, taking the Bloodhounds, boarded the next train in the same direction. At each stop, they took the hounds up and down the tracks, with no success.

They were about to give up when the train reached a station in wild and

Captain Volney G. Mullikin, a legend in his own time.

hilly country. The hounds had hardly left the train before they picked up the trail. They tore off with such eagerness that there was no doubt in their owners' minds. The men followed them the balance of the day and well into the night, when after about twenty miles of trail, the hounds led them to a cabin on the mountainside. Against the resistance of the owner, they entered and searched the cabin. The wanted man was asleep in a loft, too exhausted by his escape to hear their arrival. He was returned to jail, where he was later hanged.

After that two-day trip with its hazards and many miles behind the hounds, the men would have been well entitled to a holiday. It had to wait. While they were eating a long-delayed meal, the call reached them that they were wanted in a town down the road. A jealous lover had shot a young woman and made his escape. The hounds were taken to the spot outside her window from which the murderer had fired, and without hesitation found him, hiding in a shed several miles away. Rural justice was quick; he was hanged from the tree near which he had fired the shot.

Mullikin was described in this contemporary account as being a man of high reputation for integrity and grit. He was a nondrinker, a man of few words but amiable and well liked.

Not all his work entailed capturing criminals; he was frequently called upon to aid in finding lost persons. Shortly before his death from pneumonia at age sixty, he was called to Indiana, where he and his hounds found a baby girl who had strayed from her home and been lost in the woods for more than a day. The lives he and his Bloodhounds saved, as well as the criminals captured, will always keep their memories green.

J. L. WINCHELL AND SPIGGIE

Mr. J. L. Winchell, who reintroduced the Bloodhound to the United States after their 1888 showing by Mr. Edwin Brough, was an enthusiastic supporter of their use in mantrailing. He retained as trainer and handler a Mr. Andy Wilson, who was later to become famous for the finds made by his own hounds. He also trained Bloodhounds for some of the prisons, and was highly regarded for his knowledge of the breed. Among his mantrailers was a hound known as Spiggie; and there was debate as to whether he and others owned by Mr. Wilson equaled or surpassed those owned by Captain Mullikin. Certainly these men and their Bloodhounds did much to make the lawman's work easier.

Unfortunately, Mr. Wilson must not have had the attention from the press that made Captain Mullikin's life so well-known, as we have been able to find only brief references to what must have been an equally exciting career. Possibly, considering the fact that many handlers of mantrailing Bloodhounds, together with their hounds, were ambushed and murdered by the desperate and lawless men they often trailed, he felt it the part of wisdom to keep a low profile.

Wherever mantrailing Bloodhounds are used the name of Nick Carter will be held up as the ideal. Nick Carter was Captain Mullikin's most successful hound and held the record for the successful conclusion of the oldest trail (105 hours) for over twenty-five years.

DR. J. B. FULTON AND X-RAY AND JO-JO

Another of the earlier breeders to follow Mr. Winchell in introducing the mantrailing English Bloodhound to the United States was Dr. J. B. Fulton, of Beatrice, Nebraska. A 1902 edition of *Century Magazine* reported that at that time he had thirteen trained animals. They were famous in a wide area west of the Mississippi River, with their services called upon by law officers in Iowa, Kansas, Nebraska, Colorado, Wyoming and South Dakota. It was claimed that they had never failed to run down their man when placed on the trail within a reasonable length of time after the crime was committed.

One highly celebrated case in which Dr. Fulton's Bloodhounds took part was the robbery of the Union Pacific train in Wyoming a few years prior to this magazine report. The Adams Express company safe was robbed and a considerable sum of money was stolen. In a daring surprise attack, the robbers seized their plunder and escaped.

Posses were immediately organized, but the robbers made for the "hole in the wall" country where there was little hope of following a trail. The officers of both the railroad and the express company were outraged, and determined to run them down and make an example of them. They were willing to spend three times the amount stolen to capture and convict the thieves.

The decision was made to call in some Bloodhounds. A special train was sent after Dr. Fulton's hounds, with the request that he send his best, in charge of skilled trailers.

Realizing that the outlaws were desperate men, Dr. Fulton demanded a promise from the companies that armed posses should follow within a few feet of the hounds. He had no desire to lose his four best hounds. The promise was made, and the hounds and handlers were soon on the train to Casper, Wyoming. From here, they were taken to a ranch which the bandits were known to have passed. The trail led over rocky ground—not the best for retaining a scent—and it was more than fifty hours after the robbers had passed before the hounds arrived.

In spite of the handicaps of the case, the dogs, after circling a few times, found the trail and followed with such enthusiasm that they almost pulled the handlers off their feet. They ran toward the mountains, with the posse close behind. The case continued for thirty-six hours, pausing only long enough to allow the dogs to have a drink, or the men following them to rest briefly. At last the dogs cornered two men, who were immediately surrounded by the posse.

The men offered no resistance; in fact they were so agreeable that the posse began to doubt their involvement in the case. They protested innocence, saying they were herders looking for stray cattle, and had not even heard about the train robbery.

The Wyoming lawmen had been contemptuous of the railroad's plan to use Bloodhounds in the case, and now they ridiculed them, insisting that they had followed two innocent men. The trainers were sure, knowing their hounds, that they had the right men. They did not feel, however, that they were in any position to argue the case with an unfriendly posse. They merely predicted that someday the men might change their minds, and loading up their Bloodhounds, they went back to Nebraska.

They were right. Eventually it was discovered that the two men Dr. Fulton's hounds tracked down had indeed been involved in the robbery.

Another sensational case involving the use of Dr. Fulton's hounds was the murder case of a G. W. Barker and his wife, who lived in a little town in Nebraska. The couple were murdered in their own home by Mr. Barker's brother. Dr. Fulton's dogs X-Ray and Jo-Jo were sent to the town, and practically the entire population went to the depot to see the dogs arrive. They were taken to the suspect's home, given the scent of a coat, and without any hesitation, they picked up the trail through town, across a wheat field, and down the main road to the home of the murdered couple. There they circled the house, and then led off across the field. They stopped nearby and sniffed at a shotgun shell. The posse was now certain they were on the trail of the murderer, and knowing the man was desperate, they discontinued the search until they were able to gather reinforcements.

The hounds then led the men a couple of miles to a farm, and straight to the barn door. It was now past midnight. The dogs and handler withdrew, and the posse circled the barn. As they were watching it, they saw the wanted man come to the window and look out. Apparently he saw them, and realized escape was impossible. A few minutes later they heard a shot, and rushing in, the men found the murderer dead on the floor by his own gun.

This same pair of Bloodhounds set the all-time record for following the longest trail in distance. This took place in the early 1900s when a burglar at Oneida, Kansas, made his getaway by stealing a horse and buggy. The dogs were given the scent of the horse from the currycomb that the owner had used on him, and the hounds set out after the horse.

The handler followed the hounds in a buggy, and eventually, as the trail continued mile after mile, he lifted the hounds into the buggy also, putting them out again each time a crossroad was approached. Each time the Bloodhounds again picked up the trail and continued down the road, verifying the fact that the criminal was still continuing that way. With only short rest periods, they continued on the trail from Wednesday morning until Friday night, when they reached Elwood, Kansas, 135 miles away. Here they led police to the wanted man.

This dedication to the trail was later to lead Jo-Jo to her death. When police in Pueblo, Colorado, were unable to solve a series of burglaries, they called for some of Dr. Fulton's Bloodhounds, and this same team was sent with a handler. They followed the trail of a thief, which led across a trestle high over a river. Halfway across, the handler was horrified to hear a train speeding around a curve and coming straight at them. He jumped into the river, pulling X-Ray with him. He was unable to drag Jo-Jo off her feet, and she was struck and killed by the train.

X-Ray and the handler fell thirty-five feet into the shallow, rocky river. The water cushioned their fall sufficiently to prevent broken bones, but they were dreadfully bruised, indeed fortunate to have survived. When an investigation was demanded, the train engineer freely admitted to having seen the man and hounds on the trestle. He indifferently dismissed the matter with the statement that he thought it was someone stealing a couple of valuable dogs, and "figured I'd teach him a lesson, so didn't apply the brakes."

This could be cited as an example of why many people prefer dogs to their own kind.

Another of Dr. Fulton's famous hounds was named Miss Columbia, and it was claimed that she had never failed on a trail. In May of 1900 a store was robbed in Sabetha, Kansas, without a clue being left. The Bloodhounds were called out, and Miss Columbia and another hound named Beauregard (for some reason, a name universally popular for Bloodhounds) were taken to the job. The trail was over twenty-four hours old, but the hounds followed it without difficulty, crossing a river to reach Salem, Nebraska, where they caught up with four men eating breakfast. One was convicted; the others escaped on technical loopholes.

In another case, Miss Columbia showed her ability by trailing a man who had been vandalizing the beautifully landscaped grounds of a prosperous Nebraska farmer. The victim appealed to Dr. Fulton for help, and was told to send a telegram immediately if it occurred again. The next Sunday Dr. Fulton received the message; while the family was attending church, the criminal had struck again, chopping down a row of beautiful evergreens and destroying flower beds. Miss Columbia and her teammate immediately took the trail, leading their handler to the home of a neighbor about three-quarters of a mile away. He settled out of court, grimly stating that they'd never have gotten him if it hadn't been for the hounds.

It was claimed that this bitch had successfully followed an eighteen-hour-old trail when less than six months of age; and though she was always eager for a trail, she seemed to have reasoned there was no point in working harder than necessary. When she was put on the trail of a horse, or other stolen animal, she seemed to know it was likely to stay on the road, and would follow it far enough to get the direction. Then she would sit and wait for the handler, following in a buggy. She was the only hound Dr. Fulton allowed to trail off lead, as she could be trusted to wait for her handler. When the buggy arrived, she would jump in and ride until the next crossroad, when she would jump out, pick up the trail again, and then once more wait for her transportation.

One report stated that of the last twenty-three cases on which Dr. Fulton's hounds had been called, they had run down every trail, with eighteen of the cases resulting in convictions. Their reputations were well-known through the midwestern states, and well deserved.

DR. CECIL FOSGATE AND HIS HOUNDS

Dr. Cecil Fosgate, a veterinarian of Ashland, Wisconsin, owned, bred and trained mantrailing Bloodhounds from the time he was thirteen years old until

Texel of Oxford, a five-month-old liver and tan, bred by the English Bloodhound Kennels of Smithfield, West Virginia. This puppy is typical of many bred for use in the many phases of mantrailing.

Courtesy, James Zarifis

Ledburne Beresford, imported to the United States at six months. He was sired by Dual Ch. Ledburne Barrier out of Symbol.

Courtesy, James Zarifis

his death in 1969 at age eighty-one. He was highly regarded as an authority on the breed, and his advice started many others in their training of these lifesaving animals.

Originally a native of New York State, Dr. Fosgate obtained his first Bloodhounds shortly after they were reintroduced to this country by Mr. J. L. Winchell. His King and Queen Fosgate were direct decendants of Belhus and Rosemary, the first two Bloodhounds Mr. Brough sent to Mr. Winchell. He later imported a number of other Bloodhounds from England, trained them as mantrailers, and took part in many a search in the Adirondack Mountains before his move to Wisconsin.

We are indebted to his son, Mr. Kenneth Fosgate, and to the articles of Dr. Fosgate printed in *Bloodlines Journal* and reprinted in the *American Blood-hound Club Bulletin*. He is remembered by many with respect and admiration. During a fifty-year span, to his knowledge, Kenneth Fosgate relates, there was not a hound issue of *Bloodlines Journal* printed that did not carry as its cover picture one of Dr. Fosgate's hounds. He raised over five hundred hounds during his lifetime, and as recorded by his son, never had a case of bloat. Considering the many excellent hounds which have been lost to that sad fate, this in itself is amazing.

Dr. Fosgate was enthusiastic in his praise of the intelligence of the Blood-hound; they could be trained to trail man or beast, were devoted to children, and as guard dogs had an excellent moral effect on the vagrant and criminal element in the area. Any such person found on the property during the night, he wrote, would still be there in the morning.

He encouraged his hounds to bay on the trail, as he frequently allowed them to trail off lead, following them by sound. That was before the days when traffic presented the hazard it does now; but a handler would need speed and endurance, nevertheless, to keep in touch.

While still living in New York during the late 1920s, Dr. Fosgate and his hounds took part in the filming of the movie version of *Uncle Tom's Cabin*. Three of his imported Bloodhounds were used: Dennebola of Iscold, Marlwood Madge and Ch. Ledburn Beeswax, along with two seven-month-old puppies, Fosgate's Tip and Maid, by the imported Dark's Boy ex Marlwood Madge. Fosgate considered Madge and her litter sister, Maid, two of the most intelligent dogs he had ever known. Maid died young, but Madge served him on many a search, and would faithfully guard either persons or property.

Dennebola of Iscold was fully trained when Dr. Fosgate imported him from England, and had been trained to trail both man and horse. In August of 1924, when Dr. Fosgate lived in Morrisonville, New York, he demonstrated that he could trail cattle equally well. A Mr. Hayes, who owned an Ayrshire farm, had lost some of his best heifers from an eighty-acre pasture. One had disappeared in May; but when seven more disappeared at one time, he asked Dr. Fosgate if he thought the Bloodhounds could help locate the thieves. He was sure the cattle must have been stolen, as a rail on the fence was down.

There was a large, dense cedar swamp adjoining the pasture, and Dr.

Fosgate suggested that the cattle might have broken out and gone there to escape from the flies and mosquitoes. Mr. Hayes considered that unlikely, as he said four men and two stock dogs had hunted in the swamp for three days and not seen as much as a track.

Dr. Fosgate agreed to see what help he could give, and arrived at the pasture with Dennebola that evening. The hound sniffed the rails of the fence, but gave no response to the command to find. Then Dr. Fosgate led him into the pasture, removed his harness, and pointed to a cow track. Dennebola took off like a flash this time, while Dr. Fosgate and Mr. Hayes sat on the rails and fought the mosquitoes. Mr. Hayes was doubtful as to the safety of turning the dog loose, but Dr. Fosgate confidently told him he had turned as many as thirty loose at one time, and had complete faith in them. Just twenty minutes after the hound took the trail, the waiting men heard a "Woof," and out of the cedar swamp came Dennebola with seven of the missing cattle. The eighth, missing since May, was not with them.

Another case in which Dr. Fosgate used both Dennebola and Marlwood Madge involved the search for a four-year-old boy who had disappeared at a waterfront location. What made the trailing outstanding was the fact that the trail was forty-two hours old, and was all on concrete, stone, boardwalks or brick paving, and there had been two heavy showers since the child disappeared, with hot sun between times. The two hounds, immediately upon being given the scent, led to the dock; and Dr. Fosgate was sure the child's body was in the water. The owner of the dock agreed the hounds had trailed the boy, as he said the little fellow frequently sat on the edge of the dock, but he doubted that the child had drowned. Dr. Fosgate therefore continued the search, starting at every location where the boy had been seen on the fatal day, and all trails ended at the dock. The last trail started at a local store where the child had gone to spend a nickel. Dennebola immediately indicated that he wanted to start out the door, while Madge first investigated the entire store, nuzzling around in a box of oranges and finally pushing one orange out. The storekeeper was amazed. "How could she smell his scent on that orange?" he asked, explaining that the boy had in fact picked up an orange from the crate. When Dr. Fosgate gave the hounds the command to find, they immediately dashed for the dock; and this time he un-snapped the lead from Madge. The big hound leaped from the dock and began swimming around near the end of it, never going far away, and sniffing at leaves, twigs, or foam on the surface. Dr. Fosgate then told the mother that he was certain the child was in the water, and there was nothing more he could do. The police dragged the area without results; but a week later the body came to the surface, where the keen-nosed hound had indicated.

Dr. Fosgate, in a letter written to *Bloodlines* and reprinted in the *American Bloodhound Club Bulletin*, relates some of the amazing trailing exploits of the pair of hounds, King and Queen Fosgate, previously mentioned. He was confident that King was the greatest drop trailer who ever lived, and gave an example of his trailing, in which case he retained in his memory the scent he had been following for eight days. By this time, Dr. Fosgate had raised a litter from the pair, and sold the parents to a Mr. E. M. Allen, of Little Rock, Arkansas, who was well-known at that time as a Bloodhound breeder and handler. Shortly after receiving them, Mr. Allen received a call for help in finding a man who had attacked a little girl. Mr. Allen took King to the scene of the crime, and first the hound followed the child's trail to her home. Allen then returned the hound to the site, and again ordered him to find. This time the hound picked up a trail which led to a streetcar landing in town, where it ended. Handler and hound kept scouting streetcar landings and bus depots, and eight days later King again recognized the trail and followed it to a man, who was then arrested and taken to the home of the raped child. She identified him as her attacker, and he was hanged for the crime. Mr. Allen sent a newspaper clipping relating the facts of the case to Dr. Fosgate as evidence of the excellent training job he had done.

Soon afterward Mr. Allen sent another clipping reporting a case in which both King and Queen were used. A law had been passed requiring the farmers to dip their cattle to kill ticks which spread disease. A U.S. Government inspector and his assistant were leading their horses along a road early one morning when the inspector was shot and killed from ambush. Mr. Allen was called, but the only evidence he could find in the direction from which the shot had come was a burnt matchstick. Using this as a scent article for the hounds, he started them in the area where the murderer had waited, and the dogs immediately picked up the trail, across fields, and by a roundabout way to a farmhouse about three miles away. Nobody was home, but since the door was not locked and the hounds were eager to enter, they allowed them to do so. They immediately gave their bay of identification at a pair of boots and a bed.

At the stable, evidence showed the search party that someone had driven a team and wagon away from the place. A neighbor offered the information that the resident of the home had gone to Little Rock.

The men and hounds returned to the city and visited the stables. Again, the hounds picked up a trail, leading to a hardware store, where they identified a man. Thus confronted, the man confessed, and implicated two others.

In another case, Queen Fosgate trailed a thief after having taken his scent from a tub of hamburger. The man had broken into a store, entering and leaving through a ventilator in the roof of the cooler, and stealing some poultry. When Queen was taken outside, she picked up the trail and followed it to the subject. This example of ignoring the delights of hamburger to concentrate on the man scent must rank as one of the outstanding cases of devotion to duty in canine records.

This pair of mantrailers was personally trained by Dr. Fosgate, and he wrote of them with pride, as an example of what purebred Bloodhounds, trained with firm kindness, could accomplish. They served their owners in the 1920s, and gave Dr. Fosgate an outstanding litter to continue their work.

Dr. Cecil Fosgate did not limit his interest to Bloodhounds. His writings on Otter Hounds were also of much interest to owners of that rare breed. His interest is being carried on by his grandson, Bruce Fosgate, who now breeds Bloodhounds in Colorado Springs, Colorado.

BOB GANT AND RED EAGLE AND LADY BESS

While Dr. Fosgate was making believers in the North, Bob Gant, of Crystal Springs, Mississippi, was spreading the message in his state. He became interested in Bloodhounds when an elderly citizen was murdered in his city, and the Bloodhounds from the penitentiary were brought out to aid in the case. Their speedy success amazed Gant, and led to his eventual purchase of the pair of puppies who became famous as Red Eagle and Lady Bess. By the mid-1930s they were the veterans of over one hundred searches, and their owner proudly recorded an 85 percent success rate.

Gant and his Bloodhounds became so famous that crowds would gather when he appeared on a case, sometimes making the situation downright embarrassing. As an example, after a series of burglaries, the police became suspicious that a professional ring was operating in the area. When the drugstore was robbed, they promptly called Bob Gant, and the druggist made sure nobody went near the door through which the burglar had presumably left.

The hounds checked over the store, and indicated they had the trail. They led their owner down the street, followed by an eager crowd, and insisted upon entering the home of one of the most respected ladies of the town. In spite of the jeering and indignant protests of the townspeople, Gant and his hounds requested entry, and here the dogs led to this highly regarded lady herself. Fortunately for the reputation of the hounds and their owner, in the midst of this hostile atmosphere, the lady broke down and admitted to drug addiction, which had led to her burglary of the drugstore.

In another case, in which a postmaster was killed, what seemed to be a mistake of the hounds was caused by the groups of curious who trampled the area and muddled the scent for the hounds. With no scent article of the murderer to go on, Gant's only choice was to start his hounds from the scene of the crime, and hope for the best. Four times he started them from the post office, and four times they led him to different men who were able to establish their innocence. However, the hounds were not wrong; each of those men had been in the post office after the murder, and they naturally left the freshest scents.

Red Eagle and Lady Bess made warm friends after a search for a lost four-year-old boy in a Louisiana area known as Sicily Island. The message that reached Bob Gant said in part, "We have lost a child and no money to pay for the search." Bob got there as fast as his car allowed, bringing the two hounds. The trail was eighty-two hours old by that time, and for the past three days and nights the farmers in the area had been searching the woods and swamps for the child. The area was pretty well trampled.

Gant instructed the mother to bring the last piece of clothing the child had worn—not touching it herself, but held on a stick. She brought a little nightgown, and starting at the spot where the father had put the little boy down from the wagon and told him to go home, Gant gave the hounds the scent. Almost immediately, they were on the trail, zigzagging along the way the little boy had wandered. Soon evidence of their accuracy was discovered in bits of the child's clothing, as the pair trailed through the night. By sunrise Lady Bess, working

Trooper William W. Horton with one of the early Troop "K" Bloodhounds.

Courtesy, New York State Police

free, was out of sight when she gave a yelp that said, "I've got him!" And that dog never told a lie, Gant said. The little boy was lying there, almost naked, but alive, near the edge of the river, with Lady Bess licking his face.

Gant had his share of the murder cases too—desperate men whose greatest hatred was for the men and hounds who hunted them. One of his best was shot not far ahead of the posse on the trail. She was worth $10,000, he said—and that was in the depression days.

The movies still confuse the public with scenes of convicts eluding the hounds by taking to a stream, and Gant joins many others in scoffing at that one. "All they'll do is get their feet wet," he said. "The hounds will pick up the trail where they come out."

In one case, they did something even more amazing; they trailed a burglar from the store he had robbed to a southbound freight train; then picked up his scent again where he left it, twenty-five miles away, and caught him with the goods.

TROOPER WILLIAM W. HORTON AND TROOP K

The first police Bloodhound kennel in the East was founded about 1934, when a private citizen, Joseph Russell, became interested in Bloodhounds and gave two named Ki-Ki and Red to the New York State Troopers at Hawthorne. They were the founding stock of Troop K, and rapidly made a name for themselves. In a 1939 newspaper account, they and the later additions to the kennel were credited with a 98 percent accuracy rating in finding the persons—criminals or lost citizens—on whose trails they were started.

In addition, Ki-Ki presented the troopers with two litters of six puppies each. Some of these puppies were given to the troopers at Batavia and Oneida, where they were trained and bred, with the expectation of eventually establishing a Bloodhound kennel at each of the state troopers headquarters.

Troopers William W. (Cy) Horton and Jerry Dershimer were the handlers of these first Bloodhounds at Hawthorne, and together they took part in many a lifesaving search. One which received wide publicity in the fall of 1938 was their rescue of a former prizefighter, Frank Genero, together with his two small daughters and sixteen-year-old nephew. They had become lost in deep wilderness area near Rockland Lake.

The Bloodhounds were rushed to the area, arriving in the early evening. The trail led for five miles through dense brush and forest, until the missing group was found at about 2:30 A.M. The little girls were huddled together, their father's coat around them, while he and the youth tramped about, swinging their arms and trying to keep from freezing. Suddenly a large animal burst through the brush and leaped up on Genero, startling him considerably until it began licking his face, and he saw the grinning face of Trooper Horton at the other end of the leash which held it. They were barely in time. The doctors who treated the two children for frostbite said they would not have lasted another hour in the bitter weather.

Once the Bloodhounds weren't requested until five days after a twenty-one-month-old child had been lost. A hound named Old Monk was put on the trail, and promptly made the find; but that was the oldest trail they had had occasion to follow at that time. In another case, Horton and his hound found a four-year-old girl who had wandered away from the resort hotel where her family was vacationing. When a thunderstorm broke, she took refuge under a tree and remained there, by this time two miles from the hotel.

Troop K was supplied with a trailer which could be quickly attached to any of the police cars when a search was called. On its side in large letters was the identification, TROOP K, STATE POLICE, BLOODHOUNDS. In this portable doghouse, equipped for four hounds, they sped to many a search for a suicide victim, strayed child, or senile wanderer, as well as to the usual criminal searches.

The hounds were frequently called on lifesaving missions outside their own state, in one case trailing a twenty-one-month-old Vermont child for three miles to the rescue. This was an example that pointed up Trooper Horton's experience that a missing child would walk much farther than search parties considered possible. A child would usually walk the first day, he found, and then remain near the place he stopped. Frequently the hounds successfully trailed, in a few hours, a missing person whom a search party of a hundred had been unable to find in a day or more. Each summer would bring an average of sixty of these cases, and the Bloodhounds almost never failed in the rescue.

Convicts making their escape have waded through miles of swamp or flooded land, thinking they would lose the hounds. Scent, however, drifts like a fine mist from the entire body, and hanging over water, or on the marsh grass, would lead the hounds on the trail. One criminal carried a box of red pepper, thinking that by sprinkling it on his tracks he could foil the pursuers. That didn't work either. Often the scent will cling to grass or shrubs, breast-high to the hounds; or it will drift with the air movement, so that the hound is rarely nosedown on the exact track of the person trailed. Repeatedly, the troopers' hounds scuttled old myths about Bloodhounds as they followed their time-honored profession.

In one case, the dogs seemed to have missed. Three children had been playing near a summer cabin in the hills, but only two returned. The father gave Trooper Horton a pair of gloves as a scent article, but somehow the hound, Smarty, couldn't seem to go anywhere but back to the cabin. Later the child was found, and the father wrote to apologize. In his distress, he had given Horton the gloves of one of the children who had returned, and naturally, the hound also kept returning to the cabin.

A hound named Sappho was one who made some outstanding finds, including finding eleven lost skiers who had missed a turn on a mountain trail. Once, however, her speed almost proved too much for Horton and Police Lieutenant Frank Carlson of the Ossining Police. Two convicts had escaped prison, and forced a man in a rowboat to take them across the Hudson River. Sappho was taken to the spot where they had left the boat. A steep bluff rose above the river, and by the time the officers had followed the Bloodhound to the top, they were exhausted and stopped for a rest. It was fortunate that they did, or they would not have heard the twig snap ahead of them. Pulling their guns and separating to come at the men from opposite sides, they duped the convicts into believing themselves surrounded. They threw down their guns and gave up. Sappho had trailed so quietly and at such speed that she had almost pulled the officers up to the criminals.

Sappho performed one trailing feat which was almost unbelievable to the troopers, and thereby solved a murder case. There were no clues to this Long Island murder, but there was a suspect, who had been taken into custody. The troopers hoped that Sappho might find some evidence that would connect him with the crime. They took her to the scene, and gave her the man's sock as a scent article. Perhaps, they thought, he had hidden a weapon or other material under the bushes nearby.

Instead, Sappho began trailing along the highway, not on the road itself, but in the grass at the edge of the road. For three miles she continued, then turned off the highway and led to a house where the suspect's sister lived. Here she investigated a topless old automobile, and then led to the house. When the suspect was faced with this performance by the hound, he confessed that he had committed the crime, and driven the distance to his sister's house. His feet had never touched the ground; yet his scent, drifting from the car, had settled on the grasses at the roadside, and guided the Bloodhound.

Repeatedly, the hounds have displayed their ability to shorten a criminal case even when they could not lead the troopers up to the subject, as in the 1936 robbery of the bank at Pine Bush, in the Catskills. While the men had escaped in a car, they had been caught by a roadblock and forced to take to the woods. Trooper Horton's Bloodhound was able to trail far enough to indicate the direction of their flight, and to locate the heavy overcoat worn by one of the men, which was identified by a witness to the bank robbery. In another case, a hound named Old Red actually ran down the murderer of a woman who had rejected his advances, and his fear of the hound led to a speedy confession.

"Cy" Horton, in his retirement, contributed his memories to the first edition of *The Complete Bloodhound*. Although now deceased, he is remembered as one of the pioneers of mantrailing Bloodhound use in this country.

DR. WHITNEY'S MANTRAILERS

Dr. Leon F. Whitney, mentioned previously as one of the early breeders who helped make Bloodhounds famous by his breeding and writing, was equally well-known for the work of his mantrailers. In 1935, according to his article in *Popular Science Monthly*, there were only 167 owners of registered Bloodhounds in the country. They owned about four hundred registered animals, of which less than one hundred were trained in mantrailing.

Originally the English Bloodhounds were encouraged to bay on the trail, as they still do when allowed to run in a pack in England. Dr. Whitney soon learned that all this noise on the trail not only brought out half the county, getting in the way of the hounds and adding to the problems of trailing, but it alerted the criminal being hunted. After a bank robber in Massachusetts ambushed him one night and tried to kill him, Dr. Whitney resolved to train his hounds as silent trailers, as they have remained to this day when worked on lead.

In one difficult case, Dr. Whitney was asked by the Connecticut State Police to find a fisherman who had disappeared in the woods. Dr. Whitney let Sappho, one of his best hounds, sniff a shirt the fisherman had left behind. She hardly hesitated, but headed out rapidly for a nearby mountain. Four hours later she led the searchers to the body of the man, who had died of a heart attack.

"She never even stopped to sniff," an impressed trooper remarked. "She must have found him by instinct."

Dr. Whitney gave the man a short education on the properties of scent, and the Bloodhound's ability. Many of the best mantrailers never lower their heads to the ground, but pick up the scent chest-high, where it clings to grass and shrubbery.

In another case, Dr. Whitney was called upon to help find twelve insane and potentially dangerous patients who had escaped from an institution. He brought two experienced hounds, who trailed to the edge of a river, and then apparently disagreed. One started down the bank, while the other plunged into the river and began swimming across.

The posse split up, half of them following each hound. Before long, each group had been led to a party of the missing patients.

Several of the hounds of the New York State Police Troop K came from Dr. Whitney's kennel.

GEORGE BROOKS—MANTRAILER BEHIND A SODA FOUNTAIN

George Brooks, of La Crosse, Wisconsin, bought his first Bloodhound in 1932. It was a four-month-old female named Lady, and came from England. George had had her for only a few days when the sheriff called. Three men had attempted to rob a bank in a nearby town. One was killed, and the other two had abandoned their car and taken to the woods. Sheriff Woll wanted Brooks to bring the Bloodhound.

"She's only a puppy, she's not trained yet," Brooks explained.

"Give her a try anyway," the sheriff pleaded. An hour later, Brooks and Lady were on the scene. Ignoring the car, the puppy went to work like a veteran, and led down to the river. They took her across the river, but no trail could be found there, and the search was finally abandoned. Later that year the men were caught after another crime, and George had to satisfy himself regarding his puppy's work. He visited the men in jail, and learned a valuable lesson.

"They were southerners, and had been chased by Bloodhounds before," he explained. "They had gotten into deep water and were breathing through hollow reeds. If I'd let Lady go, she'd have found them right then. From that day on, I learned to believe my Bloodhounds."

George Brooks worked as a soda fountain assistant at a La Crosse drugstore, and had an arrangement with the owner that he could leave anytime he received a call for Bloodhound work. During the years, he took his hounds out on more than two thousand cases, one of them lasting three weeks, until a murderer was captured. He found little children, escaped convicts, the senile and insane, and POWs escaping from the nearby camp during World War II. Stories of his hounds' exploits have been published in national magazines. Throughout the forty years or so that he left that soda fountain on a moment's notice he never took a dollar for his services.

George had the trunk of his car converted into a mobile kennel for his dogs on the way to searches. A flashing red light on the roof of his car warned drivers that he was in a hurry, and he always carried a gun on searches. His many hair-raising experiences justified it.

If foresight were as good as hindsight, perhaps George might have changed history. Going through his memoirs he once found a 1958 letter from Cuba. It contained a request from the then-dictator Batista that he come to Cuba with his hounds and help track down the guerrillas hiding in the hills. Fidel Castro was the leader of at least some of those guerrillas, and by the end of that year he replaced Batista as the head of the Cuban government.

Brooks turned the job down. There was enough for him to do in his own territory.

Sgt. James Zarifis of the Malverne (New York) Police Department with Ch. Patriot John Quincy Adams. Many like Sgt. Zarifis have blended the ancient talents of the Bloodhound with techniques of modern law enforcement to create a better life for their communities.

Mermon

3

The Mantrailers— The Lawmen

MODERN LAW ENFORCEMENT finds much use for the Bloodhound just as did Volney Mullikin and many of his contemporaries. Better means of communication have given rise to a freer exchange of information that has proven beneficial to all. Here are the stories of today's law officers and their steadfast hounds—the knights behind the nose.

THE RISE OF PROFESSIONALISM

As law enforcement entered a new era, professionalism became more than ever a requirement in the training and handling of Bloodhounds. To achieve this end, a seminar was held at the Bethany Barracks of the Connecticut State Police in 1962, and a new organization was born. It was known as the Eastern Police Bloodhound Association, and was sponsored by the Honorable Leo J. Mulcahey, commissioner of the Connecticut State Police, together with his department.

The association made rapid progress toward its goals. This achievement was the result of the realization of the members involved that their aims could be achieved only through participation, cooperation and education.

The prime goal was the training of Bloodhounds by time-tested, field-proven methods, and the objective examination of past beliefs regarding the breed. Those found false are to be recognized as such and discredited. As examples, it is now accepted that Bloodhounds can trail in cities; that spayed bitches will trail as well as entire bitches; and that the advent of the auto did not destroy the usefulness of the Bloodhound. The old myths to the contrary are now permanently laid to rest.

THE NATIONAL POLICE BLOODHOUND ASSOCIATION

The growth of the association was so rapid that its name was soon changed to the National Police Bloodhound Association, Inc. It includes members from California to New Jersey, and from Maine to Georgia. There is also a Canadian representative in Kingston, Ontario.

The association presents two annual awards, one for a human, the other for a Bloodhound.

The J. B. Marcum Award, in memory of Joseph B. Marcum, is presented to the individual making an outstanding contribution to the development and the use of purebred Bloodhounds in the field of law enforcement.

The Cleopatra Award is named after Cleopatra of the Big T, the first Bloodhound owned and trained by William D. Tolhurst of the Niagara County, New York, Sheriff's Department. Cleopatra made the enviable record of over three hundred successful searches during her lifetime. The award in her honor is presented to the Bloodhound that has contributed the most outstanding performance in law enforcement and/or search and rescue work for the year.

The association takes pride in having been of assistance to members of the armed forces serving in Korea and Vietnam, who employed Bloodhounds in these areas. It has also assisted in furnishing purebred Bloodhounds to many police agencies, including the Zambia National Police of Africa, as well as to search and rescue units and individual police officers who wished to handle Bloodhounds of their own. In addition to supplying the Bloodhounds, the technical information in training and handling was made available.

The NPBA considers itself the most authoritative source of information now existing on the trailing Bloodhound in the field of law enforcement. To share and increase this knowledge, they hold two seminars a year. A spring training seminar is held at which police officers and their hounds can train together under the most skilled supervision available. In the fall a seminar is held at which police officers and their guests can hear lectures from people who are acknowledged experts in their fields.

Among the current objectives of the NPBA is the preparation of a training manual for the mantrailing Bloodhound. This is based upon the experiences of police officers throughout the United States.

Another goal of the NPBA is establishment of a "Bloodhounds for Peace" program. The purpose of this organization is the furnishing of NPBA Bloodhound teams of expert hounds and handlers, available to go anywhere in the world to fight terrorism and hijacking, or to search for lost children or fleeing felons. The only requirement of the requesting agency is that it provide the transportation and pay the expenses for these dedicated men and their four-footed teammates.

The establishment of a National Police Bloodhound Hall of Fame and Museum is underway at this time. Its purpose is to preserve a record of some of the fantastic accomplishments, dedication and romance of the mantrailing Bloodhound over the years. It is designed to give him his just place in the archives of history.

(We acknowledge with thanks the assistance of Mr. William D. Tolhurst, who contributed this information, and of the *American Bloodhound Club Bulletin*, in which it was originally published.)

The 1975 NPBA Joe B. Marcum Award was presented to Corporal Weldon Wood, Charles County Sheriff's Department, La Plate, Maryland. He joined that department in 1966 after four and one-half years with the Maryland State Police. In 1968 he brought the first Bloodhound to use in that department, and as a result of its success, the Maryland State Police now have three of the breed.

Corporal Wood has acted as instructor for several of the spring training schools, and wrote a booklet for training use which is being used by many departments, including the FBI Academy, Quantico, Virginia.

The Cleopatra Big T Award for 1975 went to a hound named Sam, of the New York State Police, Poughkeepsie, New York, whose trainer and handler has been Trooper Neil Howe. This hound ran a fifty-two-and-one-half-hour-old trail on Staten Island, New York, taking his handler directly to the end of a pier. Nine days later the body of the retarded boy being sought was located under that same pier.

Sam was also responsible for the apprehension of a suspect in a double homicide in White Plains, New York. Another of his exploits involved the trailing of a burglar from the scene of the crime, and locating three places where stolen items were left, including two guns and ammunition. He then followed a six-mile trail, six hours old, to locate the suspect at the side of a road.

The first Cleopatra Award, given in 1973, went to a Bloodhound named Joker, also trained by Trooper Howe.

CLEOPATRA OF THE BIG T

Cleopatra of the Big T never saw the inside of a show ring, but she was a champion in the best sense of the word—she was a perfectionist in the work of her breed. She was never to be a brood bitch, and dysplasia troubled her increasingly as she aged. However, she had the nose and the determination that led her on over three hundred successful searches during the nine years of her life. Law officers and lawbreakers alike regarded her with respect.

BILL TOLHURST—CLEO'S WORKING PARTNER

Cleo, as she was known, was the working partner of Special Deputy Bill Tolhurst of the Niagara County, New York, Sheriff's Department. She was Bill's first Bloodhound, a marvelous combination of the best in Bloodhound ability combined with intelligent training and observant handling.

It was about 1960 when Bill Tolhurst became interested in Bloodhounds. He had been out hunting with a game warden friend when a youth was lost in the woods. The game wardens were called to take part in the search, and Bill went along. The boy was never found. Why, Bill asked, was a Bloodhound not used? A trained mantrailer could certainly have helped.

While inexperienced with Bloodhounds, Tolhurst was a keen hunter and outdoorsman, and he loved to work with dogs. The tragedy of the lost boy turned his interest to Bloodhounds, and he began seeking any information available on the subject. He heard of Dr. Leon Whitney, and studied his book on Bloodhound training. He then visited Dr. Whitney and benefited by an oral updating of the book. He had learned a good deal since he wrote that book, Dr. Whitney admitted; and Tolhurst combined his instruction with his own keen observation in training hounds. "I may be a maverick," he says, "but I do what works for me."

The results prove that what works for Tolhurst is a top-notch system, as Cleopatra, for the nine years of her life, and her half-sister Cinnamon K of the Big T (Cindy), who has taken her place, have followed trails that would be unbelievable were they not documented. They have trailed criminals who have traveled by automobile for as long as three miles, enabling the officers to make arrests and obtain convictions. The following is one such case.

A gas station in the city of Lockport was burglarized about 3:00 A.M. It was in the dead of winter, and very cold. When Bill and Cinnamon arrived they found one footprint leaving the front door, which had been jimmied, so they knew the burglar had left that way. There were only occasional spots of snow on the ground, so no direction could be seen. When Cinnamon was shown the footprint she took the trail fast. Then came a place where she indicated by her own signals that there was a car involved, and that the subject had entered the car. There were tire prints, and the deputy protected them as best he could in case he should want to make a cast of them. Cinnamon made a couple of circles to indicate pool scent, that something had happened here, and then raised her head in the way that said, "We're going up the hill."

The team started up the main street of the city of Lockport, through the downtown section, down an alley, across a parking lot, and to another street which led to Route 78, the main highway to Buffalo. By this time it was 7:30 or 8:00 A.M. The hound trailed down the highway until they reached a laundromat, and then she went into her circle that said, "Something happened here." But whatever it was puzzled her. She tried to pick up a trail again, but couldn't find it.

Tolhurst radioed the police station and asked that a car pick them up. Back at the station, he talked to the detective on the case, and detailed what had happened.

The detective said, "You mean she trailed to that laundromat?"

"Yes, she did," Tolhurst replied. "I don't know why, but Cindy indicated there was a car involved, and that was as far as she could take me."

The Cleopatra Big T Award given annually for the best performance by a Bloodhound in connection with law enforcement and/or search and rescue operations.

Cleopatra of the Big T with her human partner, Special Deputy Bill Tolhurst. Cleo and Tolhurst worked together for the Niagara County (New York) Sheriff's Department, and in the nine years of her life Cleo establilshed a record of over 300 successful searches.

Courtesy, National Police Bloodhound Association

"We've got a fellow upstairs now," the detective replied. "We had a tip, and picked him up, and we're sure he's the burglar. Come on upstairs and we'll talk to him."

The two officers confronted the man. "We know you were at that service station," they told him. "We've got the proof, because the dog followed you to the laundromat."

"I don't know how the dog could have followed me there," the startled suspect replied. "I went there in a car. I stopped to buy a bottle of pop." Caught by surprise, he admitted the burglary. He verified the fact that he had entered the car at the point the Bloodhound had indicated, and driven to the laundromat. When he came out he was picked up in the police vehicle and taken to police headquarters.

Surprise can produce a confession in many a case. One which involved Cleopatra took place in February 1964, when she and her owner were called by the Lockport Police Department to a medical building which had been burglarized. A basement window had been broken, and there was a heelprint in the snow, showing a distinctive marking. The sergeant in charge thought Cleo might give the search a direction. Although there was snow on the ground, the sidewalks were clear, and the footprint at the basement window was the only one showing.

Cleo started from the footprint, and took off without hesitation. There was no visual track, but she began trailing east through the city of Lockport as if she knew what she was doing.

A new patrolman, inexperienced with Bloodhounds, was accompanying the team. When they came to the edge of the city and Cleo started across a large golf course, the snow was ankle-deep, but there was still no visible track. "She's taking you for a walk," the new man scoffed. "You can see there's no trail. You'd have to be crazy to follow her."

"I don't care what you do," Tolhurst replied. "I'm sticking with the Bloodhound."

The team continued onward about a quarter of a mile before they saw footprints, which led to the Niagara County Infirmary. It was about 4:00 A.M., and Cleo wanted to go inside. Tolhurst opened the door, and the men followed her as she pussyfooted carefully over the slippery floors, down the hall, into a corridor. About halfway down they met two old men going to the bathroom. As Bill tells it, when they saw this big animal coming down the corridor with three policemen, they just about died. He told them to stand perfectly still and the dog wouldn't harm them, and they froze in their tracks.

Paying no attention to the frightened men, Cleo went to the end of the hall, and into a big dormitory room which held about twenty-four or twenty-eight beds. She went down a couple of aisles and without warning jumped into bed with a man. The man leaped from that bed as if the devil had grabbed at him. The sergeant bent down and picked up his shoe, and there was the distinctive heelprint. He asked, "Why did you break into that medical building?"

"I don't know," the suspect confessed, "but I'm sure sorry I did."

A well-trained Bloodhound can not only tell her handler where a subject

Cinnamon K of the Big T with her owner-handler, Bill Tolhurst, and Sheriff Anthony Villella. Cindy is a half-sister to Cleo and became her replacement. Like the illustrious Cleo, Cindy has shown herself to be a brilliant, invaluable mantrailer.

The solemn-looking mantrailer above is Boozer. He is shown with Special Deputy Dave Onderdonk (left) and Deputy Lang of the Rensselaer County (New York) Sheriff's Department. *Courtesy, James Zarifis*

is, but where he isn't. Cleo gave a fine example of that one night, solving a case which until her arrival had tied up considerable manpower and equipment.

The Erie Barge Canal runs through the city of Lockport, and is one of its major hazards. Every year there are several drownings, or animals in the canal requiring rescue. About nine o'clock one night Tolhurst received a call asking him to bring Cleo. Several hours before, a car towing another car with a tow bar had missed the bridge and gone into the canal. A man standing on the bridge had witnessed the accident, and had not seen the driver escape. The fire department was called to bring grappling equipment, the state police and skin divers were called, and the cars were located and removed from the water. However, the body of the driver was not located. The opinion was that he had tried to escape from the car, and that the swift current had pulled him away. Perhaps the Bloodhound could come up with some information.

Since the identity of the driver had been established, Tolhurst went to his home and obtained a scent article from his wife. Before he set the hound to work, however, he asked that the crowd be dispersed, and the other rescue vehicles, with their gasoline fumes, be moved away. Then he took Cleo to the bank of the canal where the car had entered the water, and gave her the scent article.

Without hesitation, Cleo started trailing upstream along the canal. If she had gone downstream, Tolhurst thought, it might have been the drift of scent from a body in the water; but upstream meant she had a trail, no doubt about it.

For about three and a half miles, the Bloodhound led her owner along the canal, almost to the village of Gasport. At that time, the search team was not equipped with radio, but had to work with a police car following. Tolhurst made contact with his escort here, and informed him that the man was definitely not in the canal. A police stakeout was then placed on the subject's home, and within two hours he was apprehended. He had planned to dump the cars for insurance. The witness on the bridge had been so shocked at the sight of the cars going over the bank that he had not seen the driver jump from the car before it left the road.

A Bloodhound doesn't need a well-worn piece of clothing to establish a subject's scent. Sometimes very brief contact with an object will leave enough scent to lead a mantrailer to the object of the search. One such case took place the night a lumberyard near Lockport was burglarized.

The lumberyard was equipped with a burglar alarm which rang at the police department, and when it sounded that night a car immediately left for the scene. When the men investigated, they found that the burglar had committed his crime in haste and made his escape. Tolhurst and Cleo were called, and arrived perhaps fifteen minutes later.

Scanning the area for something that would give Cleo the scent, Tolhurst found a spot behind the building where the burglar had picked a rock from the ground and thrown it through the window. There were three finger holes in the mud; and they started Cleo on the trail. When her head was dropped above them and she was given the command to trail, she reacted instantly, and with such speed and enthusiasm that her owner was certain that the suspect was not far ahead.

New York's famous Troop "K" is still actively using Bloodhounds in law enforcement and search and rescue. Here are Troopers Knapp (left) and Krug with their mantrailing partners.

Courtesy, New York State Police

Trooper Krug leads a mantrailer from the special carrier Troop "K" uses to transport the hounds.

Courtesy, New York State Police

Troop "K's" future with Bloodhound seems certain, as witnessed by this litter of future mantrailers with Trooper Howe.

Courtesy, New York State Police

55

One police officer, a Sergeant Daniel Harrington, accompanied the team. When Cleo led them around the building they found the area was completely surrounded by a four-and-one-half-foot woven-wire fence. Harrington went over, and Tolhurst lifted Cleo over to him and followed. Cleo was wild to go; the trail was obviously hot. It was about three in the morning, but the men ran after the hound without a light, in hopes of overtaking and surprising the fugitive.

They came to a railroad track which ran parallel to the Erie Barge Canal, and Cleo ran down the track. They had traveled about five hundred yards when they heard a noise in the brush off to the side, between the railroad track and the canal, which was about one hundred yards away. Cleo paid no attention, however, but pulled forward.

"There's something over there," Harrington said.

"Maybe there is," Tolhurst replied, "but we're not going over. It could be a deer or a dog, and Cleo isn't interested."

Soon afterward they came to a road, and then the hound turned and headed back in the direction from which they had come, trailing between the canal and the railroad. This time there was a sudden change in her attitude that told her owner, "We've got him!" As plainly as speech, she signaled with her tail when she was approaching her subject, and Tolhurst passed the warning to Harrington. "Watch out, we're close!"

They had progressed about fifty feet when suddenly Cleo froze in her tracks, raised her head and winded; then like a flash she wheeled around. There lay the suspect in the grass, right at Tolhurst's side. The men handcuffed him and took him back to the police car, but the experience was frightening. How did he ever get back there? He could have had a knife or a gun, and it could have been very dangerous.

The next morning, he returned to the scene with a detective, and they reviewed the case. "Which way did the dog face?" the detective asked. Tolhurst told him, and the detective walked forward about fifteen feet to a clump of bushes. When he parted them he found a pillowcase, containing the loot of the burglary.

Analyzing the situation, they concluded that the man had been hiding the material there when the police team went past on the railroad tracks, as that was approximately where they had heard the noise. The wind must have been blowing the other way, so Cleo did not scent him. He had crawled away and tried to make his escape after they passed, but the brush was thick, movement would have been noisy. Cleo had come in on the pool scent from the spot in which he was lying, waiting for them to pass, until his scent in the grass had overpowered it. Since then, Tolhurst never forgets that danger when he trails at night.

In addition to training his own mantrailing Bloodhounds and a little Beagle which he trained as a narcotics detector, Bill Tolhurst has helped train hundreds of Bloodhounds for members of the NPBA and others. His sons, who played the part of trail runners when he started with Cleo, grew into experienced Bloodhound trainers and handlers also, and until they moved away from home they worked as part of his Bloodhound team.

Bill sparked a controversy when he decided to develop his third Blood-hound, Tona, into a multipurpose animal, capable not only of trailing, but of protecting him, locating cadavers, and when necessary, working off lead. Traditionalists held the view that the Bloodhound was not overly intelligent and that more than one function would endanger a one-track mind. Bill and Tona proved these traditionalists wrong on both counts. It was with Tona that Bill developed the technique for training dogs to locate cadavers.

Toward the end of the 1980s, after over one thousand successful searches, Tolhurst was forced by health to reduce the amount of trailing he was involved in. He has compensated by devoting more time to conducting seminars all around the country, helping the new generation of bloodhounders acquire the necessary skills to take over the job. He became a founding member of North American Search Dog Network (NASDN) and in 1990 was elected president.

In 1984 he collaborated with Lena F. Reed in writing *Manhunters! Hounds of The Big T*, based upon the first twenty-five years of his Bloodhound work. It gives the Bloodhound fancy a source of training information not available else-where, covering drug detection and cadaver search training, as well as the mantrailing experience.

SHERIFF WILLIAM H. WEISTER AND PAT AND MAGGIE

Like many another Bloodhound man, Sheriff William H. Weister of Lewis County, Washington, became interested in Bloodhounds when a child was lost in his area. In spite of an extensive search, it was weeks later before the case was closed with the tragic discovery of the child's body. That was back in 1955. Bill Weister decided that what the area needed was mantrailing Bloodhounds. He was convinced that had one been available, that child would have been saved. Soon afterward, he bought his first Bloodhound.

Weister made an excellent choice in the selection of this hound. Pat was sired by Doc Holiday, who, with his mother, Queen Guinevere of Laureloak, and Big Nose Kate, led their owner, Norman Wilson, on the world-record fourteen-day-old trail in 1954. His pedigree traced back to several of Dr. Whit-ney's White Isle hounds, including Trooper of White Isle, famous both as a mantrailer and as a sire of BIS winners. He was a beautiful black and tan hound, with a magnificent head, and the nose that did credit to his ancestors. In honor of that first Pat, Bill Weister has named his succeeding male hounds Pat.

Pat I had originally been sold to a man in Oregon, where his education had been started. Weister's previous training experience with hounds had been in the use of animals for cougar hunting. He obtained a booklet on Bloodhound training, and combining the information it contained with his own ideas, he set to work at developing the mantrailer that sold him on Bloodhounds. In later years, he was to breed his own hounds to provide the replacement puppies he needed.

Sheriff Weister likes to start training his puppies at about eight weeks, rewarding them with tidbits and praise. After a year and a half of intensive schooling, he has a dog that he considers as foolproof as an animal can be. It will then be able to follow a trail at least three days old through a crowd of people and lead unfailingly to the one person it is hunting. He has no sex preference in his mantrailers; both sexes have performed outstandingly for him.

Bill Weister was a patrolman in the small Pacific Coast logging town of Raymond when he obtained his first Bloodhound. The region is sparsely populated, mountainous and heavily forested—the wet, junglelike forest of the Pacific Northwest. It's a great place for getting lost. Lewis County, where he later moved as a deputy in the sheriff's department before working on up to the top, is more of the same. The Bloodhounds were frequently called upon to find lost children, hunters, senile wanderers, and of course, the criminally inclined. His albums bulge with pictures and clippings, and letters from grateful parents whose youngsters were safely returned to them by Pat or Maggie. One tiny tot, he recalls, was hanging helplessly from the briars of one of those wild blackberry patches so prevalent in western Washington.

And then there were the tragedies searchers would like to forget—the victims of accident or murder. One of these cases rates in Sheriff Weister's mind as an outstanding trailing job.

An elk hunter, sixty-seven-year-old I. B. Walters, had been reported missing, in the rugged Trap Creek area of Pacific County. Search parties included trained woodsmen, forestry department men, sheriff's deputies and a Coast Guard helicopter. After four unsuccessful days, the missing man's son came to Weister, then a Raymond police officer, and asked if he would try his Bloodhounds.

Weister took Maggie, a three-year-old black and tan female. Accompanied by the son, they went to the lost man's truck. Here they found a sock which was to start Maggie on the trail.

It had rained hard for the four days since the man was known missing, certainly not the best conditions for following a trail of that age. Maggie found it, though, and led the two men by a roundabout trail about two and a half miles through dense woods to an area above a canyon. Here the trail seemed lost.

The next day the two men brought Maggie back to the spot where the trail had ended, and this time she led out onto a log over the canyon, at the bottom of which a creek flowed. She went only partway over the log, and then indicated that her interest led below. Two loggers climbed down to the creek in the canyon and found the elk hunter's body lying in the creek. Judging from the wound on his head it seemed that he had slipped from the log, been knocked unconscious by the fall, and died there.

In another case Weister's Bloodhound displayed the uncanny ability of the breed to pick up the scent of a criminal where no scent article was available to guide him. In this case, a fugitive, wanted by the FBI, had made his escape by car one night, abandoned the car, and took to the woods. By the time the Bloodhound was called the next morning, the car had been towed away and a small army of law officers had trampled over the area. "Go get 'em, Pat!" Weister ordered the hound. Pat circled excitedly, and then headed off into the woods. Within twenty minutes, he led to the base of a tall and dense fir tree, where he treed.

William Weister and Maggie at the happy ending of a successfully followed trail. This little boy was found hanging from the briars of a blackberry patch about a mile from his home.

Nothing could be seen among the branches, but Weister had faith in his hound. He called one of his deputies who was carrying a shotgun, and speaking loudly, he instructed him, "Fire a few shots up into that tree."

The response was instant. "Don't shoot!" a voice called from above. "I'm coming down." A few moments later the escapee was again in custody.

How did the hound do it? A man who is frightened, or under extreme emotional stress, Weister explains, discharges a high level of adrenaline into his blood. The result is distinctively strong scent, which attracts the hounds. This case resulted in a commendation letter from the FBI.

An interesting highlight of Sheriff Weister's Bloodhound experience took place in September 1963, when he and his hounds were asked by the army to demonstrate the possibilities of Bloodhound use in war zones. As part of army exercise "Operation Helping Hand" Weister and the hounds trailed "guerillas" and "infiltrators" through the Olympic rain forests. In one problem the trail was started after four hours of rain; yet the hounds led to an encampment where fifty "guerillas" were captured. The military men were much impressed, and the exercise ended with a special commendation from the army.

A humorous note, from the viewpoint of Bloodhound owners, was added to the exercise by the leaflets dropped by plane to urge the "guerillas" to surrender. It closed with the warning

> Ten Bloodhounds are being used to hunt YOU. The SAF Commander at first would not allow the use of these dogs because of their vicious nature BUT because of your leaders he has approved their use. The first time these dogs were used they followed and located two of your men. We regret that both of these men are now on the critical list at the Fort Lewis Hospital. PROTECT YOURSELF . . . If you see or hear these dogs following YOU, climb the nearest tree as fast as you can. These dogs will attack with little or no provocation.

Weister smiles about that. "I never had a Bloodhound that would attack anyone," he says. "Once I tried to train one to be vicious for criminal work, but I couldn't do it. They just love people."

GEORGE TALBOT AND THE HOUNDS OF DEER LODGE PRISON

Mention of "Penitentiary Hounds" may make the hair rise on the back of your neck. You've heard stories of the vicious packs that relentlessly trail Paul Newman types and return them to jail with a few pounds of flesh missing.

The hounds that served during most of the last thirty years at the Deer Lodge, Montana, prison weren't of that kind. They spent as much time and enthusiasm hunting for lost children and hunters in Montana and surrounding states, with never a nibble on the record.

George Talbot was the first to decide that trained Bloodhounds could be an asset to his region. A rancher in Corvallis, Montana, he was aware of the

George Talbot, Montana mantrailer, rests a moment with Happy and Joy.   *Peterson*

number of people lost annually in the surrounding mountains, including Yellowstone and Glacier national parks. In 1946 he laid out $400 he couldn't really afford for two Bloodhound puppies that he didn't know how to train. His children named them Joy and Happy, because they looked so sad.

Talbot thought the Bloodhounds would be a hobby, but before the pups were a year old and fully trained, he was already being called from all over the state to help in searches for lost persons. The next year his local community formed a foundation to cover his costs and help support the expenses of the hounds. Happy went blind at six months, but until he died of old age at ten years, he trailed as well as his brother, who was still working a year later. In those first eleven years, Talbot and his hounds took part in over six hundred searches in Montana, surrounding states, and Canada.

If the hounds were called soon enough—from a day to a week after the person disappeared, depending upon weather conditions—they rarely failed to make it look so easy that it was often unappreciated. However, Talbot has faced the same problem brought up by so many handlers of Bloodhounds; they are called in as a last resort, after the area has been trampled by numerous search parties, evidence has been destroyed, and too often, it is too late to save the victim.

As the fame of his hounds spread, the Montana Sheriffs' and Peace Officers' Association placed Talbot on a retainer plus expenses, so that he could always feel free to leave his work when needed. In 1955 he was made escape officer of the Montana State Prison at Deer Lodge. However, if a call came to search for a lost child, that came first with Talbot, unless a criminal had escaped who presented a danger to the community.

Talbot emphasized the importance of the partnership between the handler and his hound. While the hound is using his nose, the man should be on the lookout for visual evidence that someone has passed that way—footprints, burnt matches, candy bar wrappers, broken brush. If the trail is that of a criminal, he might observe signs that the man is nearby and be prepared to protect himself and his hound.

The greatest danger to the lost person is his own fear; time after time lost hunters have been found dead who carried with them, and often threw away, all the supplies they needed to sustain life. In searches for little children, the factor most infrequently realized is the distance even a three-year-old can travel in a few hours. In three hours a child may travel as far as nine miles, making the search area a circle eighteen miles across, or more than two hundred and fifty square miles. A ground search by human means alone could never recover the child. In forested land, an exhausted child sleeping under a tree or next to a log is invisible from the air. Only the nose of a trained Bloodhound can start the search in the right direction.

Talbot estimates it takes two years of training to make a good mantrailer, and two more to make it really a hotshot. An intelligent, willing hound is always learning something new about his trade. But the cardinal rule it must learn is never to leave the assigned scent for any other that may cross it.

Bill and Charles Nimmo with two of the hounds who kept the men home at Montana's Deer Lodge Prison.

It takes constant training to keep a hound in top condition, and the convicts didn't mind laying trails. It is an "occupational disease" with them, Talbot said, to believe that with practice they will learn some way to fool the hounds and get away. However, the only ones who ever succeeded were three who made their break while the hounds were off on another case.

One case in which George Talbot figured, and which is especially worth mentioning as it carries a warning to all who may use their hounds in mantrailing, was a murder case in 1949 in Forsyth, Montana. The victim was shot through the window as he sat in his home. A sharp-eyed sheriff found footsteps outside, and since it was late in the day, he stationed guards to protect the area until Talbot and his hounds could arrive the next morning. They were there at daybreak, and the actual trailing took only twenty minutes. The trail crossed the highway and led to a wire fence.

Since there was a gate one hundred feet down the road, Talbot took the dogs there and through the gate, returning to the place where the man had climbed the fence. The hounds went back to the trail, and followed it about a quarter mile to a house. There they identified the man who came to the door. It was the brother-in-law of the murdered man.

Based in part on the Bloodhound evidence, the man was convicted and sent to the Deer Lodge prison. His conviction was upheld on its first appeal, but the case went to the Montana Supreme Court, where a very fine point of law arose. According to the Montana law, the trail followed must be unbroken. This would have ruled out the cases of drop trailing related in chapter 2, and indicates a lack of understanding of the ability of the Bloodhound. The defense argued that when Talbot took his hounds to the gate to get them through the fence, the trail was thereby broken and evidence presented became inadmissible. Due to this judge's interpretation of a technicality, the conviction was reversed, and the accused was released after having spent five years in the Deer Lodge prison. It makes a good argument for a pair of wire cutters in the handler's pocket.

WILLIAM AND CHARLES NIMMO, RED CON AND GUY

The next Bloodhound handler at the Deer Lodge prison was William Nimmo, who, with his son Charles and a pair of Bloodhounds, helped convince the prison inmates that an attempt to leave the premises led to nothing but a good deal of rough exercise and maybe a few meals missed. The Nimmos, with Red Con and Guy in the harness, made short work of running down the would-be travelers. Their fame was spread through the prison in verse, and a letter from the warden to Bill Nimmo credits the reputation of his hounds with having a wholesome effect upon the roving tendencies of the inmates. He has also received letters of appreciation from the National Park Service and the FBI for his assistance in cases under their jurisdiction.

Bill Nimmo served as Bloodhound handler at Deer Lodge from 1963 until 1974, using four hounds during this period. By then, he said, he was past sixty, the mountains got too high and steep, and Montana terrain became too rough.

The work of the mantrailing Bloodhound can be as current as today's headlines. When James Earl Ray escaped from Brushy Mountain State Prison on June 12, 1977, it was the young Bloodhound bitch Sandy who let the search party to the fugitive's hiding place.

United Press International

THE CAPTURE OF JAMES EARL RAY

There are still people, not familiar with the Bloodhound as a mantrailer, who think that the breed's use ended with prohibition. On the contrary, the Bloodhound's ongoing service to society, as we have seen, is as current as this morning's headlines. This fact was graphically emphasized on June 13, 1977 by the capture of James Earl Ray from Brushy Mountain State Prison in Petros, Tennessee.

Fifty-four hours before Ray's memorable capture, he had escaped from Brushy Mountain with two other inmates. A massive manhunt was launched which included helicopters, radio communication and considerable firepower. In spite of all this, James Earl Ray was located and returned to custody through the efforts of a Bloodhound.

The canine heroine of this drama was a fourteen-month-old hound named Sandy. She was part of a six-dog Pikeville dog team and was handled in the pursuit by Sammy Joe Chapman, an officer at Brushy Mountain.

Sandy, with another hound named Little Red, struck the scent of Ray after being brought in as fresh replacements for the first team of hounds. They pursued Ray for three hours through some of the most rugged country imaginable. At times it seemed that the capture was imminent, but the desperate fugitive managed to put distance between himself and the pursuers at the last minute and was off again. At times the hounds and Ray were so close that the six-man force following could hear Ray crashing through the woods.

A dwindling endurance was Ray's final undoing as he collapsed on the bank of the New River, eight miles from Brushy Mountain. Before the hounds finally caught up with him, Ray covered himself with the previous autumn's rotting leaves. This vain effort at camouflage did not deter the hounds in the slightest. Soon Sandy came upon the leaf pile and moments later the convicted assassin was again in custody.

It proved again that, as in years past, the Bloodhound is one of the lawman's most valuable assets. Sandy and her kind earned front-page headlines the next day and the wholehearted thanks of a grateful nation.

MICHELE PEARCE AND MEGGUN

Michele Pearce is a police K–9 handler in DeKalb County in northeast Alabama. She has worked mantrailing Bloodhounds for eleven years (as of 1990) along with a K–9 patrol dog, and the abilities of these dogs make an unbeatable combination in criminal work. For the last five years she has been breeding Bloodhounds as well, and she is proud of the fact that her working mantrailers are also show champions. She agrees heartily with these authors that the Standard of the breed describes the hound best able to do the work of the breed.

One example of that ability was the trail run by her Ch. Windy City Meggun of Shiloh, ABC Bloodhound Hall of Fame, Dam of Merit, Top Producer.

Texarkana, Arkansas, had experienced a two-year reign of terror by a serial rapist. The police had run out of options when the twelfth rape took place on a February morning. They called Michele Pearce for help. She asked them to preserve the scene as well as possible, and started out.

The weather was extremely windy after a severe thunderstorm. The temperature was about forty degrees Fahrenheit. The scene of the crime was a run-down neighborhood; the victim was a sixty-nine-year-old woman. The crime occurred at approximately 3:00 A.M., and Pearce was called shortly after 9:30 A.M. She and her hound arrived at noon. The house resembled a kitty-litter box: filthy, and occupied by about one hundred cats. Meggun hates cats!

The police had already been through the house, but the point of entry, a window above an air-conditioning unit, had not been contaminated. The rapist had broken out the window, put a chair under it, and climbed from that onto the air conditioner and through the window.

Meggun was started on the chair and air conditioner. She sniffed them briefly, and off she went. Once in the harness she forgot cats and everything else, including three alleys with chained pit bulls, huge dead rats, and other distractions. Finally she came to the end of an alley at an intersection, and the trail ended. She cast in a huge circle several times, but her actions made it clear to her handler that the suspect had entered a car and left the area. Pearce advised the detectives of her interpretation. They videotaped the area of the trail and broadcast a report on Crimestoppers, giving the description of the man, time of the crime, and the area of the trail.

That same day an elderly man called the police to say he had given a ride home to a man who fit the description. He had picked him up where the Blood-hound ended the trail. When the police took the suspect into custody he confessed to the rape, and to eleven other unsolved rapes.

Michele Pearce especially cherishes the letter of thanks she received from that police department. It was the last trail Meggun ran before retiring to be the house pet who was a show champion, working mantrailer, and mother and grandmother of Group winners and mantrailers.

MARLENE AURAND AND LOPP

Marlene Aurand is a Concordia, Kansas, police officer who took her hobby of breeding Bloodhounds onto the job by training them and herself as mantrailers. She was a K–9 handler with drug-detecting Labradors, but now she also serves as special deputy with Bloodhounds for seven Kansas counties. Trained Blood-hounds are scarce in that area; the penitentiary has some, but it is a four- or five-hour drive to meet and train with her nearest-known handler-friend Bill Goodell in Anderson County, in southeast Kansas. When she first began training her hounds she had a problem finding trail runners other than her husband and children. Sometimes a local man, hungry for a home-cooked dinner, would run a trail for her hounds. Practice in the city attracted too many sightseers. The police demanded that she notify them in advance so they would know they didn't have a problem on their hands.

Aurand's mantrailers have pedigrees that go back to many of the famous old hounds, American and British. She began training Lopp when he was an eight-week-old puppy. In March of 1987 when he was just a year old he made the headlines with his first case. A sixty-one-year-old woman had become disoriented while driving, and ended up stuck in the mud several miles in the wrong direction. Fortunately, she was accompanied by her Boston Terrier. A plate of cupcakes staved off hunger for both of them, and she stayed in her car.

When the woman failed to return home, her family called the police, and a search party with four-wheel-drive pickups spent several hours that night looking in the area where she was expected to be. The next morning Marlene Aurand was asked to try the Bloodhound, and Lopp promptly indicated he had a trail in exactly the opposite direction. The sheriff believed him. A helicopter was sent ahead and the missing woman was rescued while Lopp still had his nose to the trail.

A year later Lopp and his younger half sister Sassy had aided in six arrests in four different counties, and in locating missing persons. Since then, their work has become more diversified, frequent and far-reaching. One night Aurand and her husband drove eight hours with their hounds to Sioux Falls, South Dakota, where an elderly lady with Alzheimer's disease had wandered away from her nursing home. Sassy trailed to the river, where the body was found.

In another case Marlene Aurand teamed up with Bill Goodell in locating a pair of burglars. The trail was eight miles long, the temperature was one hundred degrees Fahrenheit with 90 percent humidity. The two teams took turns, trailing for a mile each, and the two criminals went to jail for five to twenty years.

When Aurand and her hound go on a trail she carries some extra equipment: spare lead and harness, canteen, flashlight with extra batteries and a weapon. The leash is hooked to her belt to leave her hands free. The trail may lead through dangerous terrain, and a hostile subject may be anywhere. She strongly recommends that anyone doing this type of mantrailing should complete the reserve deputy course and be qualified with a weapon. It increases your own safety and that of your police escort, and it helps you understand why police act and feel as they do. She has known some civilian search and rescue people to do things which could have gotten them or their police escort killed. Another criticism she has of many beginners is that they are not in good physical condition and could not survive a lengthy trail.

While mantrailing work is exciting, many hard hours of training must precede any actual work. Consistent training with the hound is absolutely essential. Puppies in training must be taken into every environment where they may trail, so that when they are on a search, they are not distracted by something unfamiliar. The Aurand hounds love police stations, sirens and flashing red lights; those people in uniform are their buddies. They are trained to travel in their crates; they don't get flung around or injured in a speeding police car. Aurand frequently videotapes training periods; it's a great way to see where you might have failed in reading your hound while you are trying to keep your footing, or avoid a bramble across your face.

Frequently Ray Aurand runs as backup with his wife on the rescue cases. "I can't cook," he explains. "I want to be sure my cook comes back."

LARRY HARRIS AND SABLE

County Copper Able Sable was born December 17, 1986. She is a red Bloodhound, partner to Orange County, California, Reserve Deputy Larry Harris. She was only seven months old, to the day, when she made her first rescue.

The call came in at 2:30 A.M.—a young man had left a suicide note. His vehicle had been located in one of the canyons in the rugged Cleveland National Forest. When the team arrived, the pup was scented on the vehicle's seat, and she immediately took trail through the parking lot, across the highway and up the mountain to a place where three or four trails merged. Here there was pool scent; possibly the man had rested there deciding which way to go next. Presently Sable straightened out the trail and continued, until Harris and his two teammates spotted the subject, still alive. He was unwilling, however, to be approached, and it took an hour of persuasion before he agreed to let the hound approach and complete her identification. The man finally agreed to return; a week later he called to thank the team for saving his life.

Sable is owned by the county, but she lives with her trainer-handler. Harris was fortunate in having the training assistance of Keith Tolhurst, son of Bill Tolhurst, who was at that time an Orange County deputy. He grew up helping his father train and run Bloodhounds, and that may account for Sable's speedy success, after only two months of training. That first trail was nine and one-half hours old, in the middle of a cold night, and took about an hour to run. Her training had been limited to trails about twenty or thirty minutes old.

It wasn't long before Sable was successful on her second and third criminal case trails. In the second case she was scented on the seat of a chair in the office of a large apartment complex. In spite of all the other scents present, she trailed out of the office, through the complex, across a street to a restaurant that the suspect had entered. From there she went to the parking lot where she identified the man standing in a group of five people.

In her third find, soon afterward, she followed two suspects who had abandoned a stolen vehicle and fled on foot. Again, she was scented on the vehicle. Trailing down alleys, across streets, she led her handler onto a three-car ferry, which they rode across the bay. When they disembarked from the ferry Sable again picked up the trail and located the two suspects, completing the identification by jumping on them.

Larry Harris now trains and uses two additional Bloodhounds, Duke and Dutchess, and all three are deputized by the Orange County sheriff. Although Harris is a reserve deputy, he is also a volunteer. In the beginning of February 1990 he wrote that Bloodhound work was getting busier all the time. In the past month he had been out on thirteen cases.

Down the long corridors of Bloodhound history, working mantrailers and dedicated volunteers have been instrumental in countless life-saving rescues. Their amazing, true achievements are often more exciting than fiction.

4

The Mantrailers—
The Volunteers

IN OCTOBER 1954 a new record in mantrailing was established by a sad-faced trio named Doc Holiday, Queen Guinevere of Laureloak and Big Nose Kate.

A man, his wife and their thirteen-year-old son had gone deer hunting in the wet, dense forests of western Oregon. A week later they had not returned, and the sheriff's posse began a search. The family car was found, but several days later there was still no sign of the hunters.

NORMAN W. WILSON AND A MANTRAILING RECORD

In Los Gatos, California, a Bloodhound breeder named Norman W. Wilson heard about the search on the radio. Wilson, a former navy pilot, had started training Bloodhounds after a friend of his was lost in the Everglades and found by Bloodhounds. He realized that this was an old trail, but considering that lives were at stake, he contacted the Oregon authorities and volunteered to bring his Bloodhounds. His help was welcomed, and he flew north to the search scene.

By now the trail was 322 hours old, and there was little hope. Using a woman's stocking found in the abandoned car, Wilson started his hounds. The trail was difficult, and it was fifteen hours before the search party was led through the woods to the bodies of the three missing people, victims of exposure.

Since then a new record was set by a hound called Clyde, owned by Bill Grimm, a coal miner who handled his hound for the Marshall County, West

Jim Shaffer with Brandy Acres Mrs. Peel on the trail.
Courtesy, National Police Bloodhound Association

Virginia, Sheriff's Office. Clyde had a record of almost three hundred successful searches when he died. Outstanding among them was trailing a lost hunter who had been out for seventeen days after over three and one-half feet of snow had fallen. Another exceptional trail was thirty-five miles long. Bill Grimm is now retired from Bloodhound handling, but to the best of our knowledge his record still stands as the oldest fully documented trail.

JIM AND BECKY SHAFFER AND EMMA

The Silver Moon Drive-In Theater in Lewisburg, Pennsylvania, was presenting its annual Labor Day dusk-to-dawn show on September 1, 1974. The feature movie was *Cops and Robbers*.

Suddenly at 9:30 P.M. the make-believe became real when two men appeared at the back door of the ticket booth. One was holding a sawed-off shotgun, and they demanded the money. They got it, and escaped by car.

The men drove to an abandoned quarry in the country. Here they set fire to the car, which they had stolen earlier in the day, and left the scene on foot. Burning the car may have been their idea of destroying evidence, but instead it proved to be their undoing. It brought the fire department to the scene, and led to the identification of the car as the one used in the theater robbery. It was also identified as a stolen car, and evidence led to the two men, who were arrested in their homes later that night. However, the gun used in the theater holdup and the money taken were not found with them.

The county sheriff, borough police and state police searched the area around the burned car throughout the night, but found neither evidence nor money. When morning came, they called Jim and Becky Shaffer of Dewart, Pennsylvania, and requested the help of a Bloodhound. At 9:30 A.M., September 2, the Shaffers arrived at the scene, accompanied by Brandy Acres Mrs. Peel, better known as Emma, a two-and-one-half-year-old liver and tan. It was her job to trace the route taken from the car, and with luck, find the loot.

Using scent material taken from the two suspects in jail, Emma was started at the site of the car fire. The vehicle was a total loss, and had been removed.

Emma made a few casts, and promptly began working a trail away from the area. She became very aroused as she approached a clump of bushes, but one of the officers present stated that he had already checked that area out thoroughly. The hound worked on about twenty feet, but insisted upon returning to the clump of bushes, determined to explore further. Excitedly, she began creeping beneath them, and soon the loot was in the hands of the police. It had been wrapped in a towel, together with the gun, and then placed in a plastic bag to protect it from the rain of the night before.

With that bit of business off her mind, Emma proceeded to trail down a paved road toward Route 15. She lost the trail at the point where a dirt lane joined the road. Here manure had been washed from the fields and covered the road. It was later learned that the men had gone to this lane to catch a ride away from the area.

The evidence of the gun and the loot, recovered by a trailing Bloodhound using scent articles from the men in prison, convinced the suspects that they were unquestionably identified. They confessed to the car theft, armed robbery, arson and several other unsolved burglaries in the area.

Emma was only following the family trade. Her mother, The Hermitage Hello Dolly, works with the Sullivan County Sheriff's Department. The Shaffers own another mantrailer, Knightcall's Noble Obie, a black and tan male. Both dogs are on call through the Pennsylvania State Police and other law enforcement agencies in their area.

Reprinted courtesy American Bloodhound Club Bulletin and James and Rebecca Shaffer.

DR. AND MRS. WALTER MEGAHAN AND LANCELOT

Although Bloodhounds have an international reputation as mantrailers, it is only rarely that one hears of their use in trailing lost animals. Perhaps this is due to the fact that owners of mantrailers hesitate to allow their hounds to trail animals for fear that they may then not remain true to a human trail if an interesting animal scent crosses it. Yet occasionally a Bloodhound may be so used, and the results may be well worth mentioning.

One such performance was the achievement of Landrover Lancelot, bred by Charles and Frances Rowland. This took place in November of 1967, when he was a seven-and-one-half-month-old puppy. The trail he followed equaled the world record mantrailing achievement of Norman Wilson's hounds in 1954. The lost victim was a valuable racing Greyhound named Stop Loss.

On October 29, 1967, Stop Loss was on his way to Florida with twenty other Greyhounds to complete in the winter race meeting. Somehow he was lost in the vicinity of Boise, Idaho. The owners offered a reward, and an extensive search was conducted.

Dr. and Mrs. Walter Megahan, of Boise, owners of Lancelot, were approached to aid in the search. They hesitated, as the pup was young and his training was limited; and by now it was November 12. However, Biggy, as he was called, knew exactly what to do. In spite of the age of the trail and the dry desert conditions, he found the trail of the Greyhound, and followed it to the place where it had been shot and hidden in the sagebrush.

Lancelot, unfortunately, was a victim of the inhumanity of man. As the Megahans returned from a show circuit, this magnificent young hound, a winner in the show ring as well as on the trail, collapsed from poisoning.

"RANGER" THOMPSON AND THE TUNA FISH CAN

On May 14, 1974, a canine first was achieved by a big red Bloodhound named Cascade's Ranger. On that day Ranger was the guest of honor of the Hayden Lake, Idaho, Chamber of Commerce and became the recipient of the annual Smokey the Bear award. This national award for an outstanding accomplishment in preventing forest fires has always been presented to a human; but this year the bear's best friend was a hound.

Ranger is the proud possession of Larry and Virginia Thompson of Hayden Lake, in the Idaho panhandle. He was sired by Am. & Can. Ch. Boomerang of Dakota, a hound with a record of search and rescue work in western Washington. He was barely three months old when the Thompsons began his mantrailing lessons, and he was only twenty-one months old on the night of August 28, 1973, when he earned the award for which he was honored.

Ranger had already given evidence of his skill. Two weeks earlier he had been called out twice during the same day with success both times. In an early morning rescue, he saved the life of an elderly man who had gone for a walk the night before and became disoriented. The trail crossed a freeway—a difficult trailing feat due to auto fumes and dispersal of the scent by speeding vehicles. He found the missing man, by now too weak to move or call for help, lying in a ditch beside a railroad track. That same evening the hound followed a five-day-old trail of an accident victim through the dark in the rugged, mountainous area above Lake Coeur d'Alene.

The call on August 28 asked for help in locating a firebug. The suspect was a fifty-three-year-old man who had spent half his life either in mental hospitals or in prisons for various crimes. He had been hiding in the forest near Priest Lake, Idaho. During the night he would raid the summer cabins around the lake, stealing food and other goods. His carelessly abandoned campfires had started three or four forest fires. The summer was hot and dry; the pitch-filled evergreen forests were like tinder. A few smoldering coals, fanned by the hot wind, could reach the dry needles that covered the ground, and in a flash the holocaust could be raging through the treetops.

The sheriff and the forest rangers had been looking for the man responsible for the recent fires. About dusk one evening a forest ranger, driving one of the back roads, recognized the wanted man as he ran across the road ahead of him. He stopped his truck and ran in pursuit, but the man vanished into the dark forest, dropping a sleeping bag as he ran. The ranger found his abandoned campsite, the fire still smoldering.

For three days the sheriff and the rangers kept watch on the campsite, hoping the man would return, while at the same time searching the area for him. Then they called for a Bloodhound.

Larry and Virginia Thompson, and Dave Marsan of nearby Coeur d'Alene, are members of Northwest Bloodhounds Search and Rescue. This recently founded volunteer organization is dedicated to training mantrailing Bloodhounds and providing them for emergency needs. Responding to a call, the three people and the Thompsons' eager young Bloodhound drove north to the Priest Lake area. They arrived there about dusk.

The sheriff brought the sleeping bag dropped by the wanted man three days before. Marsan, a big, young logger who was to handle the hound that night, buckled onto him the trailing harness which turns him from a king-sized bundle of playfulness into 140 pounds of single-minded dedication to a trail. The sleeping

Virginia Thompson with Cascade's Ranger. Ranger was awarded the Smokey the Bear Award in recognition of his part in the capture of a dangerous arsonist. This is the first time the award was not won by a human being. The pursuit and capture are detailed in the text.

bag had been in the sheriff's office since it was found, and at least a dozen people had handled it, adding their scents. Seeking an area where the scent was not mixed with those of others, Marsan turned the sleeping bag inside out and presented it to the hound. "Find!" he commanded.

The Bloodhound seemed confused and uncertain. The men could only assume that too many scents conflicted. Finally, however, he led them through the woods to a summer cabin, where they found a stack of sleeping bags of the type the wanted man had dropped. Ranger sniffed them thoroughly and then went around the cabin, sniffing here and there. They could only guess that the fugitive had not yet used the bag, and wonder if the hound had backtrailed to the cabin from which it had been stolen.

Discouraged, Thompson asked the sheriff, "Wasn't there anything around that camp of his that we could use for a scent article?"

The sheriff thought a bit. "Well," he recalled, "there was a tuna fish can he must have eaten from. But we buried it three days ago when we put out his campfire."

"Go get it!" Thompson urged. "And be sure you don't touch it; pick it up with a stick!"

Off dashed the sheriff to recover the can, while the men returned to the spot where the forest ranger had seen the man run across the road, and where Virginia Thompson shivered in her truck. The sheriff returned with the tuna fish can, and Dave Marsan took the hound's lead and held the can to his nose. "Find!" he commanded again.

"He looked at me as if I were crazy," Marsan related later. "It took three commands before he believed me—or else worked his way down through the tuna fish smell. Then he took off like a shot."

For five hours the two men followed the hound through the dark. Deputies accompanying them fell far behind. They were led to dozens of summer cabins, where the hound sniffed the doorknobs. The suspect was to verify the hound's nose when he told them later, "I didn't do anything wrong. I didn't break into any houses; I just went into ones that weren't locked."

Finally the time came when Thompson and Marsan could hear the sound of the fugitive crashing through the brush. They thought they had him trapped when he dived into the crawl space beneath a summer cabin. Then he slipped out the other side and began running again, with the two men and the hound hard on his trail. It ended when he turned to see how close they were, crashed headlong into a tree, and fell. The long, wearying chase was over.

Today the tuna fish can that started the hound on that manhunt hangs by a binder-twine bow from the wall of "Ranger's bedroom."

Originally printed in Dogs, *November 1974, by Lena F. Reed*

TOM MURPHY AND MOSES

In spite of the invaluable services performed by Bloodhounds across the country, they are still not widely appreciated. Old myths remain: that Bloodhounds are savage; that they are of no use in cities; that snow or rain end their usefulness. All these have been proven false. Another factor not always realized is that even in cases where a Bloodhound does not complete a trail, he may uncover evidence that will enable the police to solve a crime.

An outstanding example of this was provided by Tom Murphy, of Kingston, Ontario, Canada, and his hound, Moses. In October of 1965 this team traveled more than one thousand miles by plane, truck and canoe to the north Hudson Bay area. Although the trail was covered by fresh snow, Moses followed it far enough to uncover rifle shells which changed the case from missing person to murder, and led to the conviction of the man's partner.

JERRY YELK—MANTRAILING CARPENTER

Jerry Yelk has even more reason than most Bloodhound handlers to ruffle his feathers at the Hollywood version of the Bloodhound search, wherein the fugitive loses the hound by wading a stream. Two of his hounds were responsible for a new record in trailing through water, and their performance led to a Governor's Award for their owner.

Jerome J. Yelk of Wausau, Wisconsin, is a carpenter by trade and a Bloodhound handler by avocation. His father was a Bloodhound fancier before him, and Jerry was only thirteen when he worked his first Bloodhound mantrailing case to find a suicide victim. In the thirty-some years since then he has used his dogs over two thousand times on both criminal cases and searches for lost persons. Three times he was shot at by fugitives he trailed, but luck was always with him.

If the Hollywood writers could follow Jerry and his Bloodhounds, they would probably decide they couldn't use the material—nobody would believe some of those stories. In the police records, though, and with action pictures to back them up, the report has to be the truth, like the case that won him the Governor's Award. That took place in March 1969 when a Coast Guardsman, Boatswain's Mate 1/C Dallas Johnson, suffered a fatal heart attack while alone in a boat on the Manitowoc River. His body fell overboard and sank.

For five days a search was conducted for the body. Then Jerry Yelk and his Bloodhounds, King and Tony, were called in to help. The temperature, which remained below fifteen degrees Fahrenheit, added to the difficulty of the search; and the river was sixty feet deep in that area. Yelk took one Bloodhound into a boat, and began the search at the mouth of the river. The hound showed he had picked up the scent, and the boat was steered toward the direction he indicated. When he moved to one side or the other of the boat, the boat was turned in that direction. Finally, about half a mile from the starting point, a spot was reached where the hound tried to jump into the river. Jerry noted the spot, and returned to the mouth of the river to trade hounds and try again. The second hound repeated the performance of the first, again indicating a keen interest in the same spot in the river. Jerry Yelk felt certain the victim's body lay in the water below. Official photographs taken during the search plainly show one of the hounds leaning from the boat and straining to follow the scent into the water.

Jerry Yelk receiving an award in recognition of his service to the people of Wisconsin from Governor W. Knowles.

Polly (left) and King are two of the determined mantrailers that have worked with Jerry Yelk on numerous cases.

79

Divers searched the river in the area marked, but without success. Fourteen days later, the body rose to the surface fifty feet away. The scent had done a certain amount of drifting as it rose in the moving water of the river, Yelk believes. If the hounds could have finished that last sixty feet to the body they would have been right on course, a far cry from the Hollywood stories.

Jerry J. Yelk and his Bloodhounds have served the people of Wisconsin in every county but one, as well as solving cases in other states and Canada. In one widely publicized case, his hounds led him to a fugitive who was wanted for the murder of a police officer. Hundreds of officers and deputized men, together with helicopters and light planes, had combed two counties, but the man seemed to have faded away. On the seventh day of the search, Jerry Yelk volunteered to try his hand. His two Bloodhounds picked up the trail, and in five and one-half hours, led him to the murderer, lying semiconscious in a dense swamp. They brought to an end the most expensive criminal search of the times, and presented a powerful argument for the early use of Bloodhounds in similar work. The trouble seems to be, as Jerry says, "They don't get called as soon as they should be because men don't want to admit some old flop-eared hound can outsmart them," and often they are brought in only as a last resort.

Many of the trailing cases are searches for lost children. So far, Yelk has been relatively fortunate—in all but two cases they ended happily. Once a little girl was found drowned, and one little boy's body was found in the remains of a burned barn. While he has received letters of thanks from grateful parents, none has ever tried to keep in touch with him. "I can understand why," he says. "I bring back the memory of a nightmare in their lives." For this reason, he has never visited the families afterward. This sensitive interpretation offers a reasonable explanation for the experiences of other Bloodhound handlers in cases where the families have hurried away without even a word of thanks. Under the stress of a frightening experience, their only instinct is to get their child home.

Jerry has been written about in newspapers and magazines. He has received many honors and commendations for his work as a mantrailer, but the one that pleased him the most was presented by the National Police Officers Association, and was made out in the names of two of his hounds, Polly and King. As Jerry said, it was about time someone figured out that without the hounds he wouldn't be much of a mantrailer.

THE CASE OF THE MISSING TEENAGER

All who have answered the call for a mantrailing Bloodhound know the feeling that comes when the phone rings late at night. Will it be tragedy, or the opportunity to return some lost child to a distraught family? Or will it be a night of hard work and frustration with the prime reward being knowledge that your hounds have done a fine job? Frances Rowland tells of one such experience she shared with her husband and their hounds.

The phone call came at 11:00 P.M. A teenager had not returned from school. He had told the teacher he was sick, and asked permission to go to the school nurse. He had not returned to class, nor to his home, and the parents feared that he might have gone into the hilly, rocky area of the Adirondack foothills surrounding the school and been injured there.

We gave instructions for obtaining a scent article and bringing it to the school, and asked that the crowds of searchers be kept away. The trail was already ten hours cold.

The father and one other person were permitted to accompany us on the trail. Coon-hunting lighting equipment was strapped to our gear. The hounds were started where the lad was last seen in the building, quickly picked up a scent, and trailed to a closed door. We asked to have the door unlocked, and the hounds went directly to a desk, which we later learned was the desk of the missing youth. From this point, after checking two bystanders in the hall, they continued to the rest room; then down the back stairway of the school. The trail did not go to the nurse's room.

Once outside, the trail continued down a rocky hill. Here we changed hounds, as the bitch I had been handling was too fast and eager for me, fairly dragging me down the rocky hillside. The trail continued behind the bus garage and down a paved drive. Here they dropped their heads on occasion, until they reached the grass-covered area in front of the school.

At this point the trail led across the highway to a private drive; the hounds indicated that the boy had entered the darkened house, and then continued. Again crossing the highway, they proceeded some distance along the sidewalk to the village highway intersection. A group of searchers was congregated here, and for a while the hounds were puzzled until they worked out the line to the opposite corner, when again the highway was crossed, leading out of town. The trail ended at the bridge. However, the hounds showed no interest in the bridge railing or the water, so we felt confident in telling the father not to worry about injury to his son; we were sure he had been picked up in a car.

We returned to the school as a station wagon arrived; the driver informed us that he had given the boy a ride to a nearby town. To our relief, this was our own hometown.

By this time it was 2:00 A.M. At the new location we practiced drop trailing and started the hounds where the boy had supposedly left the car. The hounds picked up a scent leading to a closed restaurant, again indicating that he had entered and left, then worked their line to the railroad tracks heading south and eventually cut off to the main highway where he had apparently hitchhiked another ride. The time now was 4:00 A.M., and we gave up the search for the night.

Later that morning the boy returned home. He had slept behind a shopping center in a town fifteen miles south after his second episode of hitchhiking. He verified our secret suspicions when the hounds failed to trail to the nurse's office; his marks had been low, final exams were due, and he had been reprimanded by his parents. Before running away, he had picked up his yearbook at the darkened house the hounds had approached. The restaurant where they had indicated his entry was where he had stopped for coffee.

The other searchers who had never before seen trained Bloodhounds working a line repeated their praises for some time to come.

THE DAKOTA MANTRAILERS

The Vincent Breys have a special interest in the mantrailing Bloodhound. Contrary to the feeling of some show dog people that a show dog cannot be expected to be a working dog, they believe that a good animal should be able to perform the work for which his breed was developed. These are a few highlights on the Dakota Kennels trailing experiences.

Our first outstanding trailing Bloodhound was Am. & Can. Ch. Miss Happy Gelert of Dakota. She was our foundation bitch, and in addition to giving us our start as Bloodhound breeders, she proved to be an outstanding mantrailer, who served the police on many occasions. At least two of her sons, Am. & Can. Ch. Rye of Dakota and Am. & Can. Ch. Boomerang of Dakota followed in her footsteps.

Happy especially loved children; if anyone came into our home with a child Happy had to be locked up before they were allowed to leave with it. She also had definite objections to my disciplining of my own children; it had to be off to the kennel with Happy before a deserved swat could be administered to a small bottom. When a search involved a child she worked with an extra zeal; and when she found it, it was hers, and nobody but Vincent Brey had better pick it up.

Happy lived to an exceptional age for a Bloodhound. She was fourteen when cancer finally made it an act of mercy to put her down. She had failing eyesight due to old age for some time; but somehow, she was always able to spot a cat that might be so misguided as to approach the house. Any so foolish as to get within her reach was an endangered species. Neither did her poor vision reduce her joy in trailing; in June of 1973, when she was already twelve, we were called one night to help search for the two-year-old child of a deaf-mute couple. They were near hysteria in their helplessness at not even being able to call for the child.

Happy had not even been in harness for three years, as due to her age we had used Rye until his death. Still, she trailed as if she had been working daily.

The family's rural home was not too far from the river, and when the trail first turned in that direction Vince felt his stomach knot up with fear that it would end there. It was with considerable relief that he followed Happy as she swung away and out across the farmland. Before long the child, sleeping on the ground, was warmly greeted by a matronly Bloodhound who required all Vince's powers to convince her that she could not take it home and keep it.

In September 1974 we received a request for help from the police. A convict on parole was suspected of murder when the nude body of a woman known to have been seen with him was found in a shallow grave in a barnyard.

The man admitted that she had been with him, but insisted that she had died a natural death after a night of drinking, and that considering his status as a parolee, he had been terrified of reporting to the police. Instead, he had made an effort to conceal the body and hide her identity by burying her purse and clothing in other locations. The police hoped the hounds could find them, or any other evidence that might aid them in the case.

It had been a month since the woman's death and burial, and we had no real expectation that the hounds could find anything at that late date. We were given a bedroom slipper from her hotel room as a scent article, but did not know how long a scent would remain after an article was worn. However, we felt obligated to make an effort. Daughter Shelley took Ch. Lime Tree Libby of Dakota, Vince handled Ch. Pooh Bear of Dakota, and I took Happy, and we went to the farm where the body had been found. The dogs began casting around the area, when to my surprise, Happy began to dig. I was not at liberty at that time to give all the details, because the case was still being appealed; but each of the hounds furnished evidence which convinced the police they had grounds for arresting the man.

Although we have done some trailing work with several of our hounds, Happy and her son, Rye, were our two outstanding mantrailers. Rye lived for trailing; to the best of our knowledge, he never made a mistake. Only once was he temporarily frustrated, when the trail crossed a freshly plowed field, and then he picked it up again on the other side by circling.

Rye had been sold as a puppy to Roy and Rena Thorneycroft, in Canada. Roy had named him Rye as a companion for his cat, named Whiskey. The Thorneycrofts lived in a remote area at the time, and the mantrails were frequently crossed by trails of deer, moose, or other inhabitants of the wilderness. Nothing distracted Rye from the mantrail he had been set onto.

Rye had a bad habit of digging. Once when Roy left him in his pen and drove the few miles to town, Rye dug his way out. Thorneycroft was coming out of a store sometime later when he was amazed to see Rye racing down the road toward him. He had managed to trail either his master or the car, and he was moving fast.

There were other citizens in the area who did not appreciate the big Bloodhound: the Sioux Indians who were frightened by the unfamiliar breed of dog, and failed to understand his relationship with his owner. They regarded dogs as working animals. This huge one, and his friendly association with the family, was something unnatural to them. Knives were thrown at him, shots fired at him and he was wounded more than once.

Finally, in fear for the hound's life, Thorneycroft regretfully sent him back to the Dakota Kennels, where he became the joy of Vince's heart. Later, when the Thorneycrofts moved to another area, they returned for a new Dakota puppy.

Rye was always a fast trailer, and he trailed with his head high. He would make shortcuts across trails that curved. People watching him found it hard to believe that he was really trailing until he made the find. When I wanted to give a demonstration at a school, I would always use Happy, who trailed slowly with her nose to the ground, giving every impression of great seriousness.

Rye was a trailing genius, but he had his own little peculiarities in that pointed head. While Vince was the one who handled him, he had his mind made up that "Mama" must come along for the ride, or he wouldn't go. When the phone calls from the police came in at 2:00 A.M., this was far from appreciated. Rye had another individual signal; unlike some male dogs who will stop frequently to leave their scent along the way, Rye never stopped on a trail until he was within a short distance of the subject. Then he would stop and urinate, marking his claim, so to speak, and Vince would know that if the trail was a criminal case, he had better keep his eyes open.

Once we were attending a dog show in Wisconsin, and stayed at a motel on a riverbank across from an old people's home. We had Rye with us. When we saw a group of nurses searching around the area we asked them if someone was lost. They replied that an elderly inmate had been missing for about an hour and a half. Vince told them to bring a scent article, and we'd put the Bloodhound on the trail. They looked doubtful, but finally did bring a slip. Rye took a sniff and immediately led down the bank and along the river to the little old lady, who was sitting on a rock.

She knew that the dog was a Bloodhound, and petted him, telling us that her father had had Bloodhounds when she was a little girl. The episode made believers of the local police, who were amazed at the fact the Rye had found the woman in a matter of a few minutes, when they had been searching for her for an hour and a half.

Rye made history in the state of North Dakota as the first Bloodhound whose evidence was accepted as testimony in a court of law. This was a case in which two girls were murdered in the apartment in which one of them lived. Vince and I brought Rye to the room, and I gave him the pillowcase used to strangle them. Rye jumped up on the bed and went over it carefully. Since he knew he was not allowed on beds at home, we were sure that the fact that he did this now indicated he was picking up the scent of the murderer. Then he trailed through the kitchen door of the apartment and out of the building, and stopped in the alley behind it where the trail ended.

In the meantime, the police had been rounding up all known sex offenders and taking them to the jail for questioning. They asked us to bring Rye down there and see if he might identify one of the men. When we arrived, and stepped out of the car, Rye was again given the scent. He trailed through the front door to a fingerprinting room, then to a room where the suspects were being interrogated. Rye immediately went to one of the men, sniffing him up and down, and then sat down before him and looked at Vince with a single "Woof" that said it all.

The Bloodhound's evidence was entered as part of the record. It was corroborated by the blood and hair on the man's clothing, which matched those of the victims, and scratches on his body, and led to his conviction for the two murders.

Rye died of cancer on May 8, 1970. It was a long time before Vince could bring himself to pick up the trailing harness and train another hound.

While most Bloodhound trainers we know use basically the same methods, each may have his own preference in certain details of working. The subject on which they agree is that whatever method you use, you must be consistent if your dog is to understand you. For instance, although we learned much about handling Bloodhounds from a well-known trainer, we do not agree with his theory that the dogs should never be taken from their kennels except to trail. We feel that this lack of socializing with humans contributed to the fact that some of this man's hounds were vicious, to the degree that even he was cautious in handling them.

It is also important that you pay attention to your hound and understand his signals. A stranger cannot simply borrow your hound and go out on a search. An example of this which I remember with some amusement occurred in a nearby state where friends of ours had a mantrailing Bloodhound. They had often worked with the police, and the husband would wear a motorcycle belt with a ring on the front to which he would snap the end of the leash. The hound was a fast trailer, and this was the safest way of staying with her, as well as having his hands free for other activity.

One day a bank was robbed by a man who was seen to leave the area on foot. The police sent an officer to our friends' home, hoping that the Bloodhound could follow the robber. The husband was not home, and the officer asked if he could take the hound himself. However, he was too large a man to fit into the owner's belt. "Don't worry," he assured the wife. "I'll hang on to her."

Unfortunately, he was not prepared for the speed and power with which the hound took the trail; and the leash was jerked from his hand. Horrified, the officer and his partner saw this valuable dog for which they were responsible streak off down the street.

Making their best efforts, the men panted along in the direction the Blood-hound had taken and eventually came to a large park. There they found the hound, sitting in front of a man who was relaxing on a park bench and feeding her tidbits of hotdog from a sack of groceries. Not understanding the reward method by which the hound had been trained, they assumed that she had lost the trail of the criminal and found herself an understanding friend. They thanked the man for keeping the valuable dog for them and took her home.

About a week later, another bank was held up, by a man answering to the same description. This time the police arrived in time to catch the robber. To their chagrin, they discovered it was the friendly man with the "bag of groceries" who had fed hot dogs to the Bloodhound the week before.

Occasionally you run into a case that gets you a bit discouraged with the human race. For instance, the midnight we were wakened by a call to help search for a missing two-year-old girl. It was bitterly cold, as winter can be in North Dakota, but daughter Shelley and I got out there with one of our bitches, Tink (Ch. Aria of Dakota).

The house was full of policemen and buddies of the airman who had been keeping company with the mother. Shelley and I went for a scent article, and found a pair of the child's underpants.

Tink went all over the child's bed, then to the front door. She acted uncertain, but led us to a neighbor's house. We woke them up, and they said the child had been playing there during the afternoon. We restarted the hound three times, and she would go to the door, and that was the end of it. I told the police that I felt sure the child must have been carried out of the house. For one thing, I did not see how a two-year-old could have reached the doorknob and been able to turn it.

We spent an hour and a half in the freezing weather trying to find a trail and got no farther. The police decided to call the German Shepherds from the air base. We decided to wait around and see what they would do; but before they arrived some friends of the mother appeared, carrying the baby. They had taken her home after the mother and her boyfriend passed out on drugs.

Well, that's life.

CLYDE AND LENA REED AND BOOMERANG

Clyde and Lena Reed bought their first Bloodhound puppy from Dakota Kennels in February 1969. This was the puppy who was to become Am. & Can. Ch. Boomerang of Dakota.

We became interested in Bloodhounds after hearing stories about the man-trailing exploits of the Breys' Bloodhounds from our daughter, then living in the Grand Forks, North Dakota, area. During past years there had been several tragic cases of lost children and adults in our area (State of Washington), many of them never found or found too late. We wondered why trained Bloodhounds were not used here, where the dense forests and thick underbrush could hide a body from searchers a few feet away. We decided to train a Bloodhound. The experience has been a highlight in our lives.

Cathy Brey gave us a brief introduction to training, and we visited Sheriff William Weister, who gave us the benefit of his experience. Aside from that, we followed Boomerang, and let him teach us. He seemed to know what it was all about from the first. Later, we wrote and talked to others using Bloodhounds for mantrailing, and gradually learned more tricks of the trade.

We discovered, however, that the hardest part of using a Bloodhound was being given a chance to use him. Search and rescue operations in this state are conducted by the sheriffs or other law officers, and the local view seemed to be that Bloodhounds were an old-fashioned tool, superseded by the German Shepherd, which could be worked off lead and trained to respond to signals from its handler. Their system was to have a large number of dogs and handlers grid-search an area, combing it by means of teams spaced perhaps fifty feet apart, and looking for anyone in the area. It was a problem to convince them that one man with a Bloodhound, if given a scent article from the missing person, could save hours and manpower by following that person only and eliminating the need

Ch. Boomerang of Dakota (Ch. St. Hubert Blondel ex Ch. Miss Happy Gelert of Dakota), owned by Clyde and Lena Reed, has achieved success in mantrailing and the show ring, and is the sire of, among others, the Thompsons' Cascade Ranger.

for foot-by-foot examination of a large area. Although Boomerang did not make a large number of finds as compared to Nick Carter or Cleopatra, he struck a blow for the breed in making the Bloodhound a known and appreciated member of search and rescue teams in Washington State.

The first time Boomerang was called for a search, the victim was a retarded boy who had run away from his classroom at the state school. Boomerang promptly followed across the fields of the school farm, to a large cesspool, about one hundred and fifty feet across, in the barnyard area. He circled it, and then attempted to enter it. The stench was overpowering; it was difficult to believe that even a retarded person would be attracted there. Clyde pulled him away, and reported it to the search headquarters.

The sheriff was doubtful, and refused to drag the cesspool. The search party continued scouring the mountainous countryside through most of the night and the next day. Five days later the missing boy's body rose to the surface of the cesspool. Boomerang's report was entered in the sheriff's record, and there was a slight thaw in the attitude toward Bloodhounds. In time, the feeling became definitely friendly.

Boomerang has debunked a couple of the myths we had heard about Bloodhounds—one, that they would not approach a dead body. In the first case in which he trailed a murder victim, this seemed to be true. He had followed a trail about twenty-eight hours old, on a rainy, stormy night, through a wooded area, until finally he refused to go further, and showed signs of distress and confusion. Clyde returned with him to the truck, and then decided to go back for another look. Just ahead was a ravine, and by the dim light of his headlamp he saw evidence that something had gone through the brush. He looked down from the edge of the ravine and saw items of feminine underclothing partway down the bank, and knew what to expect at the bottom.

Twice after that, however, Boomerang did trail to a body, went directly to it, and had to be dragged away. One was a suicide; the trail was more than twenty-four hours old, and the temperature was over ninety degrees. Clyde took Boomerang into the missing woman's bedroom for the scent, and within twenty minutes the hound led him up a mountainside into a heavily forested and brushy area, where the woman's body lay. The rest of the search party was not yet out of camp, and the chief of police in charge of the case was amazed. ''I could have had a hundred men out in that woods for four days and not found her,'' he said later. To start with, nobody had any idea of the direction she had gone.

Six months later, they were called out on another search which led to a body. It was Christmas night; a blustery night of wind and rain. A diabetic man had left home that afternoon to go steelhead fishing in the Carbon River. When he had not returned by evening, his family and neighbors started a search. His truck was found parked near the river, but the man could not be found. They asked the sheriff for a search party, and Clyde and Boomerang arrived at the scene about midnight. Boomerang was taken into the subject's pickup for the scent, and promptly picked up a trail along the levee road beside the river. Every so often he would go down the steep bank to a spot on the riverbank, where the man had evidently fished for a while, and then go back up to the road and continue the trail. The fourth time he went down to the river, he refused to return. The bank was covered with large, sharp chunks of rock, wet and slippery on the stormy night, and Clyde had remained on the road, holding the hound by a long lead, to avoid the hazard of a fall. At first he thought Boomerang had stopped for a drink; then, as he refused to respond to tugs on the leash, he began to fear the hound had found a dead salmon on the bank and might be eating it. Raw salmon is poisonous to dogs, so he made his way down the bank to the narrow strip at the river's edge.

The hound was standing there quietly, but Clyde could see nothing, and tried to encourage him to continue the trail. Boomerang refused to move. Then Clyde saw a narrow white line—the white beading around the edge of the missing man's wading boot. Boomerang was standing over him, and he was lying at the water's edge, dead of a heart attack. His dark green rain gear matched the color of the river on that stormy night, and even from a few feet, he was invisible. It took a nose to find him; three human search parties had already passed that way and missed him.

We had read that in the past when horse thieves were common, Bloodhounds were famous as horsetrailers. The reports said, however, that it was rare that a hound could be trained for both man and horse trailing, as it would then be inadequate in either. We had always advised owners of Bloodhounds, therefore, not to allow their animals to trail anything but the human scent. In June 1975 Clyde received a call to help search for a woman who had left a stable in a rural area, riding her stallion. She had been gone for over twenty-four hours.

When man and hound reached the stable, there was no scent article available on the missing person. Facing the fact that she might have been thrown from her horse, and be lying in the woods gravely injured, Clyde felt that speed in beginning the search was vital. Her home was a considerable distance away, and it would have been an hour and a half or more before a scent article could be brought.

The wrangler at the stable pointed out the brush which had been used on the horse, and Clyde gave it to Boomerang, who promptly went to work. The trail led through the forest to the Stuck River, which was flooded out of its banks. In the wet dirt at the edge was an unusual horse track, with the hoof making almost a complete circle. Clyde called the search base on his radio, and described the track to the wrangler. "That's the stallion," the man replied. "There's no other horse track around here like his."

The river was deep, swift, and rocky, too dangerous to try wading. The sheriff called for a helicopter from nearby Fort Lewis, and one arrived, and transported ground searchers across the river. There they found the stallion grazing in the brush, and the woman's body caught in an eddy a short distance downriver. Although supposedly an experienced rider, she had apparently been reckless enough to ride her horse into the flooded river, where he must have lost his footing on the rocks and thrown her.

Boomerang has assisted in several criminal cases, leading to where the suspects entered cars, and in three of those cases he furnished evidence. Twice he first led to the man's home, and another time he crawled underneath a bramble, while trailing from the scene of a supermarket robbery, and pulled out the shirt and wig the holdup man had worn as a disguise. He has found a child lost overnight in the mountains, and on a few sad occasions has led to lakes, where the bodies were later recovered. His shortest trail was about fifty feet—from the roadside spot where an old man in ill health had parked his pickup to the middle of the bridge over the Nisqually River. There he stood up against the bridge railing and looked over, and Clyde felt confident in telling the deputy in charge that the body was in the water. It was, and later the old man's farewell note was found in his pickup.

Boomerang suffered later from arthritis as a result of a back injury caused when his crate was tossed upside down while on a plane trip to Iowa to help search for a missing Boy Scout. Six hundred searchers had spent three days combing the area before they arrived. The trail, sadly, led to the river, on which the ice had broken the night the boy disappeared, about the time he was last seen. Reading his hound, Clyde was sure in that first half hour; but nobody wanted to believe it. In spite of a limp from his travel injury, Boomerang covered sixteen miles that day, completely circling the park area involved; but the only trail again led to the river. The boy's jacket was later found caught on a snag downstream, but the body was never recovered.

It was a tragic journey; but as a result of it, that Iowa county organized a search and rescue team, complete with Bloodhound. It was gratifying to receive a letter from them several months later telling us that thanks to Boomerang, they were now better prepared for the next time; and that their ten-month-old pup had already made his first find.

A handler can learn from every hound. Clyde had delayed using our next hound, Ch. Cascade's Melody of Dakota, on an actual search, thinking he should not risk a life to an unproven hound when he had Boomerang. One night a police chief called to say he was sure the victim would be dead. The elderly subject had a heart condition and had gone fishing, and a large search party had been unable to find him. The officer was sure he must be in the river and wanted a probable location to drag. Might as well wait until morning, he said. In the morning the fog was so thick that visibility was near zero, and it had rained all night. In a fast, fifteen-minute trail Melody led her owner to the man's body, and it was not in the water. He had been dead only a short time; the body wasn't even cold. That was when Clyde decided that next time he was told to wait until morning he would say, "I'm coming out right now."

The first trail for the next hound, Ch. Snohomish Chocolate Candy, led from a nursing home, across a busy highway, and to the unconscious but still-living woman, concealed in dense brush. That trail gave him increased respect for the ability of the Bloodhound nose to overcome the contamination of heavy traffic.

The Reeds' current mantrailer (1990) is Ch. Cascade's Maccabee of Dakota. Maccabee's first trail, run at about fifteen months of age, was that of a three-year-old boy who had escaped from his mother at a clinic, dashed off into a city park, and disappeared. The hound took trail eagerly, forcing his way through the crowd of onlookers, and across the park. He led to a deep pond, and to the end of a dock over murky water. There he crouched, peered down, and suddenly dived as deep as the eighteen-foot-lead would allow. Clyde pulled the dog out of the pond, and reported to the police coordinator that the child was in the water. The coordinator refused to accept it; he had no prior experience with Bloodhounds and continued a ground search through the night and another day before bringing in divers. They found nothing; the water was so dirty that visibility was limited to inches. The following day the body of the child surfaced exactly where Maccabee had indicated it was.

A few years later Maccabee ran the oldest search of Reed's experience, when he followed a seven-day-old trail of a woman who had been kidnapped, forced into a wooded area, and murdered. He ran the trail as if it were five minutes old.

Maccabee helped solve another case when he couldn't find a trail. An unwed teenage mother reported that her five-month-old child had been kidnapped. She claimed that he had disappeared between the time she left for school in the morning and the time the other person in the house woke up. Clyde scented Maccabee, and the hound carefully vacuumed the crib with his nose, but did not lead out of the room. Clyde took him outdoors, and circled the house, but there was no trail leaving it. He told the deputy he was confident that the child had left that house in a plastic bag, as he knew even a babe in arms left a scent trail a Bloodhound would follow. The deputy found that hard to believe, and called Lena Reed to question the statement. She assured him that it had been proven. The mother was questioned further. Eventually she broke down and led the deputy to a wooded area, where the body was found in a plastic bag, concealed under brush.

JOE AND NORMA HIBLER AND MANDY

Maccabee's daughter Mandy (Slomoshun Cascade's Glacier) is the beloved search partner of Joe and Norma Hibler of Olympia, Washington. She gave that same department another eye-opener. A young woman failed to come home after leaving work on Saturday evening. When her husband found her car in a parking lot early Monday morning he called the police and reported her missing. Joe Hibler and Mandy responded to the police call, and Mandy trailed from the car, about fourteen blocks down the city streets, making turns, to the parking lot of a tavern. About then the woman returned home, and the husband told her to call the police. It developed that she had a boyfriend who had picked her up where her car was parked, driven her to the tavern, and thence off for the weekend. How could a Bloodhound trail a passenger in a car—especially with a trail over thirty hours old?

The police set up tests in which one of their employees walked half a mile down the street, entered a car, and drove home at about thirty miles per hour, a distance of about one-quarter mile more. All the windows were closed. The next day Mandy trailed her, turning at all the right corners. Later, another test was run with Norma Hibler. She was shut in the trunk of a car, which was then driven off and parked. Two other hounds were started on her scent, and both of them trailed about a mile down the highway to where the car was parked.

HARRY ANDERSON AND HOLLY

A major problem for beginning Bloodhound handlers is the inability to "read" their hounds. Harry Anderson of Aberdeen, Washington, and his Blood-hound, Holly, gave a fine example of proper team communication on a memorable trail. Anderson was called after midnight when an elk hunter failed to return to his camp in the snowcapped Olympic Mountains. This high country is danger-ous even in the daytime, and the man needed medication he had not taken with him. Holly took trail confidently. When she crossed two creeks, one about fifteen feet across and one fifty feet across, others were doubtful. Most lost people will follow a creek. Anderson was supremely confident. He knew Holly; she hated water and would never go into it except on a trail. After six hours of exhausting work she overtook the man and delivered his medicine.

Those are a few examples of the work the volunteers with Bloodhounds do. Sometimes they get credit, as when Armando Nigro's Daisy led to a tot trapped overnight in a neighbor's garage; but another time she did not. She led to a Puget Sound beach after a little child disappeared, and the high tide had rushed in. There were little footprints along the way and on the sand, but the police would not commit themselves without a body.

The growing number of volunteer SAR (search and rescue) groups across the country accounts for the rapid increase that has taken place during the 1980s in the use of mantrailing Bloodhounds. One of these is Illinois-Wisconsin Search Dogs, centered in Woodstock, Illinois.

On the Sunday morning of July 10, 1988, a sixty-one-year-old woman was walking down a country road near Cary, Illinois, wearing a headset radio, when she was seized from behind by a man who came out of the woods and held a hatchet to her throat. Along with robbery, the man seemed intent on sexual attack, and the woman put up a fight. She was saved by the appearance of two cars, and when the drivers stopped, the man released her and ran into the woods. Although a suspect was arrested within thirty minutes, the witness and the terrified victim did not agree on his identification.

On Monday the state police dogs were called in, and they located the radio and a knife. Unfortunately, the prints on the items were too smudged for identification. On Tuesday police dogs were called in from the sheriff in a neighboring county. No luck. The hatchet used in the attack was not found.

On Wednesday, four days after the attack, the sheriff sought help from Illinois-Wisconsin Search Dogs. Patti Gibson responded with her Bloodhound, Grace, and teams of air-scenting Labradors and Golden Retrievers, trained to locate and retrieve objects bearing human scent. If the Bloodhound could pick up that trail, and the trail could be flagged, this would reduce the search area which would have to be combed. It was a ninety-seven-degree day, not a choice one for prolonged activity. As it turned out, thanks to Grace, they were spared that job.

The sheriff provided the scent article, underwear from the man being held in jail, and Grace hit the trail at a run. Cutting through the woods, she came out at the spot where, unknown to her handler, the suspect had been taken into custody. "Get him again!" Gibson ordered, and Grace whipped about, raced back at a diagonal to the edge of a ravine, down a heavily wooded bank to a creek about nine inches deep. Without hesitation, she entered the water and with her nose to the bottom she ran upstream for seventy-five feet—where she lifted the hatchet out of the water by the head! Upon command from her owner, Grace dropped the hatchet and lay down beside it in the water, only to be commanded to lift it again when the humans failed to see it. A police sergeant on the scene when the crew arrived had been a man with little faith in dogs; now he went down on his knees in the creek to kiss the Bloodhound.

The breed is not well-known in the Illinois-Wisconsin area; most people do not even recognize it and old myths have been a handicap in their use. For instance, Gibson had heard that "Bloodhounds don't swim." She remembers the amazement in an old sheriff's voice as he watched Grace do a water demonstration. "Why, that dawg swims just like Esther Williams," he said, as he watched the submerged dog swim with a diver. Grace has been trained to recover drowning victims and to follow a trail in water. She brought another conviction when she recovered a gun.

The citizens of the victim's village awarded the SAR team a plaque mounted with the infamous hatchet. For Grace, there was a big rawhide bone tied in ribbon.

That hatchet, still bearing fingerprints after four days in the creek, sent the attacker to jail for three years.

Illinois-Wisconsin SAR Dogs can be reached through the McHenry County, Illinois, Sheriff's Office.

Like many others who were introduced to mantrailing Bloodhounds through witnessing a tragedy, Bill Goodell of southeastern Kansas bought Bloodhound puppies Jack and Jill after taking part in a search for a baby lost in a flood. Glen Rimbey, who handled Bloodhounds at that time for the Kansas State Penitentiary, and other Bloodhound teams from Missouri, took part in the search. They inspired Goodell and his son Tadd to become Bloodhound handlers. Glen Rimbey has since moved to New Mexico, where he and his hounds work at the New Mexico Penitentiary. By the time Rimbey moved, Goodell and his hounds were trained

Patti Gibson and Grace of Illinois-Wisconsin Search Dogs and the hatchet with the fingerprint that was retrieved from the creek.

and active in search and rescue. Along with helping to find lost persons, Bill Goodell conducts Hug-A-Tree programs which teach youngsters how to avoid becoming lost and what to do if they do get lost.

Jack and Jill have led their owner on many successful searches not only in Kansas but in Santa Fe, New Mexico, Missouri and south Texas. While many were cases of lost persons, Goodell has also successfully trailed criminals. In one case, a man attempted to murder his wife, and then kidnapped his son. He didn't get far; Jack located him hiding in a pile of debris, and he offered no resistance. Not many people argue when they see a Bloodhound, and that is a joke to Bill Goodell. The movies have slandered the breed by depicting them as bloodthirsty, whereas the average Bloodhound is interested only in winning the game. Still, Goodell has no wish to endanger them or his family by having his home known. In time of need he can be reached through the Anderson County, Kansas, sheriff.

Ginger Branyon lives in Yorktown, Virginia, where Lord Cornwallis surrendered to George Washington. She and her husband, John, had owned Bloodhounds for many years during his army career. Their frequent moves made dog shows her way to make friends, but after John retired and they settled near the Chesapeake Bay, Ginger was able to take her hounds a step further by training them for search and rescue. This led to the formation of the Tidewater Trail Search and Rescue Team in 1986. It is registered with the Virginia Department of Emergency Services, and has attained recognition as a valuable community resource. While most members limit themselves to SAR work, Ginger Branyon also works with the police on criminal cases.

When North American Search Dog Network (NASDN) was established, Tidewater Trail joined the network. Branyon became a member of the board of directors, where she hopes to increase the recognition and use of the King of the Scent Hounds.

Across the country in coastal northern California's redwood forests CARDA (California Rescue Dogs Association) gained a new member when Noreen Ward's three young children and nephew began an unplanned exploration of the big trees. They walked out safe after twenty-five hours, hours filled with fear and suspense for their parents. No SAR dogs were available within hundreds of miles, and the young mother wanted to be sure that situation was remedied. She bought and trained a Bloodhound puppy, and when it was ten months old it made its first find of a lost child.

"I'd seen him slobber over a lot of people," Noreen Ward said. "But when he found that child, the mother slobbered over him."

It is the rare dog handler who has trained a Bloodhound to work off lead. When William D. Tolhurst of Lockport, New York, decided to try such training with his Tona, he was the object of much criticism. That has never stopped Bill, and he proved it could be done. Later Ronald Lussier, a Quebec police officer, trained a Bloodhound to work off lead carrying a two-way radio in a backpack. It was used in remote and hazardous areas especially in the search for lost hunters. The hound could be started at the place where the missing person was last seen, and without the encumbrance of a handler, the animal could work faster and more easily. The handler followed by helicopter, keeping radio contact with the hound until the victim was located.

Another of this rare breed of handlers is Deborah McMahon-Mallatt of South Lake Tahoe, high in the California Sierra Nevada mountains. She is a member of WOOF, Wilderness Finders, Inc., a volunteer search and rescue group. This scenic, wild country, with searches often at elevations of from eight thousand to twelve thousand feet, is extremely hazardous and difficult terrain for humans and hounds. It is a great advantage to both team members if the hound can work under voice control and the handler need not risk dangerous footing. Debbie McMahon-Mallatt is one of the few Bloodhound trainers who has achieved that control.

She began working with her first Bloodhound, Caledonia, in 1977. At that time she had no preconceived notions about what a Bloodhound should do, and as she had joined a team of mountaineers, who worked their dogs off lead, she began training her Bloodhound the same way. Caledonia worked successfully for five years before she died.

Then McMahon-Mallatt received encouragement from a man she had never met—Bill Tolhurst. "Deborah, you are the only person working a Bloodhound to its full potential," he said. "Get another Bloodhound, and I'll help." She got a three-month-old puppy, Georgia, and a few years later spent a week across country learning from Tolhurst. For several years she has worked on WOOF's training team, training several different dog breeds, and she feels Bloodhounds are both the easiest and hardest dogs to train and read. While their abilities of scenting are unique, their attitude is different from that of the generally accepted "obedient" breeds. You must convince them they *want* to do something. A few examples of the types of searches she has worked, literally through fire and water, illustrate the success of her training.

A series of arson fires had plagued the Lake Tahoe Basin area. A Forest Service investigator who had helped train McMahon-Mallatt's first Bloodhound asked her if she and the hound might be able to help. This was something unknown, but worth trying, so they went to where he had found matches which might have been used to start five fires in a row. The hound was started on the match package and off she went, through smoking ash and fire hoses. Her trail indicated the fires had not been started all in a row as had been believed. At the site where the third fire had started she dug up a lunch box, and from there to the remaining sites, and on to a parking area. That was the end of the Bloodhound's work on the case. The investigator used the tire prints found there, and other information uncovered by the trail, to trap the arsonist at the next fire he started. He gave credit to the Bloodhound, who worked through hot ash, fire hoses and the confusion of fire fighters and spectators.

Debbie's second Bloodhound, Georgia, quickly proved that she was as unstoppable on the trail as her predecessor. On a mid-July day, above tree level at ten thousand feet elevation, with the bare rock heated to eighty or ninty degrees, a twelve-year-old girl was reported missing in a wilderness area. She had gone fishing, and failed to return to her campsite. It was eighteen hours after she was last seen before the Bloodhound team arrived. They started from the family's tent, and with two park rangers following, began the trail. Georgia took them across an area of huge flat rocks, on a trail seven miles long, with a steep drop on one side and high cliffs on the other. She indicated what appeared to be a nest where the child might have spent the night, and then reached the main trail. All hikers entering or leaving the area had been notified that the child was missing, and as the hound led down the main trail the Rangers were sure Georgia had to be wrong; if the girl were on the trail someone would have seen her.

Four miles later they met a mule pack train. Georgia had been trained early to avoid animals, but now she started whining and insisted upon going up to one of the mules. The missing girl was riding the mule! She had recognized the area when she joined that trail, so when people had asked, she denied being lost. And yes, she had slept in that nest.

The Lake Tahoe area is famous for its gambling casinos. Each casino provides a bus which makes a circuit of the nearby motels to pick up customers. Three times buses had been hijacked, and the drivers tied up, in an attempt to collect ransom. In all cases the drivers were able to free themselves and make their way to the sheriff's office. After the third case the Douglas County Sheriff asked for the Bloodhound.

The third kidnapping occurred at 11:30 P.M., the driver returned to Harrah's Casino at 3:30 A.M. and by 5:30 A.M. the bus was towed to the sheriff's holding yard. It was 6:30 A.M. when McMahon-Mallatt and Georgia arrived, and the bus was two miles from the location where it and the driver had been left. There was no scent article, just the seat and steering wheel of the bus, which bore the driver's scent as well as the kidnapper's. Having no choice, McMahon scented Georgia on them, and the team returned to the site where the bus had been found.

Georgia immediately began trailing, first going into the woods and re-turning with a ski-mask cap, and then continuing to the road, trailing approxi-mately a quarter mile to a deserted intersection. Here she sat down and whined. McMahon-Mallatt told the deputies that the person had entered a car at that point. There was only one house on the street, and the resident confirmed that he had heard a car there at about 3:00 A.M.

The officers informed McMahon-Mallatt that about four blocks down the road there was a house that hadn't seemed quite right to them. Would she be willing to check it out? With no other clue, she started for the house. Georgia, however, had other ideas; as they reached the spot where they should have taken a right turn, she suddenly made a left turn, ran to a house which appeared to be a vacant rental, and began jumping on the garage door. Then she ran to the side of the house, jumping up in an attempt to reach a second-story window. An officer ran to open the garage door, but in his haste he locked it instead.

McMahon-Mallatt left to go to her job, and the officers went for a search warrant. They called her later to tell her that the house had indeed been used; they had found handprints on the ledge of that window her dog was trying to reach. Debbie is convinced that the hijackers were in there, watching, and that they escaped when *both* officers went after that search warrant. Since that day, there has never been another hijacking attempt.

Bloodhounds proved many years ago that they could locate the body of a drowning victim in deep water, but it was unknown if the cold water of high-altitude lakes would affect the decomposition and release of scent. When a sailboat capsized in Crowley Lake, a high-altitude cold-water lake in California, the Mono County Sheriff called Deborah McMahon-Mallatt and her Bloodhound the next day. The team was put in a flat-topped boat and they proceeded to grid the lake from the middle to the shoreline. Crowley Lake is at an altitude of 6,400 feet, the depth is five hundred feet or more, and the temperature from sixty to sixty-five degrees.

At one point in the middle of the lake the hound alerted, but did not try to jump into the lake. To Deborah's disappointment, the sheriff didn't seem interested, and announced that it was time for lunch. During lunch he admitted that what Georgia had alerted on was the boat, which had been located at a 150-foot depth. It was a different story later in the afternoon, however, when the hound again alerted with enthusiasm, and jumped into the water, pinpointing a location. Divers were sent down, but due to poor visibility and strong undercurrents they were not able to descend farther than fifty feet. The sheriff marked the spot with a buoy; and the next day a fisherman reported that the body had surfaced right there. The hound had located the body in seventy-five feet of water.

A rescue experience that combined trailing and air scenting took place after a San Francisco company took their new-to-America physicist into the high Sierras for a fishing trip. It didn't take him long to get lost, and at 2:00 A.M. Deborah, with Georgia and another dog team, began the search at the place last seen. Both dogs began trailing, but Georgia repeatedly went up to a high spot to check the wind. After about two hours, Georgia disappeared from sight above them, so the two handlers continued following the dog on the trail for another twenty minutes, when that dog also dashed off. They then heard both dogs barking and ran toward them. They found a frightened man with a firebrand in each hand warding off the dogs, who were trying to approach him. As a stranger to America, he was unprepared for friendly rescue dogs. It took the team an hour to convince him it was proper to accept the food they offered; in a country where people are hungry you do not take food away from someone else.

"Were you afraid while you were lost?" they asked the man.

"I walked through the jungle for sixty days to escape to freedom," he replied. "I didn't think there were tigers in America."

5

Training the Mantrailing Bloodhound

THROUGHOUT THE GREATER PART OF THIS CEN-
TURY, the Bloodhound remained the rare show dog, unknown and unidentifiable
by the majority of the population. While his name was a synonym for the
relentless and unfailing pursuer, very few were actually in use as mantrailers.
Since the initial publication of *The Complete Bloodhound*, with its chapter on
training the mantrailer, the use of this natural talent has increased dramatically,
and numerous volunteer search and rescue (SAR) groups using Bloodhounds
have been formed nationwide. In 1990 the majority of new members joining the
American Bloodhound Club indicated an interest in mantrailing. To better serve
this interest, the chapter is now expanded to include more detail.

SELECTING THE MANTRAILING PUPPY

You begin your mantrailing career when you pick your puppy. We have
heard people say, "I don't care what it looks like as long as it has the nose."
The *Standard of the breed* is the description of the dog *best able to do the work
of that breed*, and that should be your guide. We are aware that in a number of
breeds, field trial dogs are described as being "like another breed" from show
dogs, and we hope that never happens to Bloodhounds. Our working mantrailers
also been show champions, although a show career is not necessary for a
mantrailer. Some people seeking only a mantrailer have bought "pet quality"

A gathering of contestants and judges at an American Bloodhound Club field trial. The judges on this occassion were Lois Meistrell and Evelyn Monte (second and fifth from left).

During a training seminar for mantraililng Bloodhounds much practical work is demonstrated and help is provided for those desiring to work with their hounds. Here a training officer instructs a handler on a specific problem as the gallery observes.

Courtesy, National Police Bloodhound Association

pups with the idea of saving money. If the pup is pet quality because it has one testicle, a kink in the tail, white above the knuckle or other color imperfections, that could be a bargain. If it is pet quality for any reason that relates to *soundness*, you paid too much if you got it for nothing. The mantrailing Bloodhound must be an athlete.

Equally important to that dog is temperament, and that depends in part upon the early training it receives during the critical periods of puppy development. Our appreciation goes to the late Clarence Pfaffenberger for his chapter on that subject in his book *New Knowledge of Dog Behavior* (Howell Book House, 1963). This illustrates the research of Drs. John Paul Scott and John L. Fuller at the Jackson Laboratory, Bar Harbor, Maine, which showed that puppies during the period between three and twelve weeks of age must be socialized and exposed to the conditions of their future lives if they are to adjust successfully. The best period for bonding to a human being is between six and eight weeks of age. The ideal time for puppies to be separated from the litter and their mother is the day they turn seven weeks old, as at that time the order of dominance in the litter is established.

Mr. Pfaffenberger, in working with Guide Dogs for the Blind, learned that if puppies were kept together after the forty-ninth day, only the dominant puppy could be trained as a guide dog. If they were separated and trained individually at that age, almost every puppy could be trained as a guide dog. When separated, each puppy thus became the *dominant*, or *alpha*, dog. While the nose of the Bloodhound is not affected by the environment, its self-confidence is. You want a self-confident, friendly puppy. Our belief is that if you choose a mantrailing puppy from an older litter that has not been separated, look for the dominant pup. Many Bloodhounds have a tendency to be shy, and as a mantrailer that dog may be reluctant to approach and identify his subject. A puppy that has been confined to a kennel and not socialized by sufficient human contact and outside experience during the first twelve weeks of its life will never adjust to change or become a working dog. It will become a victim of "kennel dog syndrome."

We will assume you have that perfect seven-week-old socialized puppy and have already brought it home. During the first week your priority is to develop a strong, affectionate bond with your puppy, and accustom it to the sights, sounds and smells of its new home. Teach it its name, to come, sit and stay, and the meaning of "No." Always handle the puppy gently, and do not allow rough play. What it learns now is what it will do later. Don't allow any "cute" tricks that could be hazardous when it weighs 120 pounds and is stronger than you.

If the puppy is not already lead trained, that can be easily done now. Simply put a light choke chain or collar on it and attach a lead. Don't try to lead the puppy immediately; it will probably put on all four brakes. Drop the lead and let it drag; the pup will see it does no harm. Then pick up the lead and go with the puppy as it explores its new home. Make friends with it, play gently, and then as you walk off the puppy will go with you. It is walking on lead.

At this age the puppy learns rapidly. As it charges toward a cat or whatever, a tug at the leash and a firm "No!" will get its attention. Then a pat, and a warm "Good dog!" gives positive reinforcement to the lesson. By nipping any forbidden actions in the bud and then rewarding for obedience, you will help your puppy learn the rules.

Teach the puppy to be a good traveler; a carsick hound is useless on a search. Be aware that you should never smoke in the car with your hound. Nicotine is a narcotic, with serious effects on the olfactory ability for as much as seventy-two hours. When your hound travels be sure it is not a victim of exhaust if it rides in a trailer behind your car. A hound can be incapacitated by being transported in a freshly painted enclosed truck. If it would bother your nose, it will bother the supernose even more.

Your hound should be at ease with any conditions or animals it might meet on a search. Walk with the puppy in city and rural roads where it may meet domestic or wild animals, and teach it that it is not to follow any of those trails. A hound may be used to trail animals, but if it is intended as a mantrailer it should not be allowed to trail any but the human scent. When it is already trained it can be given the scent of an animal if the need arises, and it will trail. See Clyde Reed's case of trailing the horse when he did not have a scent article for the rider. However, while the puppy is being trained, do not confuse it.

The following training methods are based upon our experiences and what we learned from successful trainers, including Bill Tolhurst and Bill Weister, whose stories appear in preceding chapters. The personalities of dogs and owners differ, and some may use variations of these methods. Remember you can't fool Mother Nature. You must work with instinct, physical abilities and the normal mental response of the dog. The first rule in training is to make this a happy experience for the dog. Training should be something it looks forward to. Never lose your temper or get upset or harsh. Trailing is instinctive for the Bloodhound, and if it learns that this also gets it the reward of your praise and affection, it will work with enthusiasm.

MALE OR FEMALE?

Some owners have a sex preference, but there is no evidence that either has superior olfactory ability. A big male looks very impressive in criminal work, or in giving confidence to the parents of a lost child. A female does not waste as much time checking out the other dogs which may have passed through the area. On the other hand, unless she is spayed, she is out of service for a few weeks twice a year. Some people feel she is more devoted to her owner than a male is, but we have never noticed this. One advantage of females is that they are smaller and easier to control than a large, powerful male. Bill Tolhurst prefers spayed females, and trains them from puppyhood to accept being picked up, something the average person could not do with a large male. Then, when the trail comes to a fence or wall, he is able to lift her and drop her over it. In connection with this, he trains her to obey the command "Stay!" so that he will have time to climb over after her.

MANTRAILING AND OBEDIENCE

Most trainers of mantrailing Bloodhounds have been opposed to obedience training for the breed except for those commands necessary in handling it. The hound must definitely be under handler control. It has been the feeling that it should not be inhibited in its natural instinct to lead the hunt. By no means do we want a Bloodhound that looks back to his handler for guidance. Of late, a few trainers who have been willing to apply themselves have proved that the breed has a great deal more potential for obedience training than had been believed. Examples are the off-lead mantrailers trained by Bill Tolhurst and Deborah McMahon-Mallatt, whose work is described earlier in this book. Our own belief is that the previously held attitude of the Bloodhound's limited intelligence was due to the fact that old-time trainers advised against beginning training until the animal was grown, thereby wasting those critical first twelve weeks of the puppy's life. The nose and the trailing instinct were still there, but the willingness to learn noninstinctive matters was gone. It is your decision as to the need for advanced obedience training balanced against the time required to teach it, which would otherwise be spent on mantrailing.

BEGINNING TRAILING

Make the training periods short; five or ten minutes at a time to start with. *Never keep at it until the puppy becomes tired or bored.* Keep it looking forward to trailing as a game.

If you have a large yard or a field nearby, where you can play games with the pup, this is a good place to begin training. While it is small, play with it and then run from it. It will naturally run after you. If you can get ahead of it and find a hiding place, when it loses sight of you it will soon learn to use its nose and follow you. When it finds you, praise it lavishly and give it a little nibble of some kind of treat. Bits of dry cooked liver are commonly used. Let it know that you are very pleased with it, and it will be only too willing to repeat the game. Trailing will immediately become a popular sport with it.

Next have another member of the family help you by holding the puppy while you run away, for a distance of fifty or a hundred feet. Play with it for a while first, and get it excited. As you run away call to it to hold its attention. Some trainers add to this by shaking some light-colored piece of clothing they have worn. For the first day or two, run only far enough to get out of sight behind a bush, tree or building. Then your assistant should let go of the pup, which should run after you. Almost invariably, when it reaches the spot where it lost sight of you, down will go that nose. If for any reason it does not seem able to find you, help it by making a little noise, or have your helper lead it up to you. The puppy should *always* find you, so it will learn the habit of finishing a trail. Then fuss over it and give the treat. Do this perhaps four or five times at a session, always hiding in a different place. If possible, work the puppy twice a day during the first few months. If you give this training before mealtimes, when the pup is hungry, the food reward will have more value in stimulating its interest. It is also instinctive for an animal to hunt when hungry, and that may intensify its olfactory ability.

HARNESS AND LEAD

After a few days of this lesson, the puppy should become acquainted with the harness and lead. Some handlers use a leather harness; we like one of heavy nylon webbing which does not stiffen in cold weather. In the use of a lead, likewise, there is a difference of opinion. Some handlers prefer to use an eight-foot lead, so they can be closer to the hound and better observe its actions. In the Pacific Northwest, where trails are often in dense forests and tangled under-brush, we like a fifteen- to twenty-foot lead; if the hound goes through some dense brush or bramble you can drop the lead and have a better chance of grabbing it when you run around. It also gives the hound more leeway when casting for the scent. The harness should be made to put the pull against the chest, and not the throat.

In the illustration of the man with the red hound, you will notice that the lead is attached to the D-ring at the point of a V formed by two straps snapped to the harness at the sides. The lead is far enough back so that even if it slackens, it does not get tangled in the hound's hind legs; and the pull from the sides is against the chest.

The front and side view illustrations with the black puppy show a nylon webbing harness, which is excellent for a growing Bloodhound puppy. The strap dangling below the chest in the front view has three slots through which the strap around the body can be passed, expanding it as the puppy grows. Likewise, the straps joining the buckles at the shoulders can be adjusted to extend the girth. The buckles are the type used on seat belts, which close and release easily. Notice the padding under the buckles and at the Y of the harness on the chest. This is a very practical model which saves the owner the expense of a new harness every week or two. The four-and-one-half-month-old model had grown into the full size of her harness by the time she was six months old.

Start associating the harness with trailing by putting it on the puppy as you prepare to begin training. Never put the harness on at any other time. Hold the puppy by a lead fastened to a choke chain and do not change the lead to the harness until you are ready for it to begin the trail. This will then become its clue to go to work, together with whatever verbal command you may choose to use. We say, "Find!" and at the same time point to an item of clothing worn by the trail-layer, which may be on the ground, or on a bush, or in a plastic bag.

104

The trailing harness in use.

The expandable training harness (front view above, side view left) is favored by many for working with growing puppies.

This is called the scent article, and gives the hound the identity of the person to be trailed.

Instead of using a choke chain and changing the snap from it to the harness, some handlers have a loop at the end of their lead, and slip that over the hound's head when they are harnessing it up. Then when they are ready to start the trail, they slip the loop off the hound's neck, and don't run the risk that the eager mantrailer will zip off out of their grasp before they can change the snap to the harness. The snap at the other end of the lead is already attached.

GETTING THE SCENT

Some hounds will take such a quick sniff of the scent article that they don't seem to be paying attention at all. Beginners have been tempted to rub their noses in it, or drape it over their heads. This is not only unnecessary, but may be a positive hindrance. Some students of scent claim that the olfactory sensibilities are most acute during the first moment of contact, and fade or weaken gradually on continued contact. If the scent article is rubbed over a hound's nose or face, the scent will be so strong that it may blot out the scent from the ground. Imagine you had an onion rubbed over your nose and face, and consider whether you would be able to smell an onion lying in the grass. The hound is entirely capable of registering that scent in its mind in a fraction of a second. Other hounds may prefer to sniff it more thoroughly, or even take it in their mouths. Don't try to tell your Bloodhound how to smell; it knows its business better than we ever will.

THE VALUE OF CONSISTENCY

Before you try to teach anything further to your pup, there are two points which must be emphasized. First, be consistent. The pattern you start now should be adhered to strictly. To repeat, take the hound to the spot where the trail begins, holding it by the lead fastened to the choke chain. Now put the harness on, attach the lead from choke chain to harness, and present the scent article, with the verbal command. Be ready to run with the pup, trying to hold it back as little as possible while it is learning. Later you will train your hound to your speed. When it finishes the trail, reward with praise and treats, and return the leash to the choke chain until you are ready to start on another trail.

SCENT ARTICLES

The second matter you must learn is the care and selection of the scent article. This can be an item of clothing worn by the trail-layer, or it can be his sheet or pillowcase, but it must be an item which has not been laundered since

No one can teach a Bloodhound to trail a scent. However, a hound can be taught certain responses to render his talent useful to society. These people have come to a training seminar in Ligonier, Pennsylvania, to learn more about effective handling of their own hounds.   *Courtesy, National Police Bloodhound Association*

An instructor at the Ligonier seminar gives the participants instructions before starting to work the dogs.   *Courtesy, National Police Bloodhound Association*

use. Preferably it will be an item worn next to his body. In real searches, hounds have trailed from cars driven by the missing person, from sticks or tools they have handled, or a paper carton or tin can. Hounds will take the scent from a moist paper towel which has wiped down a car seat, steering wheel or typewriter keys. Some handlers carry packaged sterile gauze pads as scent collectors. If you have a choice, give your hound the best scent article available.

A major cause of trailing failure is contaminated scent articles—that is, articles with more than one person's scent on them. Hounds have used the "missing member" method, in cases where an uncontaminated scent article was not available, and the other persons who handled the article are present. The hound will check out the persons present and look for the "missing member." You face the problem that the other persons *will not* be present, and then the hound has no way of knowing which person to trail. He would waste a great deal of time trailing the wrong persons. In a criminal case this will limit or destroy the value of the Bloodhound trail as evidence.

Never take an item of clothing from the laundry hamper where it was trapped with clothing from the rest of the family. Look for an item that nobody else has handled. If someone else brings it, emphasize to him that he must not touch it, but pick it up with a stick, a fork, a pair of pliers, etc. and put it in a clean plastic bag. Do not use a garbage bag which is treated with a deodorant. If at all possible, select the scent article yourself, and do not allow anyone else to touch it. If you chose it, your scent will not distract your hound.

An unanswered question is the length of time a piece of clothing or other scent article will retain the identifying scent which a Bloodhound can recognize. Bill Tolhurst's hound successfully trailed an escaped mental patient using as a scent article a shirt which had been hanging in a plastic cleaner's bag for three months since it was worn. There is no definite conclusion to be drawn from this case, as scent may depend upon a number of variable factors, such as humidity, temperature or other scents in the vicinity. It can only be said that if nothing else is available, try what you have, and hope that your hound will come through.

At a National Police Bloodhound Association training school an interesting experiment was conducted on the retention of scent. In October 1975 a T-shirt was bagged in plastic and frozen. Another was bagged in plastic but not frozen. Two hounds were started at different times using the frozen material and both were successful. A third dog was started from the material which was not frozen, and was also successful.

In the case of a real search for a missing person, if at all possible, take the hound into the victim's bedroom and let him sniff around for a while. First, however, be sure there are no other animals in the room. Finding a cat lying on the bed can turn your hound's brain to an entirely different wavelength.

LEARNING TO READ THE HOUND

Now back to the puppy. After a few days of running after you, and learning to put its nose down and trail you to your nearby hiding place, it has learned the rules of the game. This is the time to trade places with your helper and take over the handling of the hound. Let your helper lay the trail for the pup, while you and your Bloodhound learn to work as a team.

Do not even think about sending your puppy off to be trained for you. Just as important as training the Bloodhound is training yourself to understand its signals. The second major cause of failure for beginning trainers is inability to "read" the hound. Observe that puppy closely as it trails and see how it reacts when it first finds the trail, when it is distracted by animals or other activity, when it realizes it has found or is near its runner. If possible, videotape the puppy as it works. By viewing a number of its trails later, you may see the pattern of behavior which you missed on the individual trail. If the Bloodhound stops and takes great interest in a particular spot, sniffing around for a while before continuing, it is not necessarily digressing. These actions could indicate what Bill Tolhurst calls "pool scent," which is a heavy concentration of scent where the trail-layer has rested for a time, or sat down. Pay attention. There may be an item of evidence dropped at such a place. If the pool scent occurs frequently, it could indicate the lost person was tiring or is injured.

As a rule, a tail held high and sometimes wagging means the hound is on a hot trail. When the going gets rough, the tail droops, and a lowered tail means the trail is lost. Take your hound back to where it was on the trail and start it again from there. Give it the scent article and command at the beginning of the trail, and then do not use that command again unless you are required to restart. Use an occasional word of encouragement, but do not maintain a steady stream of chatter. Just like anyone else, a hound concentrating will "turn off" a constant nag; and you will run out of breath.

Your tone of voice is important in training your hound. When you give a command, use a crisp, authoritative sound which will get its attention. We have known a few people who could not seem to understand the importance of this. They had monotone voices and the hounds ignored them as just another meaningless background noise. Your voice should let your hound know there is something exciting here.

As you work your hound you will soon see it has its own style of indicating nearness to the subject. This is called the "alert," and if you are trailing a criminal it can be of great importance in warning you. Some hounds show a very slight alert while others make it obvious, as in rapidly wagging the tail, head up and looking toward the runner, squealing, yelping, and showing excitement. The Breys' Ch. Rye of Dakota would indicate approach by stopping and "marking" the trail. The Reeds' Maccabee looks back to its owner with a big grin.

Train your hound to go directly to the runner and identify him or her. This can be encouraged by having the runner offer the reward. We do not recommend the method once used of having the hound put his feet on the subject's shoulders. Lost persons would be frightened at having a large, strange dog do this, and small persons would be overwhelmed. Nobody likes those rough feet, even when they are clean.

Deer and other dogs are two major distractions that you must train your hound to ignore. If you are able to lay a trail where you have seen animals pass, mark that spot so you can observe the hound's reaction and sharply curb any attempts to break trail to follow. Your hound must never be allowed to "riot," which means leaving the trail to chase animals, either wild or domestic. If all else fails, get an electric collar and give the hound a shock if it riots. You won't have to use it more than twice.

FOLLOWING AN UNSEEN PERSON

For the next lesson have the trail-layer leave when the puppy does not see him go. Have him leave the scent article a few feet from the actual starting place. If possible, throw it onto a bush, as the ground may hold other scents. As the puppy gains experience, leave the scent article farther from the actual trail, so the puppy has to search for the trail. Another way is to carry the scent article in a clean plastic bag. Then close the bag after the puppy scents, so that the scent behind it will not distract it from the scent on the trail. Observe its attitude when it finds the trail during this training, when you know where the trail is. It will enable you to recognize when the hound finds the scent on a real search.

Do not make the trail too hard, and do not expect the beginner to trail in the dust, or on dry pavement. Pick soft, moist ground. If it has trouble, try again, but always be patient. Gradually make the trails longer and older. Progress only as the puppy shows itself able to find the runner every time without help.

This is important! While training the puppy always use the same person for every trail in any one day. Another day you may use another person, but not more than one runner a day until the hound is well trained. We have known some people who disregarded this rule, and we have seen what happened. If a fresher trail crossed the one they were running, the puppy would change to the fresher trail, apparently deciding that it was the next runner. Hounds must know that they are always to finish the trail they start and ignore anything that crosses it. This is the "freedom from change" which has made the Bloodhound so valuable.

LAYING OUT TRAILS

At first, the trails should be more or less straight. As a hound learns the game, add a few easy turns to the trail. If it loses the trail at a turn, it may at first keep going as if it expected the trail to turn up, but it will soon learn to "cast" by circling around until it finds the trail again.

By the time your puppy has been working with you for a few months, and seems confident on trails one-quarter or one-half mile long, send two runners out together, but have only one leave the scent article. The two should walk single file for most of the trail, and then separate and hide some distance apart. You should plan ahead of time where the trail is to fork, so that if the puppy takes the wrong turn you can take it back there. If the puppy follows the wrong runner, jerk it back sharply and say "No!" and take it back to the place where the trail

First time in harness for the three-and-a-half-month-old Patriot's Frederick Douglass. He is being equipped by his owner James Zarifis and Keith Tolhurst (left), son of the celebrated Bill Tolhurst.

The puppy watches the tracklayer as the handler prepares to switch the lead from collar to harness. The command TRAIL is given when the puppy is given the scent article.

This puppy went right to work, trailing directly to the tracklayer. He was lavishly praised and rewarded upon finding the runner.

forked. Give it the scent article again and give the command to find. When it goes to the right person, it gets praise and reward. Your hound will learn that you do not want it to indulge its idle curiosity, but to follow strictly the scent you have given.

When you start training a puppy you should know as closely as possible where your trail-layer went. If the trail is not marked, you will learn to trust your hound, and avoid the temptation to lead or guide it. If the hound thinks you will help when it hits a bad spot, it will not learn to work it out independently.

Sometimes this is a difficult rule to follow, as children laying trails have a bad way of deciding to play tricks on the hound, or fail to pay attention when they receive their instructions. They may find a hazard on the trail which they avoid, thus being out of the area where you expected them. As a result, you may be tempted to pull your hound from the trail, feeling sure it is off. This will be discouraging to the hound who is following the trail, and can retard the progress of your training.

Some beginners find it much easier on their own nerves if the trail is marked. This can be done by having the runner drop a few sheets of bathroom tissues every forty or fifty feet. If they are not picked up by the handler, they will disintegrate in the first rain.

If you do start your hound on marked trails, discontinue this practice as soon as it shows it is fairly reliable. A criminal will not be so considerate of you; and as the hound learns its work you must learn to have faith in it. In addition, as you work older trails you will find that the scent has drifted with the breeze, so that it is no longer likely to be exactly on the trail the runner took. Your hound may be fifty to two hundred feet away from the actual trail; and if the trail turns or makes loops, the experienced hound will make shortcuts, picking up the scent through the air. We recall one runner who spent considerable time in his hope of giving the hound a challenge by circling, going through water, and then making a loop back so he could watch the hound struggle. The hound raised its head, scented and went right to him.

Under ideal conditions, a hound with an especially good nose can pick up the scent as much as two miles away, and will take the shortest route to reach it. This often results in dragging the handler through swamps and thickets where the less-talented handler is certain no human in his right mind would have traveled. (The lost person is not always in his right mind.) This following of the scent, rather than the step-by-step route of the runner, is the difference between the "trailing" done by the Bloodhound and the "tracking" done by a dog with less sophisticated nose, and as required for an AKC Tracking Dog (TD) title.

As you progress with your mantrailer, you will make the trails longer, older and more difficult. You may have three or four persons leaving together, and later separating. You will teach the hound to trail through areas where other animals or people have passed over the trail, as in pastures or golf courses. You should work together in suburban or urban areas, where it must work in poor scenting conditions with the pollution of industrial odors. Work the hound in both day and night conditions. As it acquires skill, trail with it in rain or snow.

112

After the puppy has been working with you for a few months, get strangers to lay the trails for it. It will become bored with following the same family members or friends.

A male puppy will often start trailing very well, and suddenly seem to forget why he is out there. He has learned to raise his leg, and when he gets out of his own yard that is all he can think of. Don't be upset; he will soon become accustomed to his adult ability and settle back to his trailing.

Have someone lay a trail for your puppy and then climb a tree. When the puppy reaches that tree it will usually go around and around it, frustrated, until the runner makes a noise to get its attention. A good hound won't be fooled that way twice. Or have the runner hide under a large cardboard carton.

THE REAL THING

When your hound can be trusted to follow a trail a mile long and twenty-four hours old, through less than perfect conditions, you may want to answer a search call. Search records in Washington State show that in 85 percent of the cases the lost person was found within one and one-half miles from the spot where he was last seen. In searches for young children the trail may be only a few hours old. If a proven hound is not available and a life is at stake, try your hound. It may be able to run a much older trail than you have ever trained it on, and scenting conditions may be especially good. However, if an experienced hound is available and on the way, don't rush in and add to the contamination. It is not usually appreciated. Offer to serve as a backup.

On searches for teenagers or adults, the trails are often much older. Unless there is a medical problem or evidence of foul play, law officers frequently will not start a search until twenty-four hours after a person is reported missing. It is assumed that the mature person left willingly; or a hunter may have hiked farther than he planned and be overdue without being in trouble. The hound used on these trails will therefore require more training.

A good way to test your hound's qualifications for search is to have a trail laid through a park or over a golf course one evening, and run the hound on it the next evening after the area has been used all day.

EQUIPPING THE HANDLER

Before you take part in a search in a forested or remote area, you must be physically qualified to follow a hound on a long trail over rough terrain. Do not be another victim. The shoes you wear are especially important. Dress for the conditions, and carry something extra for unexpected weather changes. Weather in mountainous areas especially is unpredictable, and can be deadly for the ill equipped. It does not require freezing weather for a person to die of hypothermia. You must know how to read a map and compass, and wear a compass and signal whistle on a thong around your neck. It is recommended that you have wilderness survival training, be qualified in first aid and CPR, and carry a first-aid kit along with other emergency supplies. A small backpack can carry signal flares, hard candies, jerky, raisins, a signal mirror and a snack for your hound, along with a space blanket or two. A canteen and hunting knife can be worn on your belt, and wear a hard hat with headlight or flashlight lantern on a shoulder strap. Be sure you have extra batteries and bulb in your pack. You may add sardines, granola bars, trail food and fire starter.

States have different laws regarding volunteers because of liability, so get local information. Most of you will be interested in using your hounds in search and rescue. In the late 1980s North American Search Dog Network (NASDN) was formed as an umbrella organization to help locate volunteer dog teams when needed. As the network becomes better funded it is planned that a toll-free number will be set up for emergency location of these teams. At present, information can be obtained from the secretary, Joyce Phares, at (217) 367-3800.

DROP TRAILING

When you feel your hound is ready for a postgraduate course, start it on "drop trailing." In criminal work there are often cases where a trail is lost because the escapee boarded a car, train or bus. Later someone may spot him at another location, perhaps days or weeks afterward. Even where there is no scent article to refresh the hound's memory some have been know to retain the scent in their "memory banks" for long periods of time, and when taken to the spot where the criminal was again seen, have continued on the trail as if uninterrupted. This is drop trailing. Train your hound by having the trail-layer set a trail where he comes out at a road and is picked up in a car, then is dropped off again a few miles down the road, where he can continue on foot. Have a different car available to pick you and the hound up and drop you off where the trail continues.

This is also called "leapfrogging" where two teams work a lengthy trail, with each hound having a turn for a mile or so while the other rides in the pickup and rests before changing about. This speeds up the trail for those cold-night searches for nursing home walkaways or Alzheimer patients.

THE NATURE OF SCENT

A study of scenting conditions will help you understand why some days your hound works well and other days seems unable to trail. Weather has much to do with it. A cool, moist day is good for trailing; a hot, dry day evaporates the scent and makes trailing difficult. Wind moves and disperses the scent. Heavy pollen, as in a hayfield, or a dry, dusty road, will clog up a hound's sensitive nose in a short time. Newly laid asphalt destroys scent; creosote on railroad ties will blot out the scent to a degree, as will tobacco smoke and auto exhaust

One of the top mantraililng teams in the United State is Bill Grimm and Clyde. This photo shows them on the trail in an actual case, searching for a missing child in Charles County, Maryland.   *Courtesy, National Police Bloodhound Association*

Bill Smith of the Connecticut State Police sets off on the trail with a fresh, eager mantrailer.
Courtesy, National Police Bloodhound Association

fumes and other air pollution. Flares used at search scenes give off chemical contamination which will mask the scent in the vicinity.

Freezing will make scenting difficult; thawing will bring it out. A trail the hound can't find during a subfreezing night may be there when the sun hits it in the morning. Likewise a trail it can't find on a hot, dusty day may be discernible in the cooler night hours. A freshly plowed field holds no scent. If the trail enters it, your best course is to circle the field until the hound finds the trail on the other side. If manure has been freshly spread on a field it will mask the scent. If you approach a field which you can see has been spread with lime, avoid it, as the lime will burn the hound's nose. Circle and let him find the trail on the other side. If your search leads you into a building where you are overwhelmed by a strong scent, as in a home with food cooking, the scent will temporarily block the scent of the person you may be trailing. Stop right there for two minutes. The olfactory organs will adjust to that heavy scent, and the hound will again be able to follow his trail.

When you arrive at a search site, first of all water and exercise your hound so it can relieve itself and get acquainted with the area. Try to keep other searchers from parking their cars near the place the person being sought was last seen. Especially try to keep them from parking there with their motors running, as the exhaust fumes cover the scent and affect the hound's nose.

After you have your scent article and information about the victim, try to start your trail from the point the missing person was last seen. Frequently when a person is reported missing, calls will come in from persons claiming to have seen the subject in a dozen different directions. Others will claim to have searched the outbuildings, the attic or basement, and tell you the hound is on an old trail if he heads that way. *Believe your Bloodhound.* In case after case the subject has later been found hidden in that place those other people searched. Abusive or neglectful parents will lie to you to conceal their responsibility. People with emotional problems will tell tall stories to get attention. The Bloodhound has no reason to lie to you.

Try to avoid having a family member accompany you on a search. Family scent, because of eating the same food and having clothing laundered together, has a similarity to that of the missing person, and is distracting to the hound. The emotional condition of a family member can also add stress to the handler. Institutional scent of inmates of prisons is another example of the above scent problem.

When a scent article is not available, many breeds of dogs including Bloodhounds have trailed criminals from a crime scene by the adrenaline scent given off by fear or excitement. We have heard that this may not be true if the suspect is using drugs, as drugs will inhibit the emotions which cause that rush of adrenaline. You should be aware of that possibility.

Joseph B. Thomas, in his book *Hounds and Hunting* (1928), has some interesting observations on scent. Scenting is always bad, he says, on a south wind. His statement was based upon bird- and fox-hunting experience in the eastern United States and on reports from England and other countries. This factor was observed and noted as long ago as the fifth century B.C. Scent seems to disappear under heavy clouds with a storm about to break, but improves when the rain starts. A falling barometer is believed to indicate bad scenting conditions, while plenty of moisture in the air produces good scenting. Certain soil does not seem to hold scent; an example from India was a case where animals being hunted would run to a dried-up salt-lake bottom, where the scent was entirely lacking and the hounds could not trail. We have had other reports from handlers that their hounds could not find the trail on an ocean beach. Scent seems poor on freshly fallen autumn leaves, until they begin rotting. Very keen hounds have been observed to turn over dead leaves and smell the underside, or scratch up the soil a bit when working a difficult trail. Apparently the scent to some extent sinks into the soil.

Some hounds will trail with their noses very much to the ground, and give every appearance of serious work. Others rarely or never put their noses to the ground, but trail with their heads chest-high. To the inexperienced bystanders, they seem not to be trailing at all, and astonishment is great when the hound makes the find. Ch. Rye of Dakota and Cascade's Ranger were two such hounds.

Terrain can also influence the scent line. If the trail lies across a field with a hedge on one side, the scent will often drift and pile up against the hedge, where the hounds will find it. Or they may follow a trail down a city street on the opposite side, where breeze or traffic has blown it against the buildings. In an area of cliffs and valleys, the scent may be found at the cliff top while the trail was laid in the valley, or vice versa, depending upon whether the air warmed and rose, or cooled and dropped after the trail was laid.

As you work with your Bloodhound keep a record for your own information and to help you understand what your hound is doing. Record every success or lack of it, what weather conditions were, direction of wind, temperature and other conditions affecting scent. If you ever testify in court involving your Bloodhound trailing, this record may help to substantiate the fact that it was trained for mantrailing.

An old belief was that the Bloodhound trailed the scent of the feet, and that if the subject wore rubber boots this would prevent a scent trail. This is a complete fallacy. Scent is dispersed from the entire body, and may be described as a fine mist. It is believed to rise as it leaves the body and then settle to the ground as it cools, clinging to grass and shrubbery along the way. For this reason some observers have concluded that a trail five minutes old is as difficult to follow as one five hours old, and that a trail is at its strongest at about one hour. This is hard to prove, as that length of time seems to make little difference to a Bloodhound. It accounts for the fact that a Bloodhound can trail a person riding a bicycle or horse, or a baby being carried in the arms, or the people who entered a car. Nor does a runner lose the hound by crossing flooded fields or marshland, as the scent lies above the water, and clings to grasses or reeds growing through it. In the preceding chapters of mantrailing reports there are several where the hound has trailed into the water, or indicated the location of bodies in deep water.

While in cases involving lost persons, success is usually measured by the

Ch. Wrinklebrow's Dilly O'Dale,owned by Peggy Hemus and bred by Dale and Tressie Lewis, "takes the oath" as a representative of the only dog breed whose testimony is legal evidence in court. *Hemus*

find, Bill Tolhurst and other law enforcement people emphasize that in criminal cases this is far from the total value of the Bloodhound. The evidence uncovered by a Bloodhound may be invaluable in assisting the police in making an arrest, even when the Bloodhound may be unable to complete the trail. The hound may lead to the hidden loot, to the discarded disguise of the criminal, or objects dropped which may aid in identification. It may lead its handler to the murder weapon, and can tell when the person stopped. The route taken may indicate agility or lack of it. All these could aid the police in identifying the person; and if a suspect is picked up, these bits of information can often either identify him or rule him out. If he is picked up soon enough while the hound still retains that scent in its catalog, the hound can pick him out in a lineup.

THE BLOODHOUND AS WITNESS

It was long a matter of pride with Bloodhound owners that their was the only breed of dog whose "testimony" was accepted as evidence in a court of law. In recent years there have been cases where other dog testimony was accepted. Not all states accept this testimony, but those that do have requirements, which are basically as follows:

1. The Bloodhound must be purebred. AKC registration is acceptable evidence.
2. It must trail from the scene of the crime.
3. It must be experienced, with records to prove it.
4. It must be proved reliable.
5. There must be supporting evidence.

A knowledge of these requirements might make the difference in providing effective testimony should your hound be involved in solving a criminal case. Therefore, if your hound trails and finds a lost person, it would be very helpful to you if you got a statement of the case signed by those involved, especially the law officer in charge. This, together with your own training records, could provide the evidence of experience and reliability.

William D. Tolhurst may have testified in court with Bloodhound testimony more often than anyone. It is a matter of satisfaction to him that every case resulted in conviction. He makes an important point for the handler testifying in court; be very careful not to exaggerate or misstate your report. Being detected in anything but the exact truth can put you in a precarious position. Remember that your testimony in other cases can be used against you.

Estimates of the Bloodhound's olfactory ability vary from three hundred thousand to three million times as powerful as the human sense of smell. How one could measure this, we do not know; but we are eternally grateful that Old Nosey is the one on the forward end of the lead.

119

Ch. The Ring's Imp (Ch. The Ring's Concerto ex Ch. The Ring's Donna Elvira), owned by Mrs. Robert V. Lindsay and bred by Mary-Lees and Robert Noerr, was a memorable winner in the late 1950s. His record included Group wins as well as Bests of Breed at Westminster International and the American Bloodhound Club Specialty.   *Shafer*

6

The Great Show Bloodhounds

WHILE IT WOULD BE impossible to list every good hound and breeder of the last fifteen years, we would like to give a capsule history of some prominent among those who provided the foundation stock for today's breeders and show winners.

THE ST. HUBERT "B" LITTER

Since most of these breeders and their winning hounds have felt the influence of a single litter, it is logical to introduce this chapter with the record of what is undoubtedly the most famous Bloodhound litter in the history of the breed in America. This was the great "B" Litter of Mrs. Winifred Chatfield Stout. This was a litter of eight, one of which was unfortunately killed by an auto at four months. It was whelped June 4, 1962. The seven surviving pups all became champions; and three of them, Ch. St. Hubert Blondel, owned by Steve and Marion Pruitt (Mareve Kennels), Ch. St. Hubert Britomart, owned by Nancy Lindsay (Lime Tree Kennels), and Ch. St. Hubert Basilisk owned by Nancy Onthank, became BIS winners.

Ch. St. Hubert Bathos was exported to England, where he became an English Champion. There he sired numerous offspring, many of whose descendants have returned as imports to the United States and Canada.

The other members of the litter were Ch. St. Hubert Bodaceia, Ch. St. Hubert Boojum and Ch. St. Hubert Bailiff.

A study of the pedigree of this litter shows their inheritance from the great early kennels mentioned in chapter 1. Pedigrees of current winners, in large numbers, trace back to one or more of these notable hounds.

LIME TREE

Lime Tree Kennels was founded by Nancy Lindsay in 1954, with the aid and encouragement of her husband, Robert V. Lindsay. Their first pet had been a Basset; then their interests were extended to its larger relative.

At this time Harry Manning was manager of Mrs. Ryan's Panther Ledge establishment, and they had made his acquaintance. When they learned that a litter was expected at Panther Ledge, they visited in due time, and selected a puppy, Missy of Panther Ledge, TD. She was better known as Prue, and for eleven years the queen of Lime Tree.

The Lindsays then began looking for a male, and at Westminster they saw a puppy, The Rings Imp, bred by the Noerrs. He was sired by The Rings Concerto ex The Rings Donna Elvira. They fell in love with him, and brought him home. He was an impressive show dog, who was outstanding in the breed during the late 1950s. He was handled by both Mrs. Lindsay and Al Murray to a distinguished record. Among his winnings was what is called the "Triple Crown" of Dogdom; Best of Breed at Westminster, Chicago International and the American Bloodhound Club Specialty. He earned his championship title quickly, and before his death in 1960 had sired several champions in turn.

The Lindsays shared the sorrows of breeding together with the successes. Two bitches, Bailiol Belinda and an English import, Barsheen Jade, were doing well in the show ring when they died tragically. The Lindsays then acquired their "B" Litter Bloodhound, St. Hubert Britomart, who won her Best in Show from the Specialty at Greenwich, Connecticut, on June 12, 1965. She was handled to this win by Nancy Lindsay. Britomart was one of the earlier Bloodhound bitches to win a BIS, incidentally, in the same year that her littermate Ch. St. Hubert Blondel won his.

Unfortunately, Britomart died of bloat at age three, after having produced only one litter to carry on her excellent qualities. These, however, sired by BIS-winner Ch. Hull Down's Milk Ear Willie, distributed her genes widely. Her daughter, Ch. Lime Tree Portia, bred to the imported liver and tan dog, Dandy of Brighton, became the mother of Am. & Can Ch. Lime Tree Soames, the top-producing stud dog of the breed. Soames was whelped March 22, 1968, and died April 5, 1976. In the course of his career he was a Group winner in both the United States and Canada, a Canadian multiple Best in Show winner, and top-winning Bloodhound in Canada for 1971. He was the breed's top-producing stud dog for 1971–1974, and won the Stud Dog class at the American Bloodhound Club's 20th Anniversary Specialty show in 1973 as well as the Stud Dog class at the East Coast Specialty show in 1971.

Portia's litter brother, Pendragon, was exported to England, where as Abingerwood Lime Tree Pendragon he became an outstanding stud, and sired many puppies which ultimately returned to America.

From the mating of Ch. Thor of Gunmar and The Ring's Nedda came the St. Hubert "B" litter. The dogs pictured above are all members of that litter and all are BIS winners. They are (from left) Ch. St. Hubert Blondel with owner Richard Pruitt, Ch. St. Hubert Britomart with owner Nancy Lindsay, and Ch. St. Hubert Basilisk, owned by Nancy Onthank, with Dee Hutchinson. Judge Stanley Dangerfield is shown with this magnificent threesome. *Gilbert*

Ch. Lime Tree Soames (Dandy of Brighton ex Ch. Lime Tree Portia), owned by Mr. and Mrs. Vincent Brey and his breeder, Mrs. Robert V. Lindsay, with whom he is shown. During his lifetime this hound established a record as the top sire in the breed. *Gilbert*

123

Ch. Lime Tree Portia, owned and handled by Mrs. Robert V. Lindsay, achieved fame as the dam of Ch. Lime Tree Soames and is a litter sister to Abingerwood Lime Tree Pendragon, both vital stud forces in the breed. She is shown going WB at the 1967 ABC Specialty under judge John J. Schultz enroute to her title.   *Gilbert*

Ch. Black Tommy of Huguenot, owned by Isabel and Ed Simon, was owner-shown to many good wins. He was BB at the ABC Specialty 1958 in his first appearance as a champion. Tommy is shown winning the Hound Group at the Valley Forge KC under Richard Jennings.   *Brown*

Mrs. Lindsay became well known as a dog show judge, and both Lindsays were active members of the American Bloodhound Club, with Mr. Lindsay serving for a time as AKC delegate and Mrs. Lindsay writing the breed column in *Pure-Bred Dogs—American Kennel Gazette*, and serving for a time as American Bloodhound Club president.

In 1973 Mr. Lindsay's business responsibilities led to the family's move to England, and the Lime Tree hounds were mainly dispersed among new owners or coowners. The Lindsays returned to the United States in the fall of 1976, and Mrs. Lindsay resumed her place as a highly regarded dog show judge. She retired in February 1990 after judging the Hound Group at the Westminster Kennel Club show.

CH. BLACK TOMMY OF HUGUENOT

Outstanding among the Bloodhounds of Huguenot, bred by Genevieve and Cornelius Boland, was Ch. Black Tommy of Huguenot. He was owned by Isabel and Ed Simon, and was handled by Ed throughout his show career.

Black Tommy was whelped on April 18, 1956, and died June 4, 1967. He was a medium-sized black and tan with a beautiful, driving gait. During his show career he had seven BIS wins, one Best American-Bred in Show award (no longer awarded and not included in the official record), twenty-one GR 1s, nineteen GR 2s, eight GR 3s, four GR 4s, seventy-seven BBs and three BOS. Except for two BOS wins, he was undefeated in the breed as a champion. These wins were made between November 4, 1956, and September 8, 1962, when he was retired, except for coming out in Veterans classes.

At the 1958 Specialty, held with the Long Island KC, Tommy made his first appearance as a champion. He went BB under Percy Roberts and on to win the Hound Group under Harry Peters, Jr. Mrs. Albin Strudee from Toronto, Canada, was judging Best in Show that day, and Tommy was her selection for the supreme award.

Although Black Tommy was not used extensively at stud, he sired the Sinkinsons' Ch. The Chase's Perizadah, who became one of the top-producing dams in the breed's history. Black Tommy's influence was felt through her and his grandchildren.

LANDROVER

When Charles and Frances Rowland founded their Landrover Kennels it was not with the intention of breeding the most Bloodhounds, but breeding for the best quality that included the ability to carry on the traditional function. The Rowlands trained and used their hounds as mantrailers; their foundation bitch, Princess Timagami, was the daughter and granddaughter of world record mantrailers—Doc Holiday and his mother, Queen Guenivere of Laureloak. Her dam was Socrates M.T. She was trained in the Adirondack Mountains, rough and difficult terrain, and proved worthy of her lineage.

The next Bloodhound added to the kennel was Am. & Can. Ch. Short-Bred's Bouncer, who was awarded a Hound GR 1 at his first appearance in the show ring. He was a consistent Group placing Bloodhound, with three GR 1s and 10 other Group placements on his record. These awards made him number three East Coast Bloodhound in 1960.

When these two hounds were mated, the result was a litter of seven, of which five became champions: Landrover Lancer, Longbow, Liza, Madam B and Marshall Dillon. Liza and Longbow both won five-point majors at American Bloodhound Club Specialties. Heritage remained with his breeders, and Juno was sold to a young boy who saved his money to buy his Bloodhound.

Fran Rowland quotes from a letter received from this youth when the puppy was six months old. "For a dog of her age she is one of the best I have hunted over. I have taught her to be an all-around dog. She hunts coon—caught one on the ground so far—runs birds very well and in the marsh will bring back ducks. Game so far is 37 coon, 12 birds and 20 ducks. I would pay twice the price of the pup if I had it to do over again."

This must have been an astonishing sight to hunters with more conventional breeds of bird dogs, but a reminder that the Bloodhound line is present in the background of many of them.

Timagami's second mating was to Am. & Can. Ch. Big Ben of Huguenot, resulting in a litter of four. Two earned their Canadian titles, one with majors in the States. Both had Group placings in Canada, and later produced Group winners. Their owners occasionally used them with the Canadian police.

Tragically, Timagami died young. She was quite well trained to command, and occasionally was trailed off lead. On one such training trail, the trail left the woods and followed a railroad track. With single-minded devotion to her work, she ignored the approaching train and was killed.

During one decade of exhibiting (the 1960s) very few litters were whelped; an average of one per year or less. Landrover hounds were exhibited only to their championships, with several winning in the ring without fail, and awarded multiple Group wins and/or placements in both the United States and Canada. Each dog held its place as top Bloodhound in Canada when shown.

The first homebred champion for the Rowlands was Am. & Can. Ch. Landrover Madam B. She was exhibited six times, winning four majors at thirteen months. During that season Landrover Kennels attended only seven shows, winning thirteen majors.

Landrover hounds winning many of the top awards were Ch. Landrover Lancer, Ch. Landrover Longbow, Am. & Can. Ch. Eastway Rebecca, Am. & Can. Ch. Landrover Lorelei, who won her championship undefeated in five shows, Am. & Can. Ch. Landrover Madam B, Am. & Can. Ch. Landrover Lillabet, Ch. Landrover Liza, Ch. Landrover Elect, Ch. Landrover Nicolle, Am. & Can. Ch. Big Ben of Huguenot, Am. & Can. Ch. Zenith of Brighton (import) and Am. & Can. Ch. Landrover Lucid. Ch. Lucid was the one exception to the

Ch. Landrover Royal Liza and Ch. Landrover Royal Longbow, owned by L. P. Plumley, Director of the New York State Ranger School.

Ch. Landrover Lucid (left), handled by E. J. Carver, and Ch. Landrover Lorelei, handled by Charles Rowland, were BB and BOS respectively under Louis J. Murr at the 1971 ABC Specialty. Both hounds are owned by Charles and Frances Rowland.   *Shafer*

Rowlands' custom of not campaigning a champion; he was shown as a champion for about four months. In seventeen shows he was undefeated for BB in the United States and in several Canadian shows, with seven GR 1s, nine GR 2s and several thirds and fourths. These wins resulted in Lucid being named Top East Coast Bloodhound for 1970.

Landrover hounds won several American Bloodhound Club supported shows, and at six Specialty shows, a Landrover class entry won the major. Ironically, Lucid was the exception in placing RWD at one Specialty. However, following completion of his championship he was BB at the 1970 East Coast Specialty with his kennelmate, Lorelei, taking the honors as BOS.

There have been many other outstanding Landrover hounds through the years, including Ch. Landrover Magistrate II, a Midwest (International) Specialty BW. Altogether, although the Rowlands' breeding program was limited, the quality they produced was outstanding.

Shortly after 1970 Landrover retired from breeding and exhibiting until 1976, when Ch. Landrover Chorister completed his championship at Westminster. Three of his offspring, Ch. Landrover Chastity, Carthusian and Choral, were also successfully shown at that time.

THE RECTORY

The Rectory Bloodhounds are the justifiable pride of the Rev. George Sinkinson, Jr., and his wife, Jackie, of Owings Mills, Maryland. As of this time, fifty Bloodhounds of their breeding have completed their championships, and among them have been several Specialty and Westminster winners, five BIS winners, top-winning Bloodhound for the year several times and the top-producing dam of all breeds in the United States, Ch. The Rectory's Ruin.

Like several others, the Sinkinsons bought their first Bloodhound because owning one had been a childhood dream, although they were not actually very well acquainted with the reality of that dream. They grew up in Rhode Island where the state police maintained and used Bloodhounds, thereby striking the spark.

The Sinkinsons were fortunate in securing for their first Bloodhound Ch. The Chase's Perizadah. They called her Beulah, and before long decided she was too exceptional an animal to limit her talents to being the household pet. They began showing her, and giving her trailing training under the guidance of the Rhode Island State Police.

The Sinkinsons were later transferred to California, and it was here that Beulah whelped her first litter in 1963, founding "The Rectory" Kennels with a litter that saw five become champions. Included in this litter were Ch. The Rectory's Curate, Ch. The Rectory's Muldoon, a BB winner at Westminster and a multi-Group winner, and Ch. The Rectory's Ruin.

Ruin was bred only three times and produced a total of fourteen champions. These included four Westminster BB winners, two BIS bitches, and five Group

Ch. The Rectory's Ruin, owned and bred by the Rev. George and Jackie Sinkinson, distinguished herself as a superlative producer. She was the dam of 14 champions in three litters and was the top-producing dam of all breeds in 1970. *Gilbert*

Ch. The Rectory's Curate, owned and handled by Richard C. Hiett, was a litter brother to Ruin. He is shown here winning the Hound Group under Haskell Shuffman at the KC of Beverly Hills.

Ludwig

winners. Her first litter, sired by Ch. Equerry of Brighton, included Jackie Sinkinson's favorite bitch, Ch. The Rectory's Reward, a three-time Speciality winner, Westminster breed winner, and a BIS winner. Also in this litter was Ch. The Rectory's Recruit.

Ruin's second and third litters were both sired by Ch. St. Hubert Blondel, and the second litter included seven future champions. Ch. The Rectory's Rebel Yell, a BIS and Specialty winner, and Ch. The Rectory's Rabbi, BB at Westminster, twice a Specialty BB and a multi-Group winner were the most noted products of the Blondel-Ruin combination.

Reward's daughter, Ch. The Rectory's Shalom, produced the first Rectory all-champion litter. Sired by Ch. Leroy of Lansford, it includes Ch. The Rectory's Limbo, twice a Westminster BB winner, and BIS dog.

Two hounds of this line were especially outstanding on the West Coast.

Ch. The Rectory's Curate was owned by Richard C. Hiett. He was whelped April 18, 1963, and died Nov. 13, 1972.

Curate won his championship at fourteen months, and during his show career made a record of two BIS, seventeen GR 1s, seventeen GR 2s, nine GR 3s and thirteen GR 4s, in addition to eighty-eight BB wins. He was owner-handled during his entire career.

While he was used at stud only twelve times, he produced twenty-four champions, some of which went on to become Group winners.

In 1970 and 1971 he was named a Top Producer by Mrs. Irene Khatoonian Schlintz in *Kennel Review* magazine. In 1966 and 1967 he was among the Top Ten Hounds on the Phillips System.

When he was bred to a granddaughter, Ch. Highlands Baby Daphne, seven puppies resulted, of which four were shown. All finished.

When he was bred to a niece, Ch. Marse's Minstral of Cavieye, a litter of seven resulted, of which four finished. Two died when they were almost finished. One was not shown.

Ch. The Rectory's Recruit, whelped Nov. 19, 1965, died Feb. 1, 1975, and was owned and shown by James B. Trousdale.

Recruit was the winner of two GR 1s, many other Group placements, and was BB at Westminster in 1969. He was top-winning Bloodhound in the United States in 1969 on both the Phillips and *Kennel Review* systems, and top-winning Bloodhound in the United States in 1970 by the *Kennel Review* system.

He was champion at the exceptional age of ten months, and became the sire of twelve champions.

In addition to possessing the qualities of the breed Standard, one judge said to me that Recruit was a winner because he *showed* with style and flair, and obvious enjoyment in the ring, that made him outstanding.

The Rectory Kennels moved to Maine upon the Reverend Sinkinson's retirement, and continued breeding Bloodhounds which not only won in the show ring, but contributed to mantrailing activity as well. The Rectory's Vicar is the working partner of James Shaffer, 1990 president of National Police Bloodhound Association, and another Rectory champion is working with search and rescue

Ch. The Rectory's Recruit (Ch. Equerry of Brighton ex Ch. The Rectory's Ruin), owned by James B. Trousdale and bred by the Sinkinsons. Recruit was the top-winning Bloodhound in the United States for 1969 and numbers amoung his notable wins this BB at Westminster in 1969 under Ellsworth Gamble, Mr. Trousdale handling. *Shafer*

Ch. The Rectory's Buglin Alleluia, handled by Linda More, was the only Bloodhound to win Best in Show under breeder-judge Nancy Lindsay. *Charles*

The Rectory's Vicar, owned by Jim and Becky Shaffer, follows the traditional role of the breed.

Ch. St. Hubert Blondel, owned by Mr. and Mrs. Richard Pruitt, was one of America's top winners, with a record that included a BIS, 15 GR1s, and two ABC Specialty BBs. The second (pictured) was won from the Veterans class in 1968 under Hollis Wilson, Mr. Pruitt handling. *Gilbert*

132

in North Carolina. The dam of both these hounds, and of the Rectory's first obedience title winner, is Ch. The Rectory's Buglin' Alleluia. "Lulu" is a Westminster Best of Breed winner, winner of four all-breed Bests in Show, and the sires of both her litters were Best in Show dogs. Although the Sinkinsons have reduced their activities, the influence of their fine hounds will continue to be felt in the breed for years to come.

MAREVE

Mareve Kennels took its name from a combination of the names of Marion and Steve (Richard S.) Pruitt. Their interest in dogs began with Bassets, and in a few years extended to the Bloodhound.

The Pruitts' first Bloodhound, in 1963, was Luctor of Gunmar, bred by the Grundbergs. The next year they acquired Gudrun of Gunmar, a red bitch. She finished her championship early, and became their foundation bitch, mother of Ch. Winchester of Mareve, Ch. Tornado of Mareve, Ch. Colt of Mareve, and many others.

Upon entering the Bloodhound world, the Pruitts met Harry Manning, and like many others, benefited from his knowledge and advice. When he recommended a fine young male to them, they bought the young dog, who became their BIS winner and house pet. Ch. St. Hubert Blondel. "Barney" loved to swim with his owner, and in the Pruitt home, his favorite spot was in front of the fireplace.

Barney's show wins included one all-breed BIS, fifteen GR 1s and thirty-six other placements in a year and a half of campaigning. Harry Manning was his handler, showing him to his BIS win among other victories. Sadly, on the day of Mr. Manning's death, Steve Pruitt handled his hound to the coveted BB at Westminster. Barney was retired following this win, except for a few rare, special occasions.

Barney twice won the American Bloodhound Club Specialty show (1966 and 1968) with the second win being from the Veteran dog class. His get have been Winners and BW at the Specialty shows and in 1968 a daughter went BB from the Open bitch class at the Southern California Specialty.

Ch. St. Hubert Blondel died peacefully on January 15, 1973, as he slept at the foot of his owner's bed.

The Pruitts became active in the American Bloodhound Club soon after buying their first Bloodhound, with Marion serving as trophy chairman and then accepting the position of secretary. This task, which became steadily more demanding, she maintained until the end of 1975.

Bloodhounds from Mareve Kennels, in addition to their show success, served in many modeling assignments for magazines and television, keeping the breed before the public eye.

DAKOTA

Coauthor Cathy Brey and husband Vincent founded Dakota Kennels in the early 1960s with Sy's Mr. Red, whom we called Major. He was sired by Westways Diamond Dick ex Miss Happy of Triangle Acres, and of the Brighton line. Although he appears black and tan in his picture, he was a red dog. Soon afterward we bought the puppy who was to become Am. & Can. Ch. Miss Happy Gelert of Dakota, and our foundation bitch.

Major earned his Canadian championship, and was a Group winner in both the United States and Canada, before he died prematurely of bloat; teaching us early the grief that can go with dog breeding. Happy consoled us by living an exceptionally long life, and producing some of the puppies we will never forget.

We had become interested in Bloodhounds because of their unique ability as mantrailers; even on our flat North Dakota plains little children and the senile manage to find ways of getting lost. During the years our hounds have done considerable work not only with our local police, but throughout the state.

We built up our kennel, adding Abingerwood and Lime Tree lines, and the puppy who was to be our first BIS winner, Am. & Can. Ch. The Rectory's Rebellion. These lines combined to produce the many outstanding Bloodhounds carrying the Dakota name. Among these have been the multiple BIS winner Am. & Can. Ch. Pooh Bear of Dakota, Am. & Can. Ch. Incantation of Dakota, Am. & Can. Ch. Pathfinder of Dakota, Am. & Can. Ch. Rye of Dakota, Ch. Rainbow Chaser of Dakota, CDX, TD, and many more. As of this date, there have been over fifty champions bred at Dakota Kennels. I would like to tell a little about some of these dogs.

Another top-producing stud dog of Dakota Kennels, although little known in the show ring, was Ch. Lucky Strike of Brighton, familiarly known as Phillip. He was the sire of the multiple BIS winner, Ch. Pooh Bear of Dakota, as well as numerous other champion progeny. Many of these were winners in the Group and at Specialty shows. He was sired by Eng. & Am. Ch. St. Hubert Bathos, with his dam, Eng. Ch. Freesia of Brighton combining the Brighton and Barsheen lines.

One of the outstanding hounds we have been priviliged to share has been Am. & Can. Ch. Lime Tree Soames, whom we have coowned with Nancy Lindsay, his breeder. His recent death is a loss to the breed. He sired more champions than any other stud dog of this breed to date; and no doubt more of his get are still on their way to their championships. A week after his death, his thirty-eighth offspring to finish completed her championship; only a few days later the last litter sired by him, consisting of three bitch puppies, was whelped by Am. & Can. Ch. Hilltop Acres Nana Van Rinkle, owned by Laura Keating of Missoula, Montana.

Am. & Can. Ch. The Rectory's Rebellion was a large, black and tan, strong-moving hound who delighted many a judge and spectator by his insistence upon personally carrying his winnings from the ring. More than one judge received the surprise of his life when that big hound jumped up and grabbed the rosette right out of his hand.

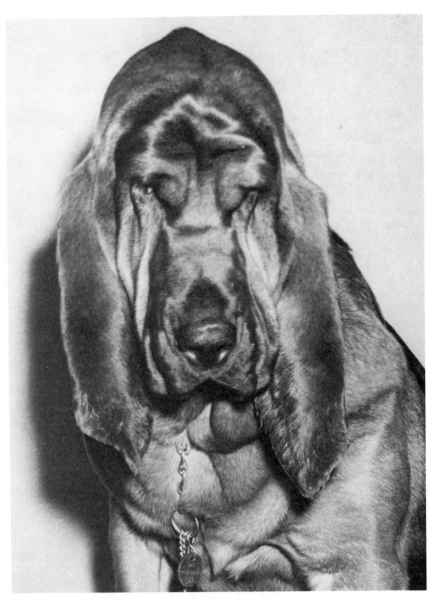

Ch. Rye of Dakota, owned and bred by Mr. and Mrs. Vincent Brey, was a respected winner and an outstanding mantrailer. *Shadow*

Ch. The Rectory's Rebellion, a Canadian BIS winner, with
owner Catherine Brey.   *Robinson*

Canadian Ch. Bugle Bay's Amos of Dakota, owned by Ernie
and Camille Danylchuk and bred by Mrs. Danylchuk and
Mrs. Brey. Amos was a Group winner and is shown here
with Mrs. Brey.   *Mattern*

Ch. Incantation of Dakota, owned by David and Pat Huff and Rita Goering (handling) and bred by Mrs. Brey. He is shown winning under judge Helen Walsh.

Francis

Ch. Bugle Bay's Rufus, a homebred owned by Ernie and Camille (handling) Danylchuk, is shown in a BIS win at Fort Garry (Canada) under judge Ellsworth Gamble.   *Colomy*

Rebel, as we called him, was a Group winner in both the United States and Canada. He made history for the breed in Canada in 1967 when he went Best in Show at the Manitoba Hound Show, under Forest Hall. On the same day, his son (later Ch.) Rye of Dakota won Best in Sweepstakes, all hounds, at the same show, under Virginia McCoy.

In 1968 Rebel made a breakthrough for Bloodhounds in Canada by winning Best in Show, All Breeds, Mid-Canada Dog Show, under the late renowned Canadian judge Thomas Joel.

Can. Ch. Bugle Bay's Amos of Dakota, a group-winning dog, was bred by Cathy Brey and Camille Danylchuk. He was sired by Ch. Lucky Strike of Brighton ex Shawnee of Dakota. His owners are Ernie and Camille Danylchuk.

Ch. Rye of Dakota was whelped Aug. 7, 1966, and was bred and owned by Vincent and Catherine Brey. There is an interesting, amusing story about the dog I'd like to relate here.

I show my dogs on a very fine chain and quarter-inch leather lead. Whenever we attended a show with Rye, any of the family who came to ringside had to remain there until Rye left the ring. His great joy in life was finding anyone who was missing; the fact that a show was in progress was of little interest to him. I had taken him to the Mid-Canada event, a prestigious Canadian show, and the large building was very crowded, with several rings going at once. My son, Kelly, about nine years old at the time, was with me. Instead of standing at ringside as he should have, he decided to go exploring. As Rye and I were leaving the ring he suddenly realized that Kelly was missing; off we went to find him. I could not pull back on the leash, as I knew Rye would break this fine choke chain he wore, and there was no telling where he would end up.

We went flying through the spectators and past the guard at the door. He called after, asking where we were going, and I yelled back, "I don't know, but I have a feeling my little boy just went out here." At high speed, we left the building and into the parking lot, and quickly corralled Kelly. As I reentered the building, boy on one hand and hound on the other, the security guard said he'd give anything to have a dog like that on the Winnipeg Police force.

Ch. Pooh Bear of Dakota was bred by Vincent and Cathy Brey and owned by Vincent and Shelly Brey.

Pooh Bear was handled to her championship and first BIS by Virginia McCoy, and campaigned as a champion by Roy L. Murray. She became the top Group-winning Bloodhound of all time, besides winning many Bests in Show.

Pooh Bear was the top-winning Bloodhound in the United States in 1972 and 1973; in 1973 she was also number nine Hound. She was the first Bloodhound ever to win BIS in both the United States and Canada, where she was BIS at the Fort Garry KC show in 1974, handled by her breeder, Cathy Brey. The Group judge was Dr. Frank Booth; the BIS judge was Maurice Baker. She was top-winning Bloodhound in Canada in 1974, and BB at Westminster in 1973. Her campaign has extended from Canada to the Gulf of Mexico, and from the Pacific to the Atlantic.

Pooh Bear's personality made many friends for the breed. She loved to

Canadian Ch. Sy's Mr. Red, owned by Mr. and Mrs. Vincent Brey, was the starting point for Dakota Bloodhound Kennels. He is shown winning the Hound Group at the Fargo Moorehead KC under Marie B. Meyer, Mrs. Brey handling.

Olson

Ch. Sims' Stormin' Norman of Dakota, owned by Lois Sims and Shelley Brey, holds the current record as the youngest Bloodhound on record to win an all-breed BIS. It is also significant that the win which gave Norman this distinction was made from the classes.

Colomy

Ch. Pooh Bear of Dakota (Ch. Lucky Strike of Brighton ex Ch. Abingerwood Wild Honey), owned by Vincent and Shelley Brey, was extensively campaigned in the United States and Canada, making good wins in both countries. She is shown in a BIS win at Town and Country KC under Langdon Skarda, Roy Murray handling. *Petrulis*

139

play with squeaky toys in the show ring, and entertained the audience with her mischievous way of managing to pop the squeakers out of them.

Am. & Can. Ch. Sims' Stormin' Norman of Dakota was whelped June 1, 1973. He is owned by Lois Sims and Shelley Brey, and was bred by Cathy Brey and Lois Sims. Norman finished his American championship from the puppy class, handled by Roy L. Murray and Shelly Brey.

He was shown as a champion for the first time at twelve months by his breeder, Cathy Brey, was BB and went on to win the Hound Group under Hayden Martin. Norman was then shown in Canada and finished his Canadian Championship by winning BIS from the classes under Bill Dawson at Portage La Prairie (Manitoba) in July 1974, thus making him the youngest Bloodhound to go BIS at an all-breed show, and breaking the record of Ch. Pooh Bear of Dakota, who won her first BIS at sixteen months, and Buccaneer of Idol Ours II, who won his at fourteen months.

Norman sired his first litter shortly after his BIS win, and his puppies are well started in the show ring at this writing.

Ch. Incantation of Dakota, bred by Catherine F. Brey, became a Texan under the ownership of David and Pat Huff and Rita Goering. He was handled in the ring by Rita Goering, and was one of the top-winning Bloodhounds in early 1975, and a Group winner, when he was struck down in the midst of his career by bloat.

One of the top-winning Bloodhounds in Canada in 1975, Ch. Bugle Bay's Rufus, sired by Ch. Lime Tree Soames ex Can. Ch. Little Eva of Dakota, was bred by Ernie and Camille Danylchuk.

Dakota Kennels has always restricted breeding to one or two litters a year, striving for quality and placement in good homes. We have seen the damage done to breeds which have become too popular, and dread the thought of the Bloodhound descending to that level.

As Mrs. Brey became more active in judging, she gradually retired from active breeding to avoid the appearance of a conflict of interest. The breed remains very special to her.

HYL-BILLIE

Another breeder with many years of experience is Hylda Owens Rose, of Wisconsin, breeder of Hyl-Billie Hounds. In addition to the many show hounds produced in her kennels, she trained and used her Bloodhounds for work with the police. It was due to this fact that she lost several of her valuable animals when they were shot in their pens while she was away from home. This tragedy was obviously an act of vengeance resulting from their use in a criminal case.

One of Mrs. Rose's outstanding hounds was Ch. Hyl-Billie's Hyrcate, CD, whelped April 7, 1961. She was a medium-sized bitch, handled during her show career by Stanley Flowers. After her official campaigning she was sometimes handled by her breeder-owner. In 1964 she was ninth in the Phillips system in

Hyl-Billie's Hyrcate, CD, owned and bred
ylda Owens Rose, was a BIS winner and
y times a Group winner in the early
's. She was usually handled by Stanley
ers, but is shown here handled by her
r to BB at the Harbor Cities KC under
rt E. Vary enroute to a GR3. *Bennett*

Ch. Cragsmoor Bacchus of Mareve, the top winner of
the breed for 1974, shown here with his co-owner,
Matt Stander. *Klein*

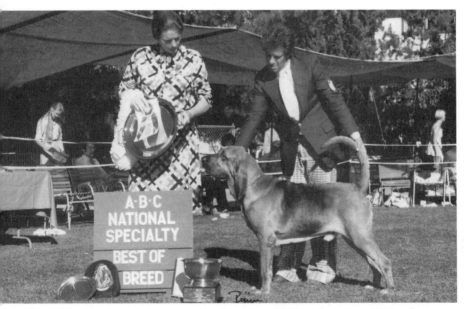

Ch. Cascade's Columbo of Dakota, owned by Cathy Brey, Eugene Zaphiris, and Debra Barber,
was Best of Breed at the 1978 National Specialty under judge Anne Rogers Clark. His dam
was Lena Reed's Search and Rescue hound, Ch. Cascade's Melody of Dakota. *Pegini*

141

the Hound Group. She was one of the first Bloodhound bitches to win a BIS in the United States. She was a multiple Group winner, and top-winning Bloodhound in the United States for several years.

CRAGSMOOR

To most people active in the dog fancy today, Matthew Stander's name is synonymous with the widely-read weekly *Dog News*. Matt Stander is also an ardent supporter of the Bloodhound and has successfully bred and campaigned several to admirable show records.

One of these was a dog he coowned. The dog's name was Ch. Cragsmoor's Bacchus of Mareve (Ch. The Ring's Zorro ex Countess Blue Chip Mara). The sole survivor in his litter, Bacchus became the top-winning Bloodhound in the United States for 1974, establishing himself as a Group winner in the process.

He was handled in the ring by Tommy Glassford and by Mr. Stander himself, winning well in the hands of both.

Bacchus was a masculine black and tan with a magnificent headpiece and overall correct breed type. He was a dog that has not only done well for his owners and breeders, but also for the Bloodhound breed.

CH. THE RECTORY'S YANKEE PATRIOT

Quite offhandedly the Bloodhound acquired a most influential admirer early in 1975. The story of how this came about is quite interesting.

Mr. Roger Caras is well-known across the land as an author, speaker and radio commentator. His *Pets and Wildlife* segment on CBS radio enjoys a large following and he has consistently spoken for humane and sensible attitudes toward all living things.

Shortly after the beginning of 1975 Mr. Caras was approached by his teenage son, Barclay, who expressed a wish to show a dog. Acting on his father's suggestion, Barclay Caras visited the Westminster show that year to look over the various breeds and decide on one that appealed to the youthful, prospective exhibitor.

Prior to visiting Westminster the younger Caras was told by his parents he could settle on a *small* breed as there were other animals in the Caras household already. Fate, however, took a hand and Barclay Caras came home from the Garden totally in love, as only a teenage boy can be, with the Bloodhound. Small breed?

Somehow the family reached an accord and the appropriate inquiries were made to locate the right puppy. In due course Barclay Caras had his hopeful in The Rectory's Yankee Patriot.

Yankee Patriot was bred by Mrs. Sinkinson and was sired by Ch. The Rectory's Wisdom out of Ch. The Rectory's Rebel Yell. The new addition's

Ch. The Rectory's Yankee Patriot, owned by Barclay Caras and bred by Rev. and Mrs. Sinkinson. Aside from being a successful show dog and sire, Yankee has brought the breed a considerable amount of favorable public attention through the various media.   *Caras*

Am/Can CH. Dominator O'Craigel Telmetrue, (Ch. Cascades Mannix of Dakota ex Ch Bonita Bonama Telmetrue), handled by co-owner Linda Winters, was the top-winning Canadian Bloodhound of all time.

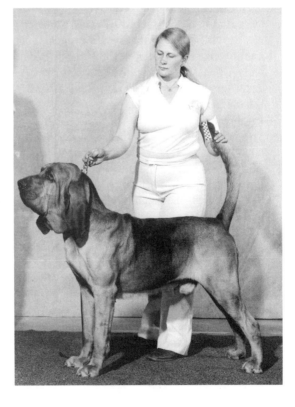

family background presaged a bright future in the show ring and this is just what came to pass. The young dog proved his mettle in competition and was a champion by the end of the year with a number of excellent wins at top shows along the way.

Yankee Patriot's life and times were the subject of a lead story in *The New York Times* Sunday magazine soon after the 1976 Centennial Westminster show. He was also a featured attraction at the Manhattan Savings Bank's annual exhibit of show dogs in 1976, proudly representing the breed with Mrs. Caras putting him through his well-rehearsed paces.

Roger Caras and his family are now confirmed Bloodhound fanciers. Owning one of the breed has caught the Carases up in the breed's singular charisma. Hopefully theirs will be a long-term involvement. It is an involvement that has already benefited the breed and all dogs in general. It can only do more to help the image of the Bloodhound, the show dog and the companion dog in the future.

JUNE PITTER AND CANADIAN WINNERS

June Pitter, of Markham, Ontario, bred only one Bloodhound litter, but out of that litter she picked a winner as her pet. He was Can. Ch. Craigallachie's Harry, and was to become the Pitters' devoted house dog until a ripe old age for the breed. He finished his championship with a BIS win from the classes, taking the award at the Progressive Kennel Club show, Don Mills, Ontario, in 1978.

In 1974 Mrs. Pitter bought a puppy cobred by the authors, sired by Ch. Lucky Strike of Brighton ex Ch. Cascade's Melody of Dakota. He was to become Am. & Can. Ch. Cascade's Mannix of Dakota, called Hector by the Pitters, and again the family pet. He was a litter brother of Ch. Cascade's Columbo of Dakota, and also went on to a notable show career, earning his Canadian title at ten months.

Highlights of Hector's career include winning the second Canadian Bloodhound Club Specialty show at Barrie. At the same Specialty, his son, Ch. Christopher Crambo Telmetrue was winner of the Puppy Sweepstakes. The following year Hector took Best Stud Dog and his son Chris was Best Opposite Sex. Although shown only five times that year, he won a Group placement each time.

Hector was bred twice to Linda Winter's Ch. Bonita Bonama Telmetrue, and from the first breeding June Pitter kept as her pet, coowned with Mrs. Winters, Am. & Can. Ch. Dominator O'Craigel Telmetrue, known as Rory. Rory died in late 1989 at the age of eleven and one-half years, leaving behind a record as the top-winning Bloodhound ever in Canada. He was handled in the ring by Mrs. Winters, finished his Canadian championship at nine months, his American championship in four straight shows, and was Best of Breed at the 1983 American Bloodhound Club East Coast Specialty from the Open dog class. His name shows in the pedigrees of many winning Bloodhounds in both Canada and the United States.

THE CHARLES SEXTONS AND CH. THE VIKING'S THOR

A dazzling star in the Bloodhound ring was Ch. The Viking's Thor, lovingly known as Sid, and owned by Charles and Inger Sexton. He finished his championship at eleven months, and soon afterward, in the hands of Vic Capone began compiling the record of the most Best in Show wins—thirty-three—of any Bloodhound in history. Among his 137 Group firsts were back-to-back (1987 and 1988) victories at the famous Westminster Kennel Club show. His perfect movement and obvious enjoyment in the show ring added to his elegance in the ring.

Tragically, he was lost to cancer at only six and one-half years of age. He sired many champions who continue his quality for the betterment of the breed. One of them, Ch. Legacy's St. Patrick of Viking, has started in his father's footprints. At less than two years he had two all-breed Best in Show wins, plus the 1989 National Specialty. While a new love never replaces a true love, he brings a bit of the old Sid into the Sexton family's life.

THE CHARLES ROBBS AND CH. ROCLIN'S IMAGE OF PINE HOLLOW

An outstanding West Coast Bloodhound of the later 1980s is Ch. Roclin's Image of Pine Hollow, lovingly known as Ace in his home with Charles and Judy Robb of Walnut Creek, California. Ace was exclusively handled in his show career by coowner Edith Hanson, and his lovely deep shade of liver and tan, together with his beautiful movement and structure, made him truly eye-catching in the ring.

Ace was preceded in the Best in Show ring by his great-grandfather Ch. The Rectory's Curate and his grandfather Ch. Pine Hollow's Yankee Doodle. He was shown 147 times as a Special, winning 8 all-breed Bests in Show, 4 Specialty shows, 140 Bests of Breed and 85 Group placements.

KATHY EVANS (KAMILOT)

At a time when most people stay with a breed for five years, Kathy Evans has owned, and occasionally bred, Bloodhounds for twenty years. The puppies she breeds are not lightly sent forth into the world; she would rather see prospective purchasers change their minds before they buy than six months later, and resists those impulse buyers. So many things can go wrong in the life of a dog, but that ''once in a lifetime'' dog can also be a source of lasting remembrances. For Kathy Evans that dog was the last one left of a twelve-puppy litter, and by then she knew he would never be for sale. He was Am. & Can. Ch. Augustus of Kamilot, a 135-pound lapdog. His untimely accidental death in 1988 left his owner heartbroken, and ended what should have been an outstanding show

Ch. Viking's Thor, owned by Charles and Inger Sexton, was the only Bloodhound to win back-to-back Group firsts at the Westminster Kennel Club Show. *Ashbey*

Ch. Roclin's Image of Pine Hollow (Ch. Roclin's High Noon of Witsend ex Rocklin's Hot Pepper of Selonky), owned by Charles and Judy Robb and Edith Hanson, an outstanding West Coast Bloodhound. *Callea*

Am/Can Ch. Augustus of Kamilot was that special dog for breeder-owner Kathy Evans. He is shown here being presented with a Group first at Jefferson County under judge Walter Shallenbarger. *Ernst*

Ch. The Rectory's Micah, owned by Drs. Stephen and Susan Harper, was the top Bloodhound on the Phillips System for 1979, 1980, and 1981. He was handled during his campaign by Jim Rathbun. *Alverson*

147

career. During the six months he was shown in 1988 he earned a spot in the top ten of the Phillips System, and was number sixty-four on the list of top 100 Hounds. "Gus" left behind his daughter Sarah to carry on the dream of Kamilot.

DRS. STEPHEN AND SUSAN HARPER

Any breed fancier would feel blessed by owning a truly outstanding winner. Drs. Stephen and Susan Harper of West Virginia have been doubly blessed. Ch. The Rectory's Micah was shown extensively during 1980 and 1981. During his show career he won three ABC Specialties, twenty-two all-breed Bests in Show, one hundred Hound Group firsts and many Group placements. In 1981 he won fifty-one Hound Group firsts on his way to the coveted Ken-L-Ration Show Dog of The Year award—the first time this award was won by a Bloodhound.

Ch. Baskerville's Sole Heir, known as Rocky, like many "second children," must have felt the need to resist being lost in the "first child's" shadow. While he won "only 20" all-breed Bests, he won 127 Hound Group firsts in addition to many Group placements, plus winning the Hound Group and Gold Medal at the American Kennel Club Centennial Show. This was said to be the largest dog show held in North America. He was entered in only one ABC National Specialty in 1985, and was Best of Breed there. He then went on to equal his predecessor by winning the Ken-L-Ration Show Dog of The Year award—only the second Bloodhound to win this honor. Out of the ninety-four shows he entered that year, he won eighty-one Hound Group firsts, thus breaking the record for the most Group wins in one year by any hound breed. This record of eighty-one Hound Group firsts also set a new record for dogs of all breeds in the United States. This record was set in 1985, beating the record formerly set by a German Shepherd, who had won eighty Group firsts in one year.

Unfortunately, both these marvelous hounds died at the early age of five years.

SPECIALTY ACTIVITY

Bloodhound fanciers were treated to the most outstanding display of the breed in the United States when the American Bloodhound Club held its 20th Anniversary Specialty on June 16, 1973. It brought together an entry of over ninety hounds from all parts of the country. This was a show and obedience trial, held in the strikingly beautiful settings of Wild Rose Farm, St. Charles, Illinois. The show chairman for this event was Mrs. Richard L. Natanek and the obedience chairman was Mrs. Elaine N. Brown. The show secretary was Mr. S. Edward Simon. Puppy Sweepstakes judge was Mr. Robert DiVita, and regular class judge was Mr. John Cook. Obedience classes were judged by Mrs. Aldythe Comstock.

Best of Breed went to Ch. The Rectory's Reward from the Veterans Class,

Ch. Baskerville's Sole Heir, owned by Dr. Stephen and Susan Harper, was the second Bloodhound, after Ch. The Rectory's Micah, to win the Kennel Ration Show Dog of the Year Award for hound breeds. Among his wins was this Best of Breed at the Westminster Kennel Club in 1985 under judge Dorothy Hutchinson; handler is Tom Glassford.

Charles Tatham

Specialties have their fun sides and their serious sides and offer fanciers the chance to enjoy each other while observing the dogs. This group includes (from left) Trooper Howe of New York State's troop "K," former ABC president Cornelius Boland, Club historian Clarence Fischer, Nancy Lindsay, and Thomas Sheahan. The Club banner is proudly carried by the ABC "mascot."

149

handled by her breeder-owner, Mrs. George Sinkinson. BOS was Ch. Snowden's Muhldune, bred and owned by Cecelia R. Smith. The Stud Dog class was won by Am. & Can. Ch. Lime Tree Soames, based upon a showing of his get which included in part Ch. The Rectory's Shalom, Ch. Lime Tree Justin of Dakota, Ch. Aria of Dakota, Ch. Evinrude of Mareve, (now Ch.) Tanglewoods Commedienne, Ch. Amos Moses of Wrinklemoor and Ch. Cascade's Melody of Dakota.

Ch. The Rectory's Reward also won the Brood Bitch class.

Best Brace was Betty R. Trumbo's homebreds Ch. Old Acres Lady Velvet and Ch. Old Acres Flame. These red littermates were whelped Feb. 6, 1972, sired by Ch. Hemoglobin II out of Riverview Farms Dagmar.

Trailing Dog and Bitch class was won by Phyllis Natanek's Ch. Dutchess Alder of Edgebrook, CD, whelped March 30, 1968. She was sired by Ch. Greenway's Fakir of St. Hubert out of Bridget Ann Quidder, and bred by Shirley A. Cruickshank.

Best in Sweepstakes was Happy Trail Geraldine owned by John and Nicolie Carpenter, and bred by Mary Sims. She was sired by Ch. Amos Moses of Wrinklemoor out of Winnie the Pooh of Edgebrook, and whelped Dec. 20, 1971. BOS in Sweepstakes was The Rectory's Atheist, owned by The Rev. George E. Sinkinson, Jr., and bred by E. Lengel and J.S. Sinkinson, whelped Nov. 20, 1972. He was sired by Allyn of the Hermitage ex Ch. The Rectory's Charisma.

Another example of the growth of the breed in this country is a comparison of the first American Bloodhound Club Specialty in 1955 with those of 1976. In 1955 that first Specialty was the only one for the country, and was held at the Somerset Hills KC show in Far Hills, New Jersey. There were twenty-five hounds entered, less one absentee. The judge was Fairfield P. Day; his selection for BB was Ch. Giralda's King Kole, owned and bred by Mrs. Dodge.

In 1976, coincidentally, Mr. Day again held the position of East Coast Specialty judge at the April 24 show held by the Wilmington KC at Stanton, Delaware. This time eighty-two Bloodhounds were entered; and his selection for BB was Ch. Gossamer of Dakota, sired by Ch. Lime Tree Soames ex Optimist of Brighton, bred by Dr. J. Heezen and Cathy Brey, and owned by Dan Chaffee. "Goss" then went on to a Group third.

The Midwest Specialty, held with the Spring 1976 Chicago International Show, had an entry of eighty-one Bloodhounds, judged by Marion Mangrum. The BB here was Ch. Sims' Son-of-a-Gun of Dakota, sired by Ch. Lime Tree Gordon ex Am. & Can. Ch. Lime Tree Quiz; bred by Cathy Brey and Lois Sims and owned by Lois Sims and Owen and Linda Nelson. This was the second consecutive Chicago International win for this young dog, not yet three years old.

The West Coast Specialty was held at Fresno, California, on March 27, and drew an entry of fifty-eight. Judge Gerda Kennedy chose as her BB a bitch, Ch. Pine Hollow's Old Glory, sired by Ch. Leroy of Lansford ex Ch. The Rectory's Welcome, and owned and bred by Judy and Myron T. Robb. "Glory" then continued on to a Group third.

In 1978, after the first edition of *The Complete Bloodhound* was in print,

Ch. The Rectory's Reward, shown here with Mrs. Sinkinson, has won three ABC Specialties, including two from Veterans class. A BIS winner and the top Bloodhound for 1971, she was GR3 at Westminster in 1971. Reward is a third-generation top producer with eight champion offspring. *Gilbert*

Ch. Gossamer of Dakota (Ch. Lime Tree Soames ex Optimist of Brighton), owned by Dan Chaffee, was BB at the Eastern Specialty of the ABC in 1976 in an entry of 82. From there he went on to GR3, handled by Robert J. Stebbins. *Ashbey*

151

the American Bloodhound Club National Specialty was held in Los Gatos, California. At this show, judged by Mrs. Anne Rogers Clark, the authors received special satisfaction when she selected as Best in Show Ch. Cascade's Columbo of Dakota. Columbo was bred by the Reeds, his dam being Ch. Cascade's Melody of Dakota, a search and rescue hound, and his sire the Breys' Ch. Lucky Strike of Brighton. Columbo's early life had been spent on a waterfront estate near Seattle, as the companion of his owners' children. He left there for his show career, coowned by Cathy Brey, Eugene Zaphiris and Debbie Barber, and was handled by Eugene Zaphiris. During this time he won three Bests in Show and several Group placings.

Best Opposite Sex at the 1978 Specialty was Ch. Sue-Z-Q of Snohomish, another Northwest hound. She was a black and tan bitch, bred and owned by Dan Chaffee of Snohomish, Washington, and sired by his Int. Ch. Gossamer of Dakota.

Bloodhounds seem destined to increased activity in the show ring, and National Specialties have been increased from once every four years to an annual event. In addition, at the 1987 National, held in the Northwest, a two-day trailing trial and seminar was conducted preceding the show. This event took place in the forested foothills of Mt. Hood, Oregon. William D. Tolhurst of Lockport, New York, conducted a seminar on training and working the mantrailing Blood-hound, and twenty hounds were entered in the four-hour-old, twelve-hour-old and twenty-four-hour-old trails. This project was sponsored by the search and rescue club founded in the Northwest by Clyde and Lena Reed in 1973. Trails offered a simulation of the wilderness experience faced in actual cases.

These were received enthusiastically, and in 1988 the National Specialty in New York State also included a trailing trial on a reduced scale. The 1989 Specialty in Oklahoma at Lake Murray State Park continued the event with an entry of ten; and it seems probable that the working mantrailer will continue to receive recognition at the National Specialties.

Mrs. Patricia Bingham of England judged the Sweepstakes, and selected as her Best in Sweepstakes Kamilot's So Fie on Goodness, owned by Niki Ganns and Kathy Evans, and Best Opposite in Sweepstakes was Sir Baron of Kamilot, owned by Kathy Evans.

Mr. Kent H. Delaney judged the regular classes, and chose as Best of Breed Ch. Legacy's St. Patrick of Viking, owned by Inger M. Sexton, and Best Opposite from the Veteran Bitch Class, Ch. Quiet Creek's Chamealeon, CD, owned by Stacy Mattson and Susan LaCroix. Winners Dog and Best of Winners was Sir Baron of Kamilot and Winners Bitch was Ridgerunner Lucinda, owned by Susan LaCroix and John Hamil.

There was an entry at the show of one hundred hounds, with seven absent.

Because of space limitations in this book, it is impossible to go into the detail we would like, but the following listings from the Phillips System will give a broad view of the outstanding hounds in the show ring in recent years.

Acknowledgment is made to Jacqueline P. Root as the statistician who compiled these records. In addition to conformation shows from 1960 through

1989, she shows that 192 hounds have earned CD titles, 35 earned CDX, 4 earned UD, 149 earned TD and 5 earned TDX.

In computing the Phillips Point System, the figures are arrived at in the following way: one point is allowed for each dog defeated at shows throughout the year for a Best in Show win. For a first in Group, one point for each dog in competition for those breeds in that Group. For second, third and fourth in Group, the entry for the breeds winning over a particular dog is deducted. No Specialties are included.

The numbers of Bloodhounds showing and winning can be compared through the years by the total points earned by the number one Hounds. The first Bloodhound listed in the Phillips Point System in 1956 was number nine in the Group, Ch. Lucifer of Giralda with 1,583 points. In 1966, Ch. The Rectory's Curate won 4,573 points, in 1967 the same hound won 3,120 points, and in 1968 he was still number one Bloodhound with 2,145 points. In 1969 Ch. The Rectory's Recruit was number one with 1,070 points; in 1970 Ch. Hyl-Billies Hystepper won 1,577 points; in 1971 Ch. The Rectory's Reward won 3,891 points; in 1972 Ch. Pooh Bear of Dakota won 5,192 points, and again in 1973 she was number one with 6,752 points. First in 1974 was Ch. Cragsmoor's Bacchus of Mareve with 2,494 points. Ch. The Rectory's Limbo then took the lead for three years, with 2,150 points in 1975, 3,699 points in 1976, and 6,095 points in 1977.

Starting with 1978, we list the top ten Bloodhounds by the Phillips System to show the current generation of show winners.

1978	Points	BIS	GP 1	GP 2	GP 3	GP 4
Ch. Pine Hollows Yankee Doodle	4,057	1	5	2	4	3
Ch. Cascade's Columbo of Dakota	3,853	1	2	8	8	0
Ch. Sue-Z-Q of Snohomish	1,885	0	1	2	7	3
Ch. The Rectory's Prodigal Son	1,783	0	2	2	3	4
Ch. The Rectory's Limbo	1,207	0	1	2	4	2
Ch. Noels Frisco Sam of Homestead	1,139	0	1	3	1	3
Ch. Rhinoceros of St. Valentine	1,076	0	1	1	1	2
Ch. Blue Acres Abigail	774	0	0	1	1	1
Ch. The Rectory's Micah	621	0	1	1	2	1
Ch. Sim's Wrinklebrow Lyam Beri	567	0	0	1	2	2

1979	Points	BIS	GP 1	GP 2	GP 3	GP 4
Ch. The Rectory's Micah, Group #10	7,790	1	16	12	13	8
Ch. Cascade's Columbo of Dakota	3,374	2	6	1	0	2
Ch. Trail Songs Claim Jumper	1,345	1	1	0	1	0
Ch. Rita's Dominator of Slo Poke	1,206	0	4	2	2	0
Ch. The Hermitage Perseus	662	0	2	1	1	0
Ch. Roamingwood Belles Starr	515	0	1	0	1	0
Ch. Pine Hollow's Blue Print	499	0	0	0	1	1
Ch. Leaping Bear Tracks	478	0	1	1	0	0
Ch. Winter Sunshine of Edgebrook	449	0	0	0	0	3
Ch. Serendipity's The Deacon	436	0	0	1	1	0

1980

Ch. The Rectory's Micah, Group #5	18,233	8	27	18	12	4
Ch. Serendipity's Nick Chopper	3,347	0	6	7	8	4
Ch. Pine Hollow's Blue Print	3,000	0	3	4	7	6
Ch. Rita's Dominator of Slo Poke	956	0	1	2	2	3
Ch. Ramblewood Sir Abraham Fish	826	0	3	2	1	2
Ch. Sherick's Flinthills Pride	683	0	1	0	2	3
Ch. The Rectory's Bishop	625	0	1	0	6	1
Ch. Chief Leaping Bear Tracks	609	0	2	1	0	1
Ch. Musicmaker's Gimme Your Hand	575	0	1	0	1	1
Ch. Roclin's Bubba Laru of Selanky	249	0	0	0	1	0

1981

Ch. Rectory's Micah, Group #2	23,459	13	51	17	13	1
Ch. Serendipity's Nick Chopper	8,275	2	15	12	7	12
Ch. The Rectory's Bishop	2,628	0	4	3	9	4
Ch. Hyl-Billies HyHoncho	2,377	0	3	7	5	5
Ch. Buglin's Tom Collins	1,717	0	0	2	4	2
Ch. Sherick's Flinthills Pride	1,693	1	5	4	0	3
Ch. Trailsongs Admissability	429	7	0	0	1	2
Ch. Cragsmoor Roughrider	423	0	0	1	1	1
Ch. St. Valentine's Sapata	383	0	0	1	0	0
Ch. Double R Gerocies Girl D'Limier	358	0	0	0	2	1

1982

Ch. Serendipity's Nick Chopper, Group #8	13,424	3	15	16	35	14
Ch. Hyl-Billies HyHoncho, Group #9	11,157	3	21	19	12	9
Ch. The Rectory's Bishop	3,068	0	5	5	6	5
Ch. The Rectory's Micah	1,431	0	19	6	6	0
Ch. Double R's Grand Slam D'Limier	1,281	0	0	2	4	2
Ch. Sherick's Flinthills Pride	1,205	0	1	2	5	1
Ch. Houndstooths Malicah	521	0	0	3	0	1
Ch. Wrinklebrows Khamsin, CD	458	0	0	0	1	1
Ch. The Celts Dixie Piper, CD	357	0	0	0	1	0
Ch. Brandeds First One to Sink, CT TD	325	0	1	1	1	1

1983

Ch. The Rectory's Bishop	10,519	2	19	19	10	5
Ch. Hyl-Billies HyHoncho	6,595	1	16	13	11	3
Ch. Serendipity's Nick Chopper	3,698	3	7	5	7	4
Ch. Hedmans Shelley	1,433	0	2	1	1	3
Ch. Shericks Flinthills Pride	1,270	0	0	3	2	2
Ch. Brandywine of Soala	937	0	0	1	0	5

154

Ch. The Rectory's Limbo (Ch. Leroy of Lansford ex Ch. The Rectory's Shalom), owned by Patricia A. Simancek and Harriet and Richard Jack and bred by Jacquelyn S. and Rev. George E. Sinkinison, Jr., has been actively campaigned against all competition. He was the top Bloodhound in the United States during 1975 and 1976 and was BB at the Eastern ABC Specialty in 1977. He is shown by Vic Capone. *Klein*

Ch. Hedmans Kate	579	0	0	0	3	1
Ch. Baskervilles Sole Heir	429	0	1	0	1	1
Ch. Gamens Liza Witha Z	416	0	1	0	1	0
Ch. The Rectory's Blessing	367	0	1	0	1	0

1984

Ch. Vikings Thor	12,607	4	12	12	13	10
Ch. Baskervilles Sole Heir	10,941	3	21	15	10	5
Ch. Nimrods Frankie	2,986	0	7	3	2	6
Ch. Double R's Guru D'Limier	773	0	1	3	0	0
Ch. Hyl-Billies HyHesperos	615	0	1	1	2	1
Ch. Sandlappers I Got Prime Time	420	0	0	1	2	0
Ch. Trailsongs Admissability	352	0	0	0	1	2
Ch. Arnmars Aye Aye Alvin CD	329	0	0	1	0	1
Ch. Baskervilles Godfrog	303	0	0	0	2	0
Ch. Witsends Ira Hayes	291	0	0	1	0	0

1985

Ch. Vikings Thor, Group #1	32,249	15	60	26	15	8
Ch. Baskervilles Sole Heir, Group #2	31,537	13	84	23	8	4
Ch. Roclin's Image of Pine Hollow	4,729	1	6	2	2	3
Ch. The Rectory's Buglin' Alleluia	2,236	0	7	5	4	1
Ch. Hyl-Billies Hyhestia	1,129	0	3	2	4	2
Ch. Double R's Guru D'Limier	1,041	1	1	0	0	0
Ch. Tennessee Woods About Time	439	0	0	1	1	1
Ch. Tracers Own Captain Zeke	386	0	0	1	0	2
Ch. Corywoods Jasper Briarpatch	357	0	1	0	1	2
Ch. Arnmar's Aye Aye Alvin CD	336	0	0	0	1	1

1986

Ch. Vikings Thor	17,289	8	38	19	10	3
Ch. Roclin's Image of Pine Hollow	7,281	3	12	1	3	5
Ch. The Rectory's Buglin' Alleluia	5,611	3	11	8	2	2
Ch. Baskervilles Sole Heir	4,456	3	5	4	0	1
Ch. Lord Morgan of Briarpatch	3,835	0	3	1	12	7
Ch. Pitter Patters Colorado Blue	1,007	0	2	2	3	2
Ch. Corywood's Jasper Briarpatch	873	0	1	2	1	3
Ch. Freespirit Texas Sunbonnet	522	0	0	2	0	0
Ch. Sherick's In Like Flint	382	0	0	0	0	2
Ch. Quiet Creek's Excalibur	377	0	1	1	0	1

1987

Ch. Vikings Thor	11,876	4	27	18	10	5
Ch. Roclin's Image of Pine Hollow	6,736	2	7	2	7	2
Ch. Corywood's Jasper Briarpatch	2,283	0	1	2	10	5
Ch. The Rectory's Buglin' Alleluia	1,882	1	4	3	1	1
Ch. Augustus of Kamilot	1,182	0	2	3	0	2
Ch. Briarpatch's Wichita Lineman	953	0	2	1	0	2

Ch. Legacy's Honkytonk Angel, CD TD	864	0	1	0	4	2
Ch. Pitter Patters Colorado Blue	739	0	0	3	2	1
Ch. Blue's Coronation Blue Heaven	496	0	0	1	2	2
Ch. Brewdun's Peter Quince	428	0	1	0	0	0

1988

Ch. Rocklin's Image of Pine Hollow	8,126	2	8	8	4	3
Ch. Dunwishin's Say Hey Willie	3,785	1	7	8	2	5
Ch. Be-Coz Sir I C Wellington	3,176	0	3	6	4	10
Ch. Viking's Thor	2,066	1	4	1	0	1
Ch. Augustus of Kamilot	1,786	0	2	2	5	2
Ch. Corywood's Jasper Briarpatch	1,189	0	4	1	5	4
Ch. Brewdun's Beloved Baritone	1,025	0	2	1	2	2
Ch. Island-Legacy Western Star	992	0	2	2	1	2
Ch. Blues True Blue JC	959	0	2	0	4	4
Ch. Hope's Miss America	934	0	1	6	0	0

1989

Ch. Legacy's St. Patrick of Viking	6,505	1	17	12	11	5
Ch. Sharoyt's Trackin George	4,906	0	3	11	9	6
Ch. Dunwishin's Say Hey Willie	3,443	2	4	5	0	1
Ch. Be-Coz Sir I C Wellington	2,807	0	5	4	6	7
Ch. Roclin's Image of Pine Hollow	2,243	0	0	6	2	1
Ch. Brewdun's Beloved Baritone	1,770	0	0	3	4	3
Ch. Nineveh's Moses of the Rectory	1,330	1	1	3	0	1
Ch. Brewdun's Peter Quince	770	0	0	2	0	1
Ch. Kun-Tre Blue's Budweiser	746	0	1	1	2	3
Ch. Kare-Fre Luke of Laurel	452	0	0	0	0	1

Judging by the Specialties and other show activity, combined with the increasing use of Bloodhounds in volunteer and law enforcement mantrailing, it seems safe to forecast that the breed's future is good. Breeders are increasingly fanciers who are taking personal interest in their puppies and the homes they go to. Socialization of the puppies is widely understood as a need before they go to new homes.

It is encouraging to note that most of the hounds listed on the preceding Phillips System lists are American-bred from American breeding.

The Bloodhound has about him a mystique stemming from his centuries-old calling as a mantrailer. This makes him more familiar to the general public than many other more popular breeds. Because of this, Bloodhound fanciers must consider carefully where they place their puppies and what hounds they breed from and show. Most important, all who have set aside a special place in their lives for the Bloodhound should bear in mind that the breeding and showing of this celebrated canine detective is a sporting activity and conduct themselves in a like manner.

Showing the infuence of a proud inheritance—Ch. Giralda's King Cole follows an interesting trail.   *Shafer*

7

Official Standard
of the Bloodhound

SIT WITH YOUR BLOODHOUNDS at a dog show and you will invariably hear admiring comments from those gathering around. "Gee, that's a neat dog," "Yeah, man, that's cool." "I'd like one of those." Or else you get the opposite reaction—those who are terrified by its size, or think the Bloodhound is the saddest, ugliest thing in the world, whether or not they themselves are one of the natural beauties of creation.

WHO SHOULD OWN A BLOODHOUND

Let's face it; not everyone should be a Bloodhound owner. If you want a lapdog, Bloodhounds love the challenge; but not many lonely ladies seeking that kind of companionship are provided with the lap to accommodate them. If you love delicate china and ornamental objects on your tables, one swish of a Bloodhound's tail could eliminate the results of years of collecting. If you pride yourself upon keeping a house where "they could eat off the floor" (though goodness knows, who would want to do that), a Bloodhound is not for you. The swing of a Bloodhound's head can spread saliva across a twenty-foot room.

If, however, you have a large yard or acreage, and prefer the friendship of a devoted and affectionate companion—if you appreciate the appearance of dignity and nobility combined with the spirit of a clown, consider the Bloodhound. If you want a working animal with an ability in mantrailing unrivaled by any other dog, the Bloodhound is the beginning and the end of your search.

BEFORE YOU BUY

If you are considering the purchase of a Bloodhound and are not already experienced with the breed, you will be well-advised to do some study before selecting your new pet. One of the distressing experiences of one who loves the breed is meeting the proud new owner who brings his puppy to show you, beaming expectantly as he waits for your words of praise. You stand there looking at a stunted, spindly legged monstrosity with ears growing out of the top of its apple head, frail bodied, tight skinned, with an undershot jaw, and a tail that would look good on a Norwegian Elkhound. And they want to breed her to your champion stud. How do you break their hearts softly?

The first recommendation to those intrigued by the breed and considering buying a puppy is: don't be an impulse buyer. That adorable puppy with the sweet, wrinkled face will rapidly grow into a hound that may crowd your facilities, if you have not acquainted yourself with the breed. Attend a few dog shows and study the hounds there. First of all, however, study the Standard of the breed, so that you may know what you should see in a good Bloodhound. You must keep in mind the fact that every dog has some fault(s) and a perfect specimen of the breed has yet to appear.

I am reminded of a show at which an exhibitor approached my husband and me, glowing with pride as she showed us her Bloodhound. His coat shone like black satin, his powerful body was supported by strong bones and well-knuckled-up feet, and his temperament was happy and outgoing. However, if his tail had been docked he would have scored well in the Rottweiler ring.

"What beautiful condition!" I bubbled away, trying to be tactful. "It's easy to see you don't economize on your pet's care. And such a lovely disposition!"

The lady's chest swelled another inch. Later, as I stood jostled in the crowd around the ring while the Bloodhounds were being judged, I heard voices ahead of me shredding and discarding the qualifications of the champion in the ring with their hounds. "Did you ever see such a terrible head?" one of them said. "Why, it's so out of proportion, it's ridiculous! It's so pointed it looks as if it were made of silly putty and molded in a dunce cap, and then someone played patty-cake with its face."

It was the lady with the Rottweiler-type sounding forth, and that was my champion she was criticizing. He has a weak point, but not on his head. I may be kennel blind, but it's as near the Standard as any I've seen.

Before you go to those dog shows, therefore, have firmly in your mind the illustration of the ideal Bloodhound and the explanation of the Standard, as set forth by AKC, and learn to separate the geese from the swans.

A FITTING DESCRIPTION

The general appearance of the ideal Bloodhound is well described by Charles Henry Lane, breeder, exhibitor and judge, in his book *All About Dogs*, written in 1900. It is an excellent basis for judging. Mr. Lane wrote:

> The hound strikes you as not over-large, but with great character, quality, and much dignity. Well-knit, plenty of bone, symmetrical, straight legs, wide across the back, full in body and back ribs, and game in temperament, with fine, deep-sloping shoulders, enormously powerful hindquarters.
>
> The points associated with the Bloodhound are as follows: Skull; long, narrow, and very much peaked. Square, deep muzzle. Ears thin, long, set on rather low, hanging in shapely folds close against the face. Eyes, dark in color and deep set, with lustrous lids, triangular in shape, showing the red haw. Flews, long, thin and pendulous, the upper overhanging the lower lips. Neck, rather long, and slightly arched toward the base of skull. Plenty of dewlap, wrinkled skin of face very loose and abundant. Short, close-lying coat, thin skin, sloping and deep shoulders; broad, muscular loins, well-let-down in the brisket, powerful thighs and second thighs. Strong, straight legs, feet round and hocks well-bent, stern tapering and carried high. The general appearance should be that of a high-classed, aristocratic and very dignified animal, who looks as if he considered himself fit company for emperors and would not care to associate with any except those belonging to the upper circles.

I agree that is the ideal description of the good hound.

Following is the official Bloodhound Standard, as set forth by the American Kennel Club, with comments following the various points.

The Bloodhound Standard

General Character— The Bloodhound possesses, in a most marked degree, every point and characteristic of those dogs which hunt together by scent (Sagaces). He is very powerful and stands over more ground than is usual with hounds of other breeds. The skin is thin to the touch and extremely loose; this being more especially about the head and neck, where it hangs in deep folds.

> Mrs. R. A. Oldfield, in *Bloodhound Breeders' Magazine* of England, Spring 1984, writes in explanation of the term "stands over more ground than is usual with Hounds of other breeds." This has confused many Americans. She says, "At the time this Standard was drawn up it was fashionable to breed Foxhounds, Harriers and Beagles short coupled. This has now changed and all these breeds like a nice length of body, so I suggest it should read, 'Hounds should not be short coupled.' If you say they should stand over more ground . . . we might get Bassets or Dachshunds, knowing the peculiarities of breeders."

Height: The mean average height of adult dogs is twenty-six inches, and adult bitches twenty-four inches. Dogs usually vary from twenty-five inches to twenty-seven inches and bitches from twenty-three to twenty-five inches; but in either case, the greater height is to be preferred, provided that character and quality are also combined.

> This is misleading to most people because they read here that "in either case, the greater height is to be preferred." One judge said to me, as we were discussing the Standard, something to the effect that "according to the Standard, the bigger the better." I explained that this is not the case; it says "the greater height is to be preferred, *but* it does say dogs twenty-five to twenty-seven inches, bitches twenty-three to twenty-five inches." Nowhere in the Standard does it say anything about dogs that are twenty-nine and thirty inches.

Weight: The mean average weight of adult dogs, in fair condition, is 90 pounds, and of adult bitches 80 pounds. Dogs attain the weight of 110 pounds, bitches 100 pounds. The greater weights are to be preferred, provided (as in the case of height) that quality and proportion are also combined.

> I feel that dogs probably should not be held exactly to those maximums; one should use common sense and find out what is the ideal weight for a given dog. While one should not try to hold to a set weight, a dog of twenty-six inches at 110 pounds is a fairly good weight. My twenty-seven-inch dogs usually maintain a proper show weight anywhere from 110 to 120 pounds, but no more than that.

Expression: The expression is noble and dignified, and characterized by solemnity, wisdom and power. **Temperament:** In temperament he is extremely affectionate, neither quarrelsome with companions nor with other dogs. His nature is somewhat shy, and equally sensitive to kindness or correction by his master.

> The description of expression gives a good picture of the typical Bloodhound. Temperament doesn't require explanation. It has been known that Bloodhounds in the past have been very aggressive, and I would fault, in judging, an aggressive dog more than a shy dog; a fear-biter should be severely faulted.

Head: The head is narrow in proportion to its length, and long in proportion to the body, tapering but slightly from the temples to the end of the muzzle, thus (when viewed from above and in front) having the appearance of being flattened at the sides and of being nearly equal in width throughout its entire length. In profile the upper outline of the skull is nearly in the same plane as that of the foreface. The length from end of nose to stop (midway between the eyes) should be not less than that from stop to back of occipital protuberance (peak). The entire length of head from the posterior part of the occipital protuberance to the end of the muzzle should be twelve inches or more in dogs, and eleven inches or more in bitches.

> This description is adequate, although particular attention should be paid to the word *narrow*. I have sometimes seen heads getting too narrow, and I have noticed that when they get too narrow the substance of the body bone is lost also. One must again use common sense in breeding and not try to exaggerate this narrow head.

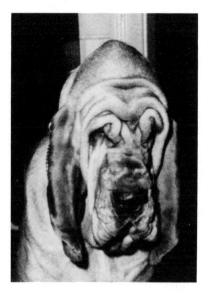

His head is a Bloodhound's distinctive hallmark and so a typical headpiece is vital if a hound is going to be a good winner. The headstudies above clearly convey what is desired in the Standard, and why so much importance is place on the head in the official document and in the minds of judges.

Skull: The skull is long and narrow, with the occipital peak very pronounced. The brows are not prominent, although, owing to the deep-set eyes, they may have that appearance.

Foreface: The foreface is long, deep, and of even width throughout, with square outline when seen in profile.

I would like to emphasize the square outline when seen in profile, because I have seen too many hounds that are lacking the proper depth of lip. An excellent example of proper depth of lip was shown by a Lime Tree puppy at a show some years back. When the judge parted his lips to examine his teeth, it was discovered that the foresighted puppy, perhaps anticipating a long, dry wait in the ring, had deftly lifted a can of beer from a bench he passed on his way into the ring. Because of his correct lip depth, it was undetectable.

Another correct example of depth of lip was given by the late Ch. The Rectory's Rebellion. An injured Dachshund puppy had been brought into the home for recuperation, and secluded in a bedroom. Rebel was tantalized by the strange scent, which he was not allowed to investigate. He waited his chance, until someone left the bedroom without pulling the door closed tightly enough to latch it. The family was soon made aware that mischief was afoot by the teasing gleam in Rebel's eyes, as he paraded around the house. Finally, he lowered his head, opened his mouth, and gently deposited an unharmed Dachshund puppy on the carpet.

The British Standard, in describing the head, includes in addition *Mouth*, and it reads, *A scissor bite with the inner faces of the upper incisors touching the outer faces of the lower incisors. The teeth should be even, very white and strong.* Although this does not appear in the American Standard, I, myself, prefer a scissors bite in my hounds; a level bite is acceptable. In judging a hound in the ring I would not judge on bite, as it is not in the AKC Standard. However, when grading my own puppies I do grade them on bite; although I am of the opinion that a fault you must look for is not as serious as a fault that is readily apparent.

Eyes: The eyes are deeply sunk in the orbits, the lids assuming a lozenge or diamond shape, in consequence of the lower lids being dragged down and everted by the heavy flews. The eyes correspond with the general tone of color of the animal, varying from deep hazel to yellow. The hazel color is, however, to be preferred, although very seldom seen in red and tan hounds.

If I were to change this in any way, I would emphasize to judges that the light-colored eye should not be penalized in the liver and tan (red and tan) hounds. It is also interesting to note that the British have added this to their Standard: *The eye should be free from any interference from the eyelash*, which is something that is definitely important.

Ears: The ears are thin and soft to the touch, extremely long, set very low, and fall in graceful folds, the lower parts curling inwards and backwards.

This needs no explanation, other than to explain that a "low" ear set should be below the level of the eye.

Wrinkle: The head is furnished with an amount of loose skin, which in nearly every position appears superabundant, but more particularly so when the head is carried low; the skin then falls into loose, pendulous ridges and folds, especially over the forehead and sides of the face. **Nostrils:** The nostrils are large and open. **Lips, Flews and Dewlap:** In front the lips fall squarely, making a right angle with the upper line of the foreface, while behind they form deep, hanging flews, and being continued into the pendant folds of loose skin about the neck, constitute the dewlap, which is very pronounced. These characteristics are found, though in a lesser degree, in the bitch.

> My only comment here is that wrinkle can be overdone, as with the lips, flews and dewlaps. When these features are exaggerated, the weight of the extra skin causes the lower eyelid to be dragged down and everted. This is the cause of some of the breed's eye problems.

Neck, Shoulders and Chest: The neck is long, the shoulders muscular and well sloped backward; the ribs are well sprung; and the chest well let down between the forelegs, forming a deep keel.

> Particular attention should be paid to the statement that the neck is long—I think the British Standard is worded a bit better in that they say the *neck should be long* and if a dog is to be suited for his work he must have a neck long enough so that he can drop his head and pick up a line without interfering with his movement. It has also been my experience that a short neck goes with straight shoulders.

Legs and Feet: The forelegs are straight and large in bone, with elbows squarely set; the feet strong and well knuckled up; the thighs and second thighs (gaskins) are very muscular; the hocks well bent and let down and squarely set.

> This is very clear. I would penalize paper feet, and consider the condition a fault. The feet should have nice, thick pads. I must mention that I have seen dogs with thin, or paper, feet, and it didn't seem to affect them in trailing. In the show ring, a better-looking hound should have a well-knuckled-up foot. The legs should be parallel from the hocks down and cowhocks or wide movement should be penalized. Feet can be ruined by letting the nails grow too long. The British Standard mentions, under legs and feet, *The shoulders muscular, well sloped back, the forelegs are straight, large and round in bone, with elbows squarely set.* They also add that the pasterns should be strong. Weak pasterns and splayed feet, besides being hereditary faults, could be caused by improper feeding during the growing period.

Back and Loin: The back and loins are strong, the latter deep and slightly arched. **Stern:** The stern is long and tapering, and set on rather high, with a moderate amount of hair underneath.

> The British Standard says, *The stern is long and thick, tapered to a point, set on high, with a moderate amount of hair underneath. It should be carried scimitar fashion, but not curled over the back or corkscrew at any time. The stern should have a thick root, and should be carried high when the hound is moving, showing confidence and overall balance. A stern carried over the back generally goes with faulty movement.* There is a great deal of controversy about the tail. Certainly while judging I would fault a bad tail, but not as severely as some other faults. I feel, as a British breeder said to me, in his opinion, "If you had to get back to the tail of

165

the hound to fault it, there really isn't that much wrong with the animal." There is something to be said for that viewpoint. I have seen some hounds with extremely good tails that had a multitude of faults ahead of the stern. I definitely want a good tail. Very often the tail in a young puppy is not what it will be when grown; sometimes tails don't settle until a hound is six or seven months old.

Gait: The gait is elastic, swinging and free, the stern being carried high, but not too much curled over the back.

A good book on movement is *Dogsteps, Illustrated Gait at a Glance* by Rachel Page Elliott and will be a great help to your further understanding of this important aspect of judging. A Bloodhound moving at a moderate trot should move its forelegs in a straight line from shoulder to foot (rear legs from hip to foot), with the feet converging toward a center line, but not crossing.

Color: The colors are black and tan, red and tan, and tawny; the darker colors being sometimes interspersed with lighter or badger-colored hair, and sometimes flecked with white. A small amount of white is permissible on chest, feet and tip of stern.

There is some controversy regarding color; while the Standard says "red and tan," hounds of this color are generally referred to as "liver and tan," and where the Standard says "tawny" the common term is "red."

Webster's New Collegiate Dictionary describes tawny as a brownish orange to light brown that is slightly redder than sorrel. Our reds seem fewer and farther between of late, and this is regrettable. I have seen two of the correct color red; one owned by Marion and Steve Pruitt and the other owned by Bob and Helen Hartman.

The British Standard shows the colors as black and tan; liver and tan and then in parentheses (red and tan) and they have changed tawny to read red. Aside from that, color is described as in the American Standard.

Another point of debate is what constitutes a *small amount* of white on a Bloodhound. It has been claimed that the white on our hounds often comes from the Foxhound cross that was allowed after World War II in Britain. Some fanciers are of the opinion that we should have a disqualification written into our Standard similar to that of the Black and Tan Coonhound Standard, which states that white spots cannot exceed one and one-half inches in diameter. I do not share this opinion as I feel there are many very nice, representative hounds that have a larger amount of white on them. I can accept white on the chest or toes, but I would not want to see it up past the knuckle. A white blaze or white stockings would definitely be unacceptable.

ADDITIONAL THOUGHTS ON THE STANDARD

The British Standard continues on, to add body hair, and to say the ribs are well sprung, the chest is let down between the forelegs to form a deep keel. The back and loins are strong, the latter deep and slightly arched. The Standard requires that the body be abundantly covered by loose, pliant, elastic skin, which is also required on the head. The skin can be lifted off the neck and pushed up the head, giving the head an even more wrinkled appearance.

These characteristics of breed type are very helpful to the Bloodhound in his original work of trailing, as the wide nostrils pick up the scent, the long ears fan the scent into the nostrils, and abundance of wrinkle around the head helps hold the scent. The loose skin helps prevent his being hurt when he is trailing in rough terrain, and the drooling or saliva that is held in the flews causes a steam to bring the scent up out of the ground.

I believe the Standard would be improved by the inclusion of a list of faults and disqualifications, with perhaps a point system. The present Standard leaves much to individual interpretation, which is well described by an old saying: It's hard to get harmony among breeders, because most want to beat the drum, few will face the music, and none will play second fiddle.

In these times when so much is being said about the important things to breed to and for—soundness, type, movement, etc. etc.—the following article puts it all together. It originally appeared in the *Saint Bernard Bulletin*, and is reprinted here with permission of its author.

A Fairy Tale
by Robert Hope

Once upon a time, four Saint Bernard exhibitors were coming home from a big show. They were driving over a mountain pass in the middle of a violent snowstorm when, suddenly, their car went into a skid, hit a guardrail, and went careening down a slope about a mile into a ravine. The trailer which they had been pulling, containing their four dogs, landed relatively undamaged next to their car. No one had seen the accident in the blinding storm, and, as luck would have it, the Saint breeders were trapped inside their car. The door to the trailer, however, had popped open!

The first dog out was a very "typey" Saint, as this was what his breeder cared about the most. He made it about a quarter of a mile up the slope before he was gasping for air and his nasal passages began to freeze because of his foreshortened muzzle. After another two hundred yards, he was blind and hopelessly lost because of the driving snow piling up in his haws.

The second Saint out of the trailer was bred for "important things"—like prettiness, size, color and perfect markings. He was a beautiful sight to behold but, unfortunately, he too collapsed after only a few hundred yards from the ravages of hip dysplasia.

The third dog to try and summon help had been bred for "soundness." His breeder wouldn't have dreamed of using a dog that wasn't X-rayed free of hip dysplasia. He made it halfway up the slope before he collapsed from exhaustion. He could not cope with the high drifts. His breeder hadn't realized that there was more to "soundness" than hips, and had neglected to include the head, neck, shoulders, forelimbs, feet, chest, heart, lungs, and hindquarters in his "breeding for soundness."

The fourth breeder was conscious by now and knew that, at last, all those years of breeding would pay off. He had bred for type, being careful not to shorten the muzzle so far as to obstruct the breathing or ruin the bite. He was proud of his dog's "tight eyes." His dog had "storybook markings," a richly colored coat, and was a very powerful, proportionately tall, strong and muscular figure. He had an OFA number, of course, but he was also big boned, had a very strong and powerful neck that was loaded with muscle, and his shoulders were well laid back. He had good rib spring with ample room for heart and lungs; his forelegs were straight and strong, he had strong pasterns and strong, tight feet. He had perfect rear angulation and his hocks couldn't have been any stronger. When moving, he was absolutely flawless. With great pride, and tears in his eyes, the breeder saw his big, beautiful, perfect Saint Bernard drive off into the blinding storm just like the Hospice dogs of old!

The last Saint made it up to the road almost effortlessly. A passing State Trooper saw the dog, and stopped to investigate. As he got out of the car, the dog attacked and ate him.

Rights and Wrongs of the Bloodhound
Standing and Moving

On the next 13 pages there appears a series of drawings by Phyllis Natanek illustrating faults and virtues in the Bloodhound at rest and on the move. These originally appeared in the *American Bloodhound Club Bulletin* and are reproduced here through the courtesy of the American Bloodhound Club and the artist.

Large head, but in proportion to body; good length of neck; strong loin; stern in balance; good angulation front and rear; good depth of body.

This hound is too long in body and too high on leg. Such a specimen is said to have too much "daylight" under him. Also shows a long loin.

This hound is very short in loin. It would be difficult for such a hound to show the "elastic, swinging, and free" movement required by the breed Standard. A well-angulated, short-coupled dog will frequently be a "pacer." An overly gay stern further spoils the outline.

Out of balance; leggy; too-long stern. A "rangy" hound appears undeveloped and untypical, especially when compared to a balanced specimen. Stern should balance body—neither too long nor too short.

This hound has a short neck, a serious fault, for he could not do the job he was bred for. A Bloodhound must have length of neck for the purpose of following ground and airborne scent.

Out of balance; too short on leg. While this is not a drastic fault, a very short-legged hound is not as pleasing as a properly balanced animal.

A truly faulty specimen—this hound shows a "ewe" neck, a sway back, and a goose rump as well as a lack of sufficient "lip." The outline of this Bloodhound leaves a great deal to be desired.

This hound shows an incorrect, arched topline. Some young hounds will arch their backs in the ring due to nerves or discomfort, but if a hound possesses this fault, standing and/or moving, it is most incorrect.

Incorrect balance—straight front and rear. Such hounds may stand and move well, but they have two serious, if not uncommon, faults.

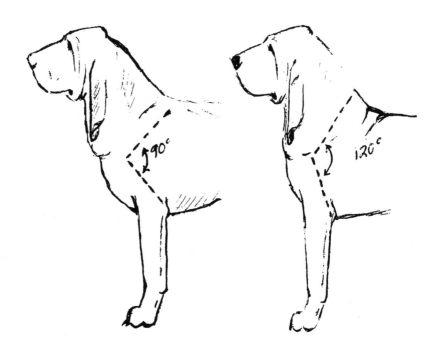

A good front. The chest forms a deep keel in front of the forelegs. The forelegs are well set under the body and the pasterns are strong, with a slight bend. The properly angulated shoulder forms a ninety-degree angle with the upper arm.

Straight shoulders—shoulders and upper arm form a 120-degree angle. Forelegs are too far forward; lack of forechest; dip behind shoulder.

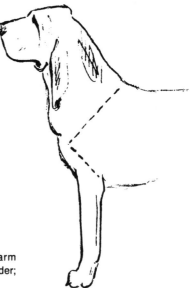

Short upper arm—length of upper arm does not match that of well-laid shoulder; forelegs too far forward.

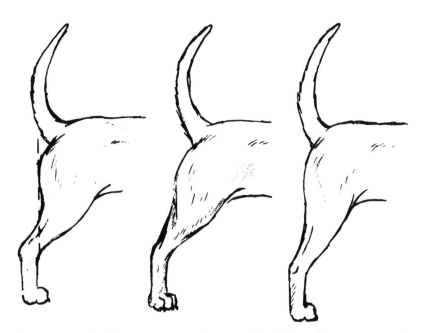

A good rear (left) Scimitar stern is well set on, with slightly sloping croup; good angulation; short, straight hocks; tight feet. With cowhocks (center), stifles and feet incline outward. With straight stifles (right), there is little or no rear angulation.

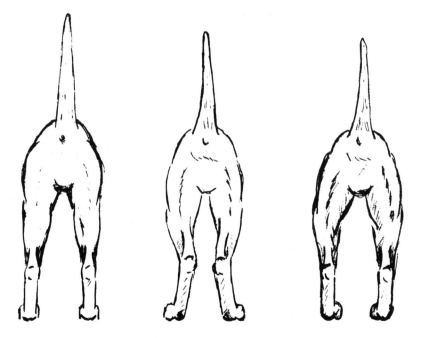

Correct hindquarters (left); Cowhocks (center); Bandy legs (right).

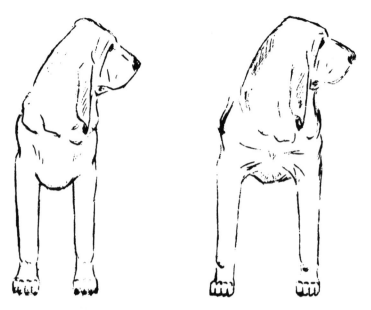

A good front (left). Elbows close to body; shoulders muscled, but not loaded; stands neither too wide nor too narrow. Forelegs strong and straight. Tight, well-knuckled forefeet, point almost straight ahead. A wide front (right). This hound has overmuscled, loaded shoulders.

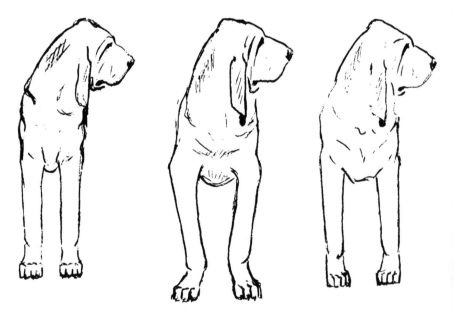

A narrow front (left) lacks breadth of forechest. Out at elbow (center); bent forearm; east/west feet. Pigeon-toed (right); forefeet turned in.

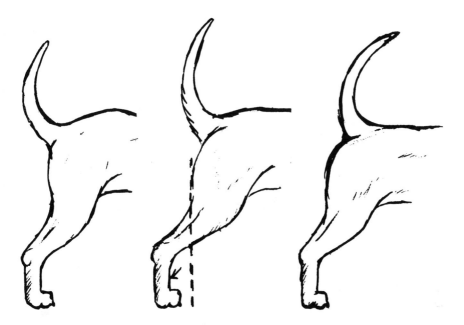

A steep croup (left), also termed "goose rump." Over-angulated rear (center). The dotted line indicates where the foot should be placed. Flat croup (right).

Squirrel tail

Ring Tail

Wry Tail

Correct movement is "elastic, swinging, and free." When all the component parts are correct there will be no constriction in action. With a good hound the topline remains level during movement, reach and drive are matched, and there is no crabbing. The stern is also well carried. Such a specimen appears to be able to go on indefinitely without tiring.

When viewed from front or rear a good mover will display a straight column of support from shoulder to pad in front and hip to pad in the rear. The legs converge on a center line of gravity as the speed increases.

A soft back can sometimes be concealed in the standing hound, but will become obvious when the dog moves. This fault lessens endurance, undesirable in show animals or mantrailers.

The pace is a fatigue gait and is objectionable in the show ring. Consistent pacers are often very short-coupled, with good angulation. The drawing also shows a gay stern.

If a hound stands and moves with an arched topline, more usually known as a roached back, something is put together wrong! Often such a hound is also very rubber-legged behind.

This hound suffers from poor angulation front and rear. When moving he shows a stilted, restricted gait completely opposite what the Standards requires. It would not take him long to drop from exhaustion in field conditions.

Overreaching, a fault, is usually caused by a slightly straight shoulder and excellent rear drive.

A dog with straight shoulders will usually have restricted reach in front and excessive movement in the shoulder blades

Hackney gait is inefficient action resulting from a too-short upper arm.

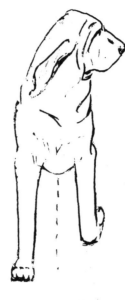

| Moving close | Moving wide | Crossing over |

| Paddling | Toeing in. Out at elbows |

Moving close   Moving wide   Cowhocks

Crabbing   Moving with hocks turned out

181

Ch. Lime Tree Swithin, at three months, owned and bred by Nancy Lindsay.   *Allen*

8

Buying Your First Puppy

$\mathbf{B}$Y THE TIME you have read this far and visited a few dog shows, we hope you are "talking Bloodhound" knowingly. You can sit at ringside and appraise the class, joining in applause of the obviously excellent judge whose selection agrees with yours; or groan in despair at the one who must have weak eyes. You can hardly wait to enter the ring with a winner of your own.

FINDING THE RIGHT PUPPY

Now you come to the selection of your first Bloodhound puppy. How do you find a good one?

The safest answer to that is, find a good breeder. A good breeder will take the time to answer your questions, and give you some knowledge of the breed. He will not try to pressure you into buying in haste, if you are unsure about your choice. Impulse buyers may take home the puppy with no knowledge of the care it requires, or its eventual size, its rapid growth, and the bottomless pit it has for a stomach. It may be neglected, abused or passed on to another home, eventually to end up at the Humane Society, or dumped along a country road.

We would recommend buying your puppy from the small breeder who has time to spend with a growing litter, giving the puppies personal, loving care during their early weeks. Zookeepers will tell you that any wild animal, if taken from its mother before its eyes are opened and raised by humans, will be permanently "imprinted." It will think of itself as part of the human race, since that is the scent which has been reaching it, and those are the creatures it sees when it opens its eyes. Without taking it from its mother, it is especially important that a young puppy have a friendly and affectionate relationship with humans, starting by the time it is three weeks old, if it is ever to develop a close and devoted attachment to them.

Ask the owners of the hounds you have seen and admired at the shows if they sell puppies, or if not, where they bought theirs. Also, ask the owners of the ones you didn't like so well, and get some hints on whom to avoid. As, "When my puppy arrived and I took it to my vet for a checkup, I discovered it had every parasite known to infest dogs; it was terrified of people, and looked half starved. It took months of care and a fortune in vet bills before it got over looking like a model for a canine CARE poster." You can take your money to better places than the breeder who shipped that puppy.

You may find advertisements of puppies for sale in dog magazines, but we would advise you to read magazines such as *Dog World* or *Pure Bred Dogs—American Kennel Gazette*, rather than sporting magazines where you might read advertisements for "hound breeds and crossbreeds" for bear, cougar and coon hunting. Stories have been heard of crossbred puppies which an unscrupulous breeder registered as part of a purebred litter. We have seen several hounds bought from these kennels, and only one of a dozen could be considered of fairly representative breed type. To give all due credit, several of the others proved to be excellent trailing dogs. However, for a little more original cost, and no extra expense in raising the animal, the owner could have had a hound which could both trail and represent the breed in a manner to do it credit. Certainly, if you intend to breed, you should breed only from the best.

If, through dog shows or advertisements, you are able to learn of a Bloodhound litter available or expected within reasonable driving distance, call the owner of the bitch and ask if you may come out and see the hounds. If the stud is also present, so much the better. In any case, the owner should have pedigrees of both bitch and stud, and should let you study them. Observe the condition in which the animals are kept, their health and general well-being. Avoid a breeder whose animals look scruffy, underfed, or are kept tied, or inadequately housed. If the parents look like hounds you would like to own, you can reasonably expect the puppies to be as desirable.

PEDIGREE AND REGISTRATION

If you reply to a magazine advertisement, ask for a copy of the puppy's pedigree. If you order a puppy through the mail, make it quite clear to the breeder whether you require a show dog or one of pet quality. If you want a show quality puppy, be prepared to pay more than you would for a pet quality pup. In either case, however, you are entitled to receive the registration form transferring the puppy to you as soon as you have paid for the puppy in full. Do not be misled

Cascade's Honey West of Dakota, a three-month-old hopeful bred by the authors.

"Sweet dreams" are one of the important things puppyhood is made of.

by a seller who tells you that you don't need that if you aren't going to breed, because it will only cost you more money. The only additional cost will be the registration fee payable to the American Kennel Club, which is only a few dollars; and the registration will be proof of your ownership. If you live in Canada, you will register your pup with the Canadian Kennel Club.

A seller who fails to supply the registration promptly and without question is very likely selling stolen puppies or puppies which are not purebred. You should be aware that there is a considerable market in stolen dogs, and it is a good idea to look for a tattoo inside the pup's ears or inside the flank, which could indicate a stolen dog. And incidentally, have your puppy tattooed with its registration number. It will give you a positive means of identification should it be lost or stolen. Research laboratories will not buy a tattooed dog as they will suspect it of being stolen; and this may save your dog's life.

Another precaution is taking a noseprint of your dog, in the same manner as fingerprints are taken, and keeping it in a safe place with his registration certificate and pedigree. In Canada, this noseprint or a tattoo is required with the registration application.

Although you may not intend to breed your puppy, you will still require AKC registration if you wish to enter it in dog shows. Registration may also be important if you use your pet as a mantrailing dog and it is involved in a criminal case. Some states have accepted Bloodhound evidence in court cases, with the requirement, among others, that the dog be purebred, as evidenced by AKC registration.

BUYING ON APPROVAL

If you buy a puppy sight unseen from a distant breeder, you should have an understanding by letter that you may look it over, take it to your own veterinarian for a checkup, and if it is not healthy or as represented, return it within a week. You must, of course, take the best of care of the puppy. You will expect to pay the airfare and cost of shipping crate when you receive it. Likewise, the breeder should expect to pay return shipping charges if the puppy does not satisfy the customer, unless other agreements have been put in writing beforehand.

It is naturally assumed that buyers are sincere and honest in ordering the puppy in the first place, and are not merely entertaining themselves at the expense of a breeder and a puppy.

WHAT AGE TO BUY

A Bloodhound puppy, with its wrinkled face radiating love and trust, is an utterly charming creature. You are tempted to cuddle it up and take it home with you immediately. But it is not wise to take the puppy until it is at least seven weeks old and has had its first distemper shot, even if the breeder is willing to part with it sooner. You may be exposing it to disease. If the puppy is being shipped from another state, your state laws may require that it have a rabies vaccination before it enters the state.

A breeder of show quality puppies would be reluctant to ship before a minimum of eight weeks and would prefer to wait at least three months, as age facilitates the ability to grade the puppies as to quality. Some factors, especially bite, may change as a puppy gets older. Puppies usually have correct bites with their first teeth; but bites may become undershot when the permanent teeth come in, and that is something which cannot be guaranteed. If the bite is not good with the first teeth, it is unlikely that it will ever improve.

THE GAWKY STAGE

Bloodhound puppies between the ages of six months and one year go through periods of uneven growth which make them look awkward and unbalanced. They will frequently go through a stage of being high in the rear, and you may wonder if you bought a kangaroo. If the puppy had a good topline at four weeks, it will normally have a good topline after it passes adolescence.

If you decide to make your own selection from the litter, the breeder cannot be held responsible if you later change your mind about the puppy you chose. Select your puppy with the Standard of the breed in mind, and with an eye for soundness and good temperament.

CHOOSING A MANTRAILER

If you are specifically looking for a mantrailer, here is a test which will help. If all the puppies can be put in a pen with a board fence (or the wire fence covered by cardboard), quietly approach the fence and observe them through a peephole. Before long, one of the puppies will catch your scent and gallop over to look for you. If possible, repeat this several times, and see if the same puppy is often the first to locate you. This will usually prove to be the puppy with the best nose.

The Reeds also have a theory that the most aggressive puppies in the litter will make the best mantrailers, as a mantrailer must be self-reliant and independent.

More complete advice on selecting puppies is given in a later chapter under "Grading the Litter." The final consideration in selecting any puppy, however, should be this: If you never took it to a single dog show, would you still want that dog? Is this a personality that matches yours? Do you and that puppy love each other?

LIFTING A YOUNG PUPPY

Now that you are ready to buy a puppy and bring it home, you should learn the correct way to pick up a Bloodhound puppy. Never pick it up by the back

How not to lift a young puppy. Sheila Brey demonstrates a common mistake. Even the puppy looks apprehensive.

"That's better." The correct way to lift a puppy is easier and more comfortable for all concerned.

of the neck, nor by the front legs. Put one arm around its brisket and the other around its rump and cradle it in your arms, giving it full body support. If you pick your puppy up this way frequently from the beginning, it will be accustomed to handling and will give no trouble when it is lifted to the veterinarian's examining table or to a grooming table.

When your veterinarian checks it, he will advise you on shots or worming your puppy may require. If the puppy was shipped from out of state, it will have a health certificate accompanying it telling which innoculations it has received.

FEEDING ROUTINES

The Bloodhound should always be fed from a raised dish, so that it stands up to its food, rather than stooping down on its pasterns. We make a little table with the center cut out to fit the size of its dish. Always use aluminum or stainless-steel dishes, which can be sterilized, which will not break or chip and which cannot be chewed up as plastic dishes can. Avoid like the plague leaving any plastics within the reach of your puppy. If it eats them, they will not digest, and will cause an obstruction in its intestines which will kill it. A case is known of an adult Bloodhound which chewed up a plastic cleaner's bag and died as a result. George Brooks lost an excellent hound to a walnut-sized bit of sponge it swallowed. Your puppy's keen nose will lead it to anything you have handled, and it will want to chew it. Use the same care you would use with your own baby.

Bloodhounds are creatures of habit, and we stress feeding at exactly the same time every day, and putting the dog's dish in the same place at every feeding, preferably in a spot where it won't be disturbed while eating. If you have more than one dog, feed each one separately, as Bloodhounds are inclined to be aggressive over food, and this can lead to serious fights. It is also important to keep hounds quiet and encourage rest after meals, as this reduces the likelihood of gastric torsion. Nor should they be fed when overtired or overheated from exercise.

A BLOODHOUND PUPPY IN THE HOME

If your puppy is to be a house dog, plan its sleeping area in a draft-free, our-of-the-way spot where it will be warm and undisturbed when it wants to sleep. A Bloodhound puppy will sleep so soundly that you can pick it up and have it hang on your arms like a wet dishrag. As it gets older, however, though you may approach it quietly you will soon see its nose working even as it sleeps, and it will wake up. It deserves its rest, and it will save training time if you accustom it to its permanent bed in the beginning.

Even if your hound is to be an outdoor dog, it is a good idea to keep it indoors with the family for the first few weeks. It will be very lonely for its brothers, sisters and mother, and needs the love and attention of the family to help it adjust to his new life. You will be able to train it faster with this extra attention, and it will rapidly learn what you expect of it.

Of course, home life means housebreaking. If you do not already have a traveling crate it is a good idea to buy one. You will need it when you go to dog shows or on mantrailing trips, and it will be a great help in housebreaking it now. If the puppy uses the crate as its bed, it will not want to wet it, and will learn to stay dry until you get up in the morning and let it outside. Of course, this precludes sleeping late on the weekends during your hound's puppyhood, as the little fellow will be quite nervous by morning. If you make a practice of taking it out several times a day, always after meals and after waking from naps, it will soon learn what is expected. It loves you and is eager to please.

Do not let the children play too roughly with the puppy. Because a Bloodhound puppy is big, people tend to forget it is still a baby and can be damaged easily. Also, with its naturally shy nature, it may be frightened and lose confidence in people from too-rough handling.

Usually when a person acquires a first puppy, and raises it in a friendly atmosphere, there are no temperament problems. Then they get their second or third puppy, and may be surprised to find this one becoming shy or spooky. This may be due to the fact that when a stranger approaches, the puppy will go bounding out to meet him, but the older dog, responding to its watchdog nature, opens up with vigorous baying. The puppy interprets this as a sign of danger and retreats, developing a fear of strangers. This can be avoided by not putting a puppy or young dog in a pen with older dogs until the puppy is at least a year old. By this time the youngster has attained confidence and social ease.

A Bloodhound should always have a fenced yard in which to exercise. There are too many hazards present for dogs roaming the streets and highways. Your bloodhound is inclined to disregard traffic, and it may be struck by a car, or cause a driver to have an accident in avoiding it. It may be stolen, or injured by vicious animals or people. Although it is normally a gentle and affectionate animal, many people are afraid of large dogs and react in a hostile manner. A female in season in the area may cause a male to roam, and some owners are likely to blame the male who does what comes naturally instead of their own carelessness in not protecting their bitch. Also, homeowners do not appreciate a Bloodhound's contributions to their landscaping.

If space is limited, a run ten feet by thirty feet will give the dog some safe exercise. However, if it is limited to a run of this size, it definitely will need additional exercise with the family, such as playing ball, going for walks, accompanying you as you ride a bicycle, etc. Bloodhounds love to swim, and if a lake is available, will benefit from it.

At about one year of age, you can start the puppy on harder exercise, such as roadwork, if there is a dirt or gravel road nearby. This should not be forced running, but a slow trot, starting at about a mile a day and working up to two miles or more. Paved roads should be avoided, as they tend to weaken the pasterns and splay the feet.

Bloodhounds, like other very large breeds, should always be fed from a raised dish. This routine should begin in puppyhood and should continue throughout the hound's entire life.

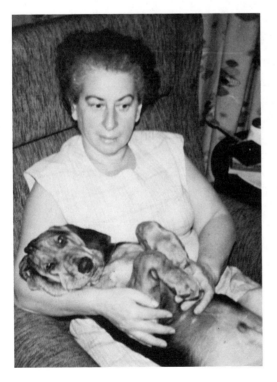

A Bloodhound puppy's natural, almost irresistible, appeal invites loving sessions in his owner's lap. This can be an unwise habit pattern to encourage, as a lap is quickly outgrown by a young hound.

An eight-week-old puppy bred by Ernie and Camille Danylchuk. How wise a countenance in one so young.

If your Bloodhound is to be an outdoor dog, accustom the puppy to this life during the summer, and as winter approaches it will grow a dense undercoat which will keep it warm in fairly cold winter weather. The puppy should have a well-built, insulated doghouse which will be cool in summer and warm in winter. A good house size for a Bloodhound is three and one-half feet wide, three feet high, and four feet long.

Keep your puppy's toenails trimmed short, but be careful not to cut into the quick. Some hounds have a hostile attitude toward nail trimming, and can make it difficult. If you accustom your hound to nail trimming during puppyhood, laying it down and having another person brush its underside while you trim the nails, it will enjoy it and give you no trouble. Long nails will cause splay feet and broken-down pasterns. Whether a hound is to be a mantrailer or a show dog, good feet and proper foot care are vital essentials. Hounds kept on concrete may wear their nails down naturally, but concrete is hard on the feet.

If your hound is to be a show dog, begin at once by leash training the young puppy and teaching it to trot at your side with its head up. Accustom your dog to strangers, other animals, and distracting sounds so that it will maintain its poise when it enters the ring. If a handling class is available in your area, you and the puppy will find it educational, and it will accustom the puppy to strange dogs and people.

THE CHALLENGE OF OBEDIENCE TRAINING

If your Bloodhound is to be a pet and companion, you may wish to try the challenge of obedience training. I do not use the word "challenge" lightly, as obedience training is the program which has mistakenly given owners of German Shepherds and Dobermans the impression that Bloodhounds are mentally retarded. This is far from the truth. If you spend three weeks snowed in with a Bloodhound puppy, as one of the writers once did, you will be very confident of the breed's high degree of intelligence. The challenge in obedience training results from the fact that Bloodhounds are independent, self-reliant animals, confident of their own good sense and judgment. As puppies, eager to please and innocently believing everything their beloved people tell them, they stampede to answer your call. At maturity, the response is likely to be a head tilted to the side and a quizzical expression that plainly asks, "Why? The fun is over here."

Susan B. Rowe, of St. Louis, Missouri, breeder of Happiness Hounds, has concentrated upon obedience training of Bloodhounds, and has many with obedience titles to her credit. She has written several articles on her training methods in the *American Bloodhound Club Bulletin*. This has encouraged other Bloodhound owners, and a considerable number now enter the obedience ring, with noteworthy success. Since there are excellent manuals on obedience training, we will not enter into the subject here, but recommend that you become familiar with the great variety of books available on this subject to find the ones most useful to you.

Caring for a Bloodhound presents some situations not usually encountered in most other breeds and are covered in this chapter. Bloodhound owners unanimously agree that their choice is worth the small amount of extra care needed for top condition.

9

Caring for the Bloodhound

SENSIBLE, DAY-TO-DAY CARE of a Bloodhound is essential to its ongoing health and well-being. Whether you have one hound that lives in the house or several that are housed in kennel conditions, comfortable quarters, wholesome food and attention to a Bloodhound's particular needs will go a long way toward helping you get the best out of your hounds at all times.

HOUSING

The most important consideration in housing a Bloodhound is cleanliness. This will apply to the hound's surroundings as well as to its own body. If it is to live in the house, continue as described in the preceding chapter by giving it a secluded spot for its bed, where it will not be annoyed when it wants to sleep. Its bed could be a rug or one of the commercial dog mattresses, as long as it is a material which can be kept clean.

Some dog mattresses are made with canvas covers, and we have seen them covered with Naugahyde. The latter is easily wiped clean, but caution is suggested in the case of puppies which are still inclined to chew, as Naugahyde is not digestible.

Even the Bloodhound that is kept as a house dog should have a fenced outdoor area for exercise. It should never be allowed to run loose where it may be exposed to danger. When it puts its head down and the wrinkles fall over its face it is virtually blind, and may not see approaching danger. It is also a convenience to have this safe exercise area and a house for its protection so that it may be outside when you are away from home, or if you have company and don't want it in the house for a time.

Be sure the run has some shade to give protection from the hot sun in summer. If you do not have shade trees, artificial shade can be provided by a canvas tarp over a part of the run. It is advisable to make the run as large as your space permits, remembering that length is more important than width.

Breeders have differing opinions as to what surface is best for a dog run. Some prefer a surface of well-packed fine cinders, claiming that this provides good drainage and is good for the feet. There is some truth to this, although good feet also depend on inheritance and proper feeding, and feet can be ruined by keeping a hound on a soft or sandy surface. We like to use pea gravel in our runs. We find this surface also gives good footing, and provides good drainage. The gravel is small enough so that if the puppies or hounds do swallow some it does not cause an obstruction. Both cinders and gravel have their drawbacks, one of which is the fact that parasite eggs and larvae can exist and thrive in them. They are almost impossible to clean from this kind of surface, although a blowtorch will kill them.

Some owners prefer concrete runs, which are easier to clean, and present a good appearance. This again is a porous surface in which the minute eggs of parasites can take refuge, and the blowtorch or scrubbing with disinfectant will be necessary. Concrete sometimes retains odors, but a disinfectant and deodorizing solution can eliminate that. A strong borax solution poured on the gravel or cinder runs or used to scrub the concrete will destroy hookworm larvae.

The ideal fencing is a heavy chain link with metal posts set in concrete. We suggest using a six-foot fence, although you read that "Bloodhounds are not jumpers, and a four- or five-foot fence is high enough." Considering the relative cost, the added protection is worthwhile. Bloodhounds have been known to be climbers, and the six-foot fence seems to discourage them. It also will keep out most other dogs which may wish to join your females in season, unless you have in your neighborhood the rare commando who climbs fences with the speed of a monkey.

A sure cure for fence climbers is an electric fence, such as farmers use to hold livestock. You can buy an electric fence charger from an agricultural supply store; and a single wire carrying an electric charge, strung about eight inches above the top of the kennel fence, will end climbing at once. The hound will not be injured, but it will learn a healthy respect for that top wire without robbing it of its natural love for standing against the fence to greet visitors.

If you can't afford the six-foot chain link fence, you can use hog wire or a two-inch turkey mesh, but whatever fencing you use, be sure it is strong enough to hold when your hound jumps up on the fence. Always put the wire on the inside of the posts, so when the hounds jump up they don't push it away from the posts. If you use wooden posts for the fence, be sure to paint the portion going underground with creosote or some other good wood preservative before you set the posts in the holes.

The next big project is the doghouse. You can make this as simple or as elaborate as you wish, and your climate will demand some adjustment in the basic plan. If you live in a warm climate you may want it larger and airier, but in a cold climate no larger than required for comfort, and it will take less body heat to keep it snug.

We suggest a house with a covered porch that gives shade from the sun and a place to lie in bad weather. The feeding table is fastened to the front of the house under this porch, so feed and hound are protected. The foundation of the house can be built of two-by-sixes, and the floor built on that, so the house is raised above the ground and the dampness. In a cold climate we recommend a double wall and insulation in the floor, walls and ceiling, and a gable roof above, with air vents at each end to keep it cooler in summer. Be sure to cover the air vents with insect screens, or bees and wasps may be attracted to the space as a home.

The doorway should be placed all the way to one side of the front of the house, making it approximately eleven by twenty inches with a sill raised about eight inches above the floor. This keeps drafts out and bedding in. Projecting inward from the front of the house beside the entrance should be a stub wall about eighteen inches wide. This will keep the winter winds from blowing directly onto the dog and provide a snug area where it is protected. During warm weather it can sprawl in front of the doorway.

The roof may be covered with shingles or heavy tar paper. It has been said that blue or blue-gray paint will discourage flies, but be sure that whatever paint you use is a nonlead type that will not poison the dog if it chews on it.

When your house is placed in the run, try to locate it so the door will be protected from the winter wind and the hot summer sun. If it is at all possible, your hound will be happier if it can lie in the doorway of its house and keep an eye on your house, your activities and guests. This also makes it easier to check on its well-being.

Some dog food companies print sensible and budget-controlled kennel plans which may be obtained for the asking.

FEEDING

This is the menu Dakota Bloodhound puppies take to their new homes at age eleven weeks. If your puppy is older or younger when you bring it home, adjust according to the individual appetite.

8:00 A.M. One cup puppy chow soaked in one cup skim milk. Add one-third pound hamburger, one teaspoonful cod liver oil and one teaspoonful calcium-phosphorus powder. Mix well and feed.

Noon: Two boiled eggs and one cup cottage cheese. Never feed raw eggs; they cannot properly digest the raw egg whites and it is a waste of half the food value.

6:00 P.M. Same as morning feeding, omitting cod liver oil and calcium. Add one teaspoonful corn oil or other vegetable oil and one Vitamin C tablet (as sold for humans), five hundred milligrams daily until over one year old.

9:00 P.M. One cup puppy chow, dry, as the puppy enjoys chewing. After this, one cup skim milk.

A vitamin and mineral supplement should be added according to your veterinarian's directions. Since bitch's milk is richer than cow's milk, fat must be added to puppies' food when they are weaned to make it equivalent to bitch's milk. Remember that puppies eat much more than adult dogs of the same size. Once they are grown, the food intake will stabilize. Bloodhound puppies gain from four to five pounds a week during the early months after weaning, and plenty of highly nutritious food and milk are essential for this rapid growth.

At age three months the late feeding may be omitted, and at six months the lunch may be omitted. Add the eggs and cottage cheese to other meals in place of part of the meat.

Increase the amounts as the puppy grows. Give him what he will clean up promptly, but never allow a pan of food to stand before a healthy dog more than thirty minutes under any circumstances. If a hound is fed at the same times each day, it will be eager to eat at those times.

It is a good idea to watch the hound as it eats and observe its appetite and feeding habits. Then you will learn what is normal for it and notice quickly any signs that may indicate illness.

A typical diet for a Bloodhound over a year old is between five and six cups of good commercial dog meal plus a pound of meat, boiled egg, half a cup of cottage cheese and a tablespoonful of corn or other oil or cooking fat. A little salt seems to reduce the Bloodhound's tendency to slobber. Add one teaspoonful baking soda, to help reduce gas which may cause bloat. Divide this into two meals, and use water or milk to moisten the food. Don't get it too sloppy and watery. Two or three times a week we add a teaspoonful of honey. Twice a week we use tomato juice instead of the water or milk to moisten the food. Three times a week we use a small carton of yoghurt.

We let the food sit for fifteen or twenty minutes to allow the food to swell and let some of the gases escape. We believe this reduces the chances of gastric torsion, as the food will already have swollen and will not be so likely to do so inside the stomach. If a hungry hound fills itself with dry food and then drinks a quantity of water, the food will swell and may be the cause of bloat.

Your hound should always have fresh, clean water available. Remember to keep the buckets clean, and scrub them with a disinfectant solution once a week or so. Common laundry bleach added to the scrub water is a good disinfectant.

It is important to remember that the essentials of a hound's diet are protein, carbohydrates, fat, vitamins and minerals. All of these elements should be included in the diet if your hound is to grow properly and maintain the "bloom" it will need to be a top show competitor or stalwart mantrailer.

If the adult hound receives a well-balanced diet and a good commercial dog food, it probably gets all the vitamins it needs. If it is in good health, showing plenty of pep and sparkle, with a shiny coat, you need not worry about supplements.

Bitches in whelp and lactating should definitely receive additional vitamins and minerals, especially calcium, phosphorus and cod liver oil. Your veterinarian should give you directions on this. Some owners seem to think if a teaspoonful is good, a tablespoonful is better, and this may result in a toxic reaction.

Occasionally we have a Bloodhound who is a finicky eater. Much of this is caused by irregular feeding and changing the diet. There seems to be less of a problem if the schedule is regulated and the diet is well balanced and not varied. A dog with a poor appetite may be helped by supplementing with Vitamin B_{12}.

Following are some recipes we have used for the hounds, which may be classed as folk medicine, or herb remedies. One in which I have faith as a result of personal experience helped a Bloodhound with an injured pancreas which was having trouble gaining weight and keeping food down. This consists of two cups of dry cooked rice, three cans strained baby meat, veal, chicken or liver, a jar of strained baby carrots, one cup cottage cheese, one teaspoonful meat tenderizer containing the papaya enzyme.

Another natural medication I have found successful, and have used on other breeds, is rose hips. If a bitch seems about to miscarry, gather all the rose hips you can find, cut them up, and steep them in boiling water for fifteen minutes. Strain off the resulting liquid and give two or three tablespoonfuls to the bitch every hour for two days. This has seemed beneficial. Rose hips are an excellent source of Vitamin C, many times richer than oranges. Rose hip tea and rose hip jelly are also frequently used as a source of vitamins for human consumption.

If puppies have diarrhea, it may cause them to become very emaciated, almost to the point of death. Take slippery elm powder, mix it with water, and feed it by the tablespoonful; or else mix it with the dog food for the puppies. This will stop diarrhea.

I know people who make a tea of raspberry leaves which they feed to the female Bloodhound during the last month of pregnancy.

We always advise, however, that you consult a veterinarian first. These folk medicines should be considered a last resort.

THE OVERPROTECTIVE HOUND

Although Bloodhounds are an affectionate and devoted breed with their owners, it must be admitted that temperament can sometimes be a problem. They are inclined to be very protective, both of their owners and what they may regard as their own property, and it is generally recognized that they can become quite testy at times. Perhaps the greatest breed improvement in recent years has been the improvement in temperament. Some of the older judges who were around when temperament was more of a problem can be spotted in the show ring because they will ask the handler to show the dog's bite, rather than parting his lips themselves. The Bloodhound's temperament is such that one should never *tell* it what to do; one should *ask* it to do something. It is a dog of much dignity.

Perhaps the pendulum has swung too far to the other side now, and for this reason we are seeing many shy dogs in the ring today. Fanciers of the breed must work on this problem to reach a happy medium.

Vicious Bloodhounds are in the minority, but it is a fact that they do exist, and this should be realized. Perhaps vicious is not the correct word in describing Bloodhounds, as they rarely attack. They simply do not back down. This is why we say you do not *tell* a Bloodhound, you *ask* it.

EYE CONDITIONS

Eye troubles are a common breed problem. The lids may be inverted, or turned in, which is called entropion. The lash will rub against the eyeball, causing painful irritation for the hound, eventually causing ulceration and even leading to blindness.

The opposite condition, where the lids are turned out, is called ectropion. Both conditions are classified as being hereditary, and may be corrected by competent surgery. When these conditions exist, they should be remedied as soon as possible, to spare the animal suffering and damage to his eyes. Dogs with these problems should not be used as breeding stock.

BLOAT

While we hope we are writing a book you can enjoy reading, there is no way of being entertaining about bloat and gastric torsion. This condition is one of the common killers of Bloodhounds and other large dogs. It has been the subject of much study and speculation, but as yet its cause is uncertain. Until the cause is definitely known, methods of prevention are speculation, at best.

It is believed that overeating, eating and drinking while overheated and tired from exercise, swallowing foreign material such as stones, etc., and possibly emotional causes may contribute to bloat. If the gas-filled stomach then turns in the body cavity, closing off both ends, this is gastric torsion. The gas now has no means of escaping, and as the food in the stomach continues fermenting, the gas increases, distending the abdomen, and if unrelieved, is a cause of painful death.

Bloat is simply a condition in which the abdomen becomes excessively filled with gas. This gas may be in the stomach or other parts of the digestive tract. This condition may rapidly become acute, so that if the owner is at home and attentive to the animal, the swollen condition will be obvious. It may be caused when a dog swallows air, as in tonsillitis or following general anesthesia, overeats or has gastric inflammation. If the stomach is in its proper position this gas buildup may be relieved by belching, vomiting or passing food and gas back into the small intestine.

As long as the animal belches or vomits, torsion is not present. Recovery may be aided by passing a stomach tube down the throat and into the stomach, which allows the gas to escape. It is also relieved by a generous dose of a product such as Pepto-Bismol, Di-Gel, Mylanta, etc. A plastic turkey baster is a convenient tool in administering these. Walking the animal seems to encourage the passing of gas.

Beware if the hound shows the signs of bloat, but tries repeatedly to vomit and is unable to do so; if it seems very thirsty, but promptly gags and loses the water; if it shows great pain, reluctance to lie or sit and labored breathing. **Rush** the animal to your veterinarian immediately, as gastric torsion is indicated. Without surgery, the animal will surely die in agony. If in doubt, assume the worst and waste no time in seeking medical aid.

There are no doubt many cases of gastric torsion deaths that are not reported as such. The animal is found dead, and no investigation of the reason is made. Other causes may be assumed; or if an older dog is involved, it may seem natural death.

The only cure for gastric torsion is immediate surgery. The stomach is emptied and repositioned, and then stitched in place. Treatment for shock and antibiotics are given. The dog must be watched carefully during the recovery period. Do not feed for twenty-four hours, and then put it on a soft bland diet. After the dog seems well on the way to normalcy, its regular food can be gradually added to the bland diet, which should be fed in three or four small meals.

The recipe for a soft bland canine diet is as follows:

One-half cup farina (Cream of Wheat) cooked to make two cups
One cup creamed cottage cheese
One large whole egg, hard cooked
Three tablespoons granulated sugar
Two tablespoons dry active baker's yeast
One tablespoon corn oil

This diet is approximately 7 percent protein, 3 percent fat, 11 percent carbohydrate, and provides about 422 calories per pound. A one-hundred-pound Bloodhound would eat approximately five and one-half cups of this mixture per day.

Another diet supplement which has given good results in cases where a dog was recovering from serious illness or surgery is a high-calorie protein supplement sold for human use. Mix it according to directions and freeze it in ice cube trays. Even if the sick dog is uninterested in eating, you can feed these to it by tucking one cube at a time between its lips.

HIP DYSPLASIA

Hip dysplasia is the number two bogeyman of the dog owner. It is a condition which occurs in all large breeds, although small breeds rarely seem afflicted. Serious though it may be, it is not the swift killer that gastric torsion is. Dogs exhibiting only a slight degree of dysplasia may well live a normal and untroubled life span. However, a dog exhibiting a swaying, wobbling gait and stiffness and pain in the rear end while still young should definitely be euthanized.

In simple language, hip dysplasia is a condition in which the hip joint is loose, accompanied by malformation of the hip socket and the joining head of the thighbone (femoral head). Abnormal development of the connective tissues results in instability of the joint. X rays show that the hip socket, instead of being a cuplike connection for the end of the thighbone, is very shallow or almost nonexistent. This poor connection results in an unstable gait and painful movement.

It is believed that hip dysplasia is a hereditary disease; however, other factors may enter into it. Pups of dysplastic parents are twice as likely to have dysplasia as those from nondysplastic parents, which would seem to indicate it is a recessive trait. However, according to Cornell University Veterinary College figures, even when two dysplastic dogs are mated, about 20 to 30 percent normal offspring may be expected; and the occurrence of dysplasia in the progeny of mildly dysplastic dogs does not appear to vary in any great extent from that of progeny of normal parents. Even when two proven, normal dogs are bred, approximately 30 percent of the progeny may be afflicted with hip dysplasia.

Many dog owners and breeders are reduced to a state of near-hysteria at the mention of dysplasia, and would sooner admit to the presence of a two-headed child in their family than dysplasia in their dogs. Cases are known of entire litters of puppies being destroyed as a result of a test of unproven validity. Many breeders refuse to use any animals not certified perfect as a result of X ray by the Orthopedic Foundation for Animals (OFA).

The Swedish Army Dog Training Center conducted a ten-year study of hip dysplasia, and the conclusion drawn was that it was in part due to the interaction of a number of genes and in part due to environment. It is established that all hip joints are normal at birth; and that dysplasia develops in pups lacking sufficient pelvic and thigh muscle mass.

While every effort should be made to breed the best and reduce defects of every kind, exaggeration of the importance of only one feature has resulted in many cases in the breeding of animals with perfect X rays and a multitude of other faults. Although Dakota Kennels X-rays its breeding stock, it has consistently been the opinion at this kennel that a fault which requires an X ray to find is far less serious than a fault which is obvious, such as a bad head, swayback or poor temperament. Keep in mind the Saint Bernard who ate the state trooper!

10

Preparation for the Show Ring

THE FIRST DOG SHOW held in America took place in Chicago in 1874. Since that time dog showing has developed into a full-time business, involving thousands, from professional handlers and show superintendents to manufacturers and purveyors of necessary equipment.

Just as evident is the fact that dog showing is for many a happy leisure activity. Often it is a family hobby with mother and dad concerned about scoring the points in the conformation ring while the youngsters test their mettle in Junior Showmanship.

In the show ring history of the Bloodhound in America, many of the most memorable winners were guided by their devoted owner-handlers to a host of red-letter triumphs. Tom Sheahan scored well with Ch. Fancy Bombardier and Ch. Essex Fancy Thomas. Ed Simon led his Ch. Black Tommy of Huguenot to many coveted awards while Nancy Lindsay frequently accompanied Ch. The Ring's Imp into the winner's circle.

More recently the Sinkinsons have been much in evidence as amateur handlers of commendable ability as has Mrs. Brey guiding the Dakota entries. There are numerous other examples of talented owner-handlers who derive the full measure of enjoyment from personally competing and winning with their Bloodhounds.

Am/Can. Ch. The Mountaineers Jacob, bred by Walter H. Elgin and owned by Sheila and Mark Bashnick of Surrey, British Columbia, was the top Bloodhound in Canada for 1985 and 1986.

Exercise and conditioning are essential for a successful show animal. Here Ch. St. Hubert Blondel and owner Richard Pruitt engage in a swim. Swimming, if the facililties are available, is a wonderful means of conditioning a hound.

BEFORE YOU START

For you who have acquired a show prospect Bloodhound puppy you stand on the threshhold of a unique experience that is like nothing else in the world of avocation. Through your hound you will meet people you would never have met otherwise. You will go places you would never have imagined traveling to before and the entire experience will enrich your life and broaden your total outlook.

Before setting out to conquer these bright new worlds, you should understand that in one important respect dog shows are like many other endeavors in life; you stand to get out of your participation about the same as you put into it. No one wants to lose, but someone always must. There are enough people showing good Bloodhounds so that you must work to develop your puppy's fullest potential. Given a good hound, good training and proper attention to good grooming, you too can win your share.

GROOMING

Your Bloodhound puppy is now six months old, which qualifies it for the Puppy class. You are looking forward to its show ring debut. First, a little advice on grooming and show training.

There is nothing more beautiful than a healthy, well-groomed Bloodhound with its shiny coat and alert eyes. Grooming is a matter of habit for both the dog and the owner. Try to make it a pleasurable occasion for both.

At Dakota Kennels we start the puppies on a grooming routine early, by putting them on a grooming table and handling, or going over them. If you are kind and firm, your puppy will enjoy this individual attention and look forward to it. We begin cleaning the puppies on the grooming table at the age of three or four weeks. This makes it easier to teach them their show stance, because when they are up on a higher level they seem to stand better. This training also makes it easier to grade the litter.

The Bloodhound can be trained to jump up on the grooming table or bench, preferably on command. Most groomers and handlers use the command "Table."

Groom your Bloodhound at least once a week; once a day is better. The more you brush the coat, the shinier it will get. Bloodhounds need not be combed before they are brushed unless they are very dirty. A hound glove, which can be purchased in a pet supply shop, is recommended. This is a glove which has little bristles on one side, with the other side being made of corduroy or velvet-type material. Do not use sharp brushes or wire brushes on your Bloodhound, as it is easy to scrape the tender skin. Brush in the direction the hair grows until it is smooth and shiny. Your dog gets much pleasure from this individual attention. Be sure the brush and hound glove are always clean before you use them.

This routine grooming should include nail clipping. Check the ears also while you have the hound on the table. The ends of a Bloodhound's ears tend to pick up food and dirt, which should not be allowed to accumulate. It is best not to poke down into the inside of the ear. More damage is done by probing into the ear than by ear diseases. If the ear does appear dirty or full of wax, take a bit of cotton and wrap it around your finger, wet it with rubbing alcohol, and use this to clean the ear. Be sure not to thrust anything into the ear canal.

If you notice your hound scratching its ears or shaking its head violently, it might have some type of irritation such as canker or ear mites. Have your veterinarian check the ears in this case. He might recommend that you fill the ear with mineral oil or propylene glycol, which is good treatment for these problems. Give this treatment while the hound is on the table so you can hold the earflap and see into the ear canal while you treat it. Then massage the base of the ear and wipe away the excess oil. This also helps dissolve wax.

Check the eyes of your Bloodhound regularly. If they exude matter, it should be wiped away with a small piece of moist cotton. There are several types of soothing eye ointments which can be obtained from the veterinarian when your hound has eye irritations.

Another routine check while the hound is being groomed is the condition of the teeth. If you see any tartar on the teeth, use a tartar scraper. Dog biscuits and bones made of animal hide, like rawhide, are excellent aids in prevention of tartar. We do not recommend giving meat bones to your Bloodhound, even to fight tartar. If tartar is excessive, it would be best removed by your veterinarian. This routine dental care will also prepare your hound for the examination of its bite while in the show ring.

While doing your grooming, check the anal glands. These are two glands situated on either side of the anus. If you think of the anus as a clock, the glands are situated at four and eight. They appear to serve the same purpose as the scent glands of a skunk, and give off an unpleasant odor if the dog is extremely frightened. If they are not discharged periodically, they will become enlarged and infected. Use a tissue or cotton to empty these glands, as the liquid is quite unpleasant. Hold the tail up with one hand, and with the other, gently squeeze each lump upward and outward. If this does not empty the glands, they will require the care of a veterinarian.

BATHING

The dog should be bathed only often enough to keep it clean. The bath should be given in a warm area, free from drafts, using a good-quality dog shampoo. Do not use human shampoo as it is too alkaline for dogs and prolonged use can damage the coat.

Be sure you do not get soap in your dog's eyes; an ophthalmic ointment put into the eyes before the bath is a good precaution.

There are also many of the so-called dry bath preparations on the market, and these serve the purpose for the "in-between" baths. Most contain a special detergent which includes insecticides, and some leave an insecticidal residue.

When you bathe your hound, a waterproof apron is a precaution, as with one shake of that loose skin a Bloodhound can spread enough water to make you wonder who is getting bathed for the show. Be sure that you rinse thoroughly and squeeze all the water out of the coat. Pay particular attention to the loose skin under the head and neck, because this does collect soap that can cause irritation if left there. A vinegar rinse is good, but be sure you do not get any into the eyes.

Drying the dog is important, especially in a cold climate. It is wise to bathe the dog in the evening, and let it remain in the house all night so it will not be chilled while wet. Towel-dry it as thoroughly as possible. We know one breeder who puts sweatshirts on her dogs after they are bathed to keep them warm, and we find this a very sound idea.

RING TRAINING

Your hound is now so beautiful you wonder how a judge could resist it. Along with beauty, however, must go ring manners and style. This means it must lead well, moving at your side at a slow trot and not diving between your legs just as the judge turns your way. It must ignore the other dogs, acting neither frightened nor hostile.

Start your puppy on lead training without putting pressure on it. Using a light collar and lead, take it out in the yard. If it is accustomed to being played with, it should be happy to go with you. At first follow it where it wants to go, so it will not become frightened at this new restraint. If you give the lead a little tug and say "Come," it will soon learn what you want. It is important that you are never harsh with the puppy, as you do not want to break its show spirit. Make it a fun time for it, and when it goes into the show ring it will have that extra "pizzazz" that often makes the winner.

It should already be more or less familiar with the meaning of "Stand" from its grooming experience on the show table. While you lead it around, stop now and then and say "Stand" so it will learn to obey this command in the show ring. At first, do not be too particular where it places its feet, as long as it more or less stands still. Use praise lavishly, and give it a little treat. Here again, the main idea is to keep up its morale.

I remember a judge telling me once that when we come to the building with our dogs in the morning there is a sign that says DOG SHOW. "That is exactly what your dog must do," he said. "He must *show* to win." In other words, you do not want to take the "show" out of your show dog.

While your puppy is standing, go over it with your hands. Part its lips in front to accustom it to the bite check, and touch the male puppy's testicles, as will be done by the judge. If your hound is not trained to accept such attentions, it may give you a very bad time in the ring, and may even be disqualified for snapping at a judge whose examination it resents.

Here are some important training tips that will help make the dog show a satisfaction to both you and your hound. First, remember that your puppy is anxious to obey you and is really trying even if it doesn't seem that it is succeeding. One unbreakable rule you must remember is everlasting patience. Be consistent in your training; use the same words for the same commands. Always react the same way to success or lack of it.

When I am showing a hound, I always try to get it into the mood from the beginning. When I take it out of the crate, I say, "Come on! Let's go show, let's go show!" I play with it just a bit to get it eager and happy. When I take it into the ring, I use the command "Stand!" for the show pose. When the judge singles us out for the individual gaiting, I touch the hound a little under the chin to encourage it to hold its head up, and say, "Let's go!" You can use other commands, but remember that you must always use the same words and the same routine, so your hound knows exactly what is expected.

It is important to teach the Bloodhound one step at a time. Reward it *immediately* when it does something right. I don't believe in physical punishment. I will use the command "No!" with a strict voice, and this does it. My experience has been that the Bloodhound is very willing to please me, and this has always been adequate.

Before going into the ring, use the regular grooming procedures given earlier. Since a Bloodhound's ears are a prominent breed characteristic which the judge will especially notice, always give them a last-minute check to be sure they are clean. Check its eyes to be sure they don't have any matter or residue around them. In past times, we always advised cutting off the whiskers to give a smooth appearance to the head, but in late years a number of fanciers oppose this. "Whiskers" in an animal are actually sensory organs, properly called vibrissae, and serve a purpose for the animal. To trim or not is now optional, but we do trim the little twist at the end of the tail. You may spray your hound with a coat conditioner of some kind that can be purchased from a pet supply house. Wipe it down afterward so you are sure it is dry and the judge will not get oil on his hands when he examines the hound in the ring. A piece of velvet or a chamois is excellent for wiping the coat. This gives the coat that extra gloss.

Teach your hound to gait on a loose lead with the head up. Many hound judges will not penalize you for letting your exhibit's head drop, because this is a natural instinct for a scent hound. However, if you have been standing ringside you will notice that when the head drops it may spoil a hound's rear action. Keeping the head up improves the gait and gives it greater style. You will find it easier to teach your puppy to gait with the head high if you use the reward system. It will then keep its head up and watching for the treat, or the pat under the chin.

Teach your puppy to gait in a straight line. Having it decide to cut across in front of you while gaiting can be both hazardous to your health and demoralizing to your dignity, as you unscramble your legs from your dog's and pick yourself up from the floor of the ring. If your local kennel club gives conformation classes, this can be beneficial in ironing out the wrinkles in its show training, and will socialize the puppy. It is also excellent training for both of you if you attend as many as possible of the local sanction matches.

SANCTION MATCHES

If you are a novice, let us caution you not to take the placings at the matches very seriously. Often the judges officiating at matches are familiar with their own particular breed, but not necessarily Bloodhounds. They are learning, much as you are. It is a training ground for judges, just as for puppies and handlers.

I know of a case in which a novice judge at a match told an exhibitor that the Bloodhound he was showing did not have a proper headpiece. Being novices also, the owners did not show the puppy again because they felt he was deficient in head type. The puppy was later seen by a Bloodhound breeder, and the breeder, being knowledgeable, commented that the puppy was of excellent quality and should be shown. Its head, in fact, was one of its better points. This dog then went on to become a well-known show dog, but valuable time was lost because an inexperienced owner had taken too seriously the remarks of a match judge.

IMPROVING YOUR CHANCES

Remember that while the match is a training ground, it is *only* a training ground, and keep this in perspective. Your hound needs the experiences of matches before it makes its big debut into the formal point shows.

Before showing your hound be sure it is in top condition, carrying the right weight, and the right muscle tone. Have it well-groomed, as detailed earlier. Arrive at the show grounds early—at least an hour before show time—so the dog can relieve itself, get used to the smells and commotion, and settle down.

Take a few minutes to stand at the ringside of the judge under whom you will be showing and observe the ring procedure he uses. This is valuable, as the judge has only a few minutes to go over your hound, and the more you can do to make it easier for him, the better for all concerned. Remember that he may be judging 175 dogs that day, he is not a teenager, and he will be on his feet for many hours, often under less-than-ideal weather conditions. Do not test his endurance or waste time by forcing him to repeat unnecessary instructions.

Many novice owner-handlers will express unkind suspicions that judges show favor to professional handlers. They fail to consider that the handlers not only know how to show the animal at its best, but know the proper ring routine and spare the judge extra wear on his throat. They realize that the armband is provided for identification, and wear it so the number is easily seen and the judge does not have to walk around behind them to note it for his record.

Pick up your armband at ringside before Bloodhounds are called, and watch your judging schedule so that you can be there with your entry when the class is called. Do not expect a judge to wait for you. When you enter the ring it usually does not matter where you are in the line, although some judges do prefer having entries in catalog order. Get into that ring and have your hound properly posed as quickly as possible. As the judge looks down the line his first impression is very often the impression he will keep, unless in looking over your dog he finds something significant that will affect his decision one way or the other.

HANDLING

Do not crowd the hound ahead of you in the ring. There is plenty of room for all. You must think of yourself almost as a used-car salesman, so to speak, and you must inspire the judge to "buy" your exhibit. You must work all the time for your hound.

On the other hand, do not overhandle. This is the value of proper training; have your hound standing and yourself relaxed, while everyone else in the ring is straining to keep their hounds under control. If the hound ahead of you does not gait as fast, do not crowd it; swing out a bit and take a bigger circle. If one behind seems to be crowding you, it is perfectly acceptable to let it get ahead of you, and then continue.

Always remember, no matter how the judge places you, thank him for the ribbon. Courtesy never hurt anyone, whether or not you agree with his placements. Judges have been known to have long memories, and your attitude may make a difference the next time you show under him.

The correct way to stand a Bloodhound in the ring is as follows. The front legs should be brought straight down under the shoulder. The back legs are stretched back a trifle, so the hocks will be perpendicular to the ground. Then hold the tail up, slightly curved, but not curled over the hound's back. I have seen frightened novices grasp the tail in a death grip and hold it straight up like a ramrod. Give it the natural curve, holding it easily by the tip. Some judges want you to bring the hound's head up and fold all the wrinkles forward, such as one sees on a Basset Hound. Personally, I prefer the natural appearance in the pose, with the head held up in its normal position. Another reason I do not like to pull all the skin over the face is that especially with males it makes it difficult to keep them standing, as this covers the eyes and they like to see what is going on.

I usually pose a hound by holding the head with my hand under the jaw. When the judge approaches, I use my left hand to push the wrinkle forward while the judge is approaching.

Once the judge has the hound's head in his hand, I move, let go of the head and hold the tail. When the judge moves to the rear, I take the head and move to the front. I again take the skin and pull it forward while the judge is at the back, so the judge can see my hound's length of neck. Sometimes one finds that in Bloodhounds with their tremendous amount of loose skin and jowls, the neck will appear to be short when it is in fact of a good length. If you will stand in front of your hound, holding the head with your left hand and pulling the skin forward, the length of neck will be emphasized. This will also enable you to control a male who may resent a judge with cold hands examining his testicles. When the judge has finished examining the rear, move back to your original place with the hound's head in your right hand, holding the tail in your left.

It is most important here to check that your hound did not shift its feet while the judge was going over it. Some Bloodhounds have a tendency to place their front feet too far forward, giving them a "rocking horse" appearance and making them seem down on their pasterns.

210

When the competition is close, skillful handling often makes the difference between winning and losing. Here judge George Beckett evaluates the merits of Ch. St. Hubert's Bailiff as handler Alfred Murray makes the most of his hound. At left, handler E. J. Carver steadies Ch. Landrover Royal Lancer for comparison with his rival for the judge's nod.

First impressions can often be lasting ones in competition. How the hounds strike the judge as they first come into the ring frequently plays an important part in how they are placed. The wise handler acts accordingly, making sure his hound litterally puts its best foot forward from the start.

RING ATTIRE

Along with proper presentation of your hound at the shows, give some thought on your own appearance in the picture. Remember that a dog show is a beauty contest of sorts, and your appearance should not disgrace your Bloodhound's. Women should not wear skirts that are too short while showing; do not try to "outshow" your hound. Skirts that are too full may blow into the hound's face. Avoid high heels for the show ring, as you will not be able to gait the hound properly and may have a misstep. There are now many stylish, attractive pantsuits in style, and these will give a woman an appropriate and dressy appearance in the ring. If you wear a color which contrasts with the color of your hound, it will make a better display in competition and in the photographs.

I remember seeing a Dalmatian exhibitor at one show who had managed to obtain a dress of a print that exactly matched the markings of her dog. In a picture it would have been hard to see where one ended and the other began.

Men should wear sports jackets, or sports suits (i.e. tweed, corduroy, etc.) in the ring. It is preferable to wear a tie while showing. In hot weather, the jacket may be dispensed with, but as a matter of courtesy it is recommended that if the judge is wearing a jacket in the ring, all male exhibitors should keep their jackets on. A well-groomed handler and a well-groomed dog always make an attractive picture.

POINTS TO REVIEW

To summarize: (1) Observe the judge; watch him judge other breeds before you go into the ring, so you will know his procedure. (2) If the class is large, decide which other hounds you want to be near, to give yours the best advantage. Most dogs of all breeds look better near those of similar type. (3) Pay attention to the judge at all times; he may change his instructions or give an award. (4) When gaiting, know what particular speed to expect from your hound. Learn to turn your hound without breaking his gait. (5) Practice stacking your hound before a mirror. The judge will see its opposite side, so you must know how that side looks. (6) Always treat the judge with courtesy, win or lose. Don't talk to the judge except to answer questions he might ask. Always thank him for the ribbon, whether you like it or not. (7) Have a positive attitude. You must believe that your dog can win, and you must act as if you believe it when you show.

SPORTSMANSHIP

Finally, remember that dog showing is a sport, so conduct yourself in a sportsmanlike manner accordingly. Win or lose, accept the results graciously. If you are truly proud of your breed and interested in its improvement, you should want your hound to win because you honestly believe it is the best specimen present; but if the judge feels it is not, congratulate the winner. Cheer the

Nancy Lindsay in the ring with Barsheen Jade. The handler presents a picture of good taste in ring attire. She is neither overdressed nor too casual. Guidelines for proper ring attire are simple for both men and women, and following them will always help the handler make as pleasing a picture as the hound.

Bloodhound on that goes into the Group, give it your support, for it represents your breed. At another show under another judge, you may be the one receiving the trophy for your hound.

COMIC RELIEF

Now that you are well schooled in the serious aspects of dog showing, and have reviewed the basic rules, we caution you that the nature of the breed being what it is, a bit of levity sometimes enters the program. As an example, when the Reeds brought their first puppy to his first dog show, daughter Bobbi handled him while Mama watched and hoped to learn. Boomerang, however, already had a few months of training as a mantrailer, and that was exactly what he wanted to do, all the way around the ring. Bobbi had had considerable experience in the show ring; but even at six months a male Bloodhound has the power to overcome any objections to what he considers his duty. Then he arrived at the table holding the trophies, and beautifully decorated with flowers. Here he finally raised his head and stopped, like Ferdinand the Bull, to carefully smell the bouquet. The audience laughed, and Bobbi turned pink.

The worst, however, was still to come. Since he was the only Bloodhound entry, he had to represent his breed in the Group. We'd have to be dreamers, of course, to have expected a puppy at his first show to place; but he did look beautiful. The fortune cookies with our Chinese dinner had said we would be lucky.

Disaster! Whatever made that placid, loveable slouch of a Bloodhound change his personality at a time like that? Suddenly he realized he had competition, and had to do *something* to get his share of the attention. Then a brilliant idea entered his little pointed head, and he lay down and rolled over. The audience roared with laughter, and with the happiness of success, Boomerang rolled over again and again. When he left the ring he walked with an almost dancing gait, his face all smiles around the wrinkles, a glow of happiness in his eyes.

Don't think it is only the beginners who get trapped by the clown behind those worried-looking faces. It has happened to an expert. No names mentioned, but there is a certain Bloodhound stud who has served with distinction in that duty, but whose ring career was brief. Fortunately, his first three shows resulted in three five-point majors and championship, as a fourth or fifth such experience might have caused severe emotional hardship to the owner who showed him.

At the first show, while gaiting individually, something caught the hound's eye as he returned toward the judge. Without warning, he leaped up, snatched the boutonniere from the lapel of the judge, and ate it to the last petal. The judge gave him the points.

At the second show, the judge was a woman. As hound and owner trotted around the ring toward her, the owner, keeping an eye open for possible pranks on the part of her dog, saw his eyes suddenly light up, and followed the direction of their gaze. Just at one point at the side of the judge's skirt, the lacy edge of her slip showed about half an inch. The handler made a valiant effort at control, but the hound was too fast. With a sudden lunge, he snatched at that bit of lace and tugged downward. The judge was wearing a half-slip; but she stepped out of it to give the sharp-eyed hound his second five-point win.

When the third show arrived, the owner was in a state of near-trauma at the thought of what might happen this time. She tried to persuade her husband to show the animal; but he had already proven his bravery in wartime, and felt no need to try for the Congressional Medal. Back into the ring went hound and owner. Perhaps by now, with a little ring experience, he might have quieted down.

For a while, all went well. Then came the time when the class was lined up while the judge made his final inspection. Our lady bent down to check the placing of her hound's feet. With a speed to put to rest all rumors that Blood-hounds are slow moving, her hound made a quick snatch and lifted her wig neatly from her head. Nor would he return it. Instead, he shook it thoroughly, to complete destruction, while the judge watched in total seriousness. "Well," he said after a while, "do you think it's dead yet?" and added the final five points needed for championship. The owner took her hound home to the kennel, determined that he had seen the last of the show ring.

Then sometimes it's the owner who is infected by the spirit of the Blood-hound.

Humdinger of Dakota, better known as Luke, is owned by Hans Van Den Heuval, of Dugald, Manitoba, Canada. Hans is a well-known German Shepherd breeder in Manitoba, and is a dyed-in-the-wool German Shepherd tracking man. He felt strongly that they were *the* breed for that job. Somehow, he became inspired to buy a Bloodhound, and Luke joined the kennel. The first time he tried Luke as a tracker, he frankly admitted that German Shepherds could never compete in Luke's league. He still breeds German Shepherds for their other excellent qualities, but he no longer has any delusions as to what breed should be used for tracking.

His wife, Joan, is a veterinarian who also owns and raises Burmese cats. She travels all over the country to cat shows, while he does his time at the dog shows. Once a dog show and a cat show happened to be taking place in the same city at the same time, so they were able to enjoy the weekend together.

Hans went to the dinner of the cat show club that night, where Luke is well-known among the cat fanciers. He often goes to the cat club meetings with Joan, where her friends seem to enjoy the contrast, and give him a good deal of attention.

The judge at this cat show was from Georgia, and he had five or six Georgia State flags which he wanted to give as special awards. Hans said he felt Luke should win one of the flags, as he had attended so many cat meetings, and was so well-known in the fancy. The judge dropped the subject with the explanation that it would not be reasonable in this case, as the next day's showing was for longhairs.

The next morning found Hans in the cat grooming area, where he gathered all the Angora and Persian hair available. With the assistance of a few friends, and that indispensable product, cellulose tape, he equipped Luke with long eyebrows, a pom-pom tail, and a variegated coat of long fluffy hair. Then he entered the show ring, picked Luke up, and put him on the table for the judge's

Ch. Smokey Blue of Blackhawk, UDT, owned by Dr. I. Lehr Brisbin, is the only Bloodhound to date to hold the Utility degree.

Ch. Rainbow Chaser of Dakota, CDX, TD (Ch. Rye of Dakota ex Nosie Rosie of Dakota), owned by Phyllis Natanek and bred by Mrs. and Mrs. Vincent Brey.

216

examination. With an enthusiastic reception from the audience, Luke left the show ring with a Georgia flag and the title of "Best Blood Cat in Show."

OBEDIENCE BLOODHOUNDS

Purebred dogs registered with the American Kennel Club may be shown in obedience and conformation classes. Obedience wins lead to the titles of CD (Companion Dog), CDX (Companion Dog Excellent) and UD (Utility Dog). There is also a TD (Tracking Dog) title. Dogs entered in obedience trials do not compete with each other, but must perform in accordance with a standard for the trial.

The first champion Bloodhound to earn a CDX in the United States was Ch. Giralda's Daniel. He was owned by Mrs. M. Hartley Dodge and won his CDX title in 1940.

The first Bloodhound to surpass this honor was Phyllis Natanek's Ch. Rainbow Chaser of Dakota, who was the breed's first champion CDX, TD. She won her CDX title in 1973, a span of thirty-three years after Giralda's Daniel and was owner trained and handled throughout. Her breeders were Vincent and Cathy Brey, and she was whelped April 18, 1969. Her sire was Ch. Rye of Dakota ex Nosie Rosie of Dakota.

This second winner was soon followed by Ch. Rebel Hentan, CDX, TD, owned by Gary E. Ott, whelped December 28, 1968. His breeder was Susan Brown Rowe; his sire was Ch. Skrymar of Nibelheim and dam Ch. Happiness is Elegance, CDX.

The first Bloodhound to win the UD title was Ch. Smokey Blue of Black-hawk, owned by Dr. I. L. Brisbin. This record-setting achievement was accomplished in 1974. "Blue" also holds a tracking degree.

Only a year later, in May 1975, this title was won by a second Bloodhound, Ch. Rebel Hentan, UDT. Rebel was a son of Susan Rowe's Ch. Happiness is Elegance, CDX, and one of several obedience title holders of her line. Since then two more Bloodhounds have won UD titles: Ch. Weltschmerz's Priscilla, UDTX, owned by Robin Santee and Pippin O'Hillock, UDTD, owned by Ruth Anderson.

One young hound who deserves special note because of the circumstances involved is Limier Hills Bramshot Pirate, bred by Mrs. Sidney Domina of Ontario, Canada. Pirate is owned by Steve Juenger, a student at the University of Missouri. What makes his achievement in training and showing a Bloodhound so outstanding is the fact that Steve is blind. Yet he was determined to introduce nine-month-old pirate to the conformation ring at one of the major shows of the nation, the Chicago International. And Pirate came through for him, in a manner which showed he understood his master as a guide dog understands his. It was a proud and touching example of what can be accomplished by love and determination.

You may obtain complete information pertaining to AKC dog shows and obedience trials by writing to American Kennel Club, 51 Madison Ave., New York, New York 10010. Canadian rules are similar, but not identical.

Am/Can. Ch. The Mountaineers Breeze, Durin Registered litter of thirteen at nine days (owned by Sheila and Mark Bashnick).

11

Breeding

W HEN ONE FIRST DEVELOPS an interest in purebred dogs, the natural inclination is to acquire a quality specimen and enter it in competition. While the shows offer pleasure and excitement to those who participate, serious students will, in due course, gravitate to breeding for their ultimate satisfaction. When you win with your Bloodhound that someone else bred it is an accomplishment to take pride in. When you win with a hound that you yourself bred, the feeling utterly defies description.

Even the greatest Bloodhound in the world eventually passes his prime and must be retired from the ring. If such a campaigner is owned by a nonbreeder, the owner can either purchase another hound to show or stop showing. The breeder, with the ability to produce successive generations of quality animals, is never faced with such a "dead end." A breeder of quality Bloodhounds makes a name for himself by reason of the dogs he keeps and shows and for the dogs winning for others that were bred by him.

As personally satisfying as breeding is, it should never be entered upon lightly. Not only does breeding involve endless hours of hard physical work, it also carries with it the heavy responsibilities of the future well-being of the breed and the security of the hounds you cause to come into the world. If you are willing to accept these truths, the world of the breeder will bring you endless fascination and satisfaction that is not otherwise possible.

GENETIC FACTORS

Since many good books on genetics, written by experts in the field, are readily available, there is no need to go into great detail here. Briefly, here is an

219

line of the dominant and recessive traits which should be considered before selecting a mate for your animal.

The following rules apply to dominant traits:

1. The dominant trait does not skip a generation.
2. On the average, a relatively large number of the progeny are affected.
3. Only affected individuals carry the trait.
4. With dominant traits there is less danger of continuing undesirable characteristics in the strain than is the case with recessive traits.
5. The breeding formula for each individual is quite certain.

The rules for recessive traits are:

1. The trait may skip one or more generations.
2. On the average, a relatively small number of individuals in the strain carry the trait.
3. Only those who carry a pair of determiners of the trait exhibit it. The presence of only one determiner can be ascertained only by mating. Hence, there is much more danger of contaminating the strain than is the case with dominant traits. The recessive trait must come from both sides of the family.

Here are some of the conclusions reached at Dakota Kennels after years of breeding Bloodhounds. The tendency to produce large litters is distinctly hereditary, and the number of puppies in the litter is determined by the bitch, not by the stud dog.

Short legs are dominant over long legs. Bad bites appear to be carried as a recessive. In all our years of breeding Dakota Bloodhounds, we have never had a puppy born with a cleft palate, so we have no opinion as to whether it is a dominant or recessive trait. However, there is a theory that a cleft palate can be caused by a deficiency early in the embryonic stage. This has been found true in baby pigs that were deprived of Vitamin A in the embryo stage.

Umbilical hernias seem to run in some families. It could be a single recessive factor or multiple factors which account for the hernia. In some cases the ring in the opening is so small that only one-half inch or less of the intestine is pushed out. This often becomes solidified as the dog becomes older, and is usually nothing to worry about. If the hernia is larger than that, one should consider having surgery performed to correct the problem.

It is our observation that a narrow chest is dominant over a broad chest. A nice, tightly knuckled foot such as the Standard describes appears to be dominant over the flat paper foot. Trailing willingness appears to be inherited, but conclusive evidence is not available as to whether it is a dominant or recessive trait.

COLOR INHERITANCE

Anyone wishing to become well versed in the genetics of Bloodhound color is advised to read the book *Color Inheritance in the Bloodhound*, by Dennis

Piper of Abingerwood Kennels in England. This book was published in 1969 and is an authoritative study. A copy may be purchased by writing to Dennis Piper, Ewhurst, Cranleigh, Surrey, England.

Bloodhounds are described in the Standard as black and tan, tawny (red) and red and tan (liver and tan). The liver and tan color was excessively rare, and great concern was felt among English breeders that it would be lost. In 1957 a group of breeders made a determined effort to preserve and increase the liver and tan Bloodhound population. This color is recessive, which means it must be carried in the genes of both parents of a litter for any puppies to exhibit it.

Much experimenting was done in breeding for the liver and tan color, using the offspring of Ch. Dominator of Brighton, owned by Lilian Hylden of the Brighton Kennels (now Mrs. George Ickeringill). Finally some liver and tan puppies were produced. The next challenge was the production of an all liver and tan litter.

Mr. Dennis Piper and the Ickeringills studied this possibility, and mated Abingerwood Saga to Snoopy of Brighton. On September 12, 1965, this union produced a litter of eight liver and tan puppies. These were Dreary, Druid, Dictator, Defiant, Desperado, Damson, Debonair and Dandy of Brighton. This was the first all liver and tan Bloodhound litter on record.

Dandy of Brighton was imported to the United States by Nancy (Mrs. Robert) Lindsay, of Lime Tree Kennels. To the best of my knowledge, he did not sire a liver and tan puppy, but did sire black and tans which carried the liver and tan recessive. This is the source of the liver and tan gene which Ch. Lime Tree Soames, who became one of the top-producing Bloodhounds of all time, passed on to his puppies. Credit must go to Mrs. Lindsay for importing Dandy of Brighton and maintaining the quality of the liver and tan Bloodhound in the United States.

Liver and tan is the only color that always passes on only liver and tan genes, since it is produced by a recessive gene on both sides. Black and tan mated to black and tan will yield black and tan puppies or black and tan and liver and tan offspring, provided the parents are both carrying a liver and tan recessive. Black and tan mated to red will produce puppies of either color. Black and tan bred to black and tan that does not carry liver and tan recessive genes will produce only black and tan puppies.

A liver and tan bred to a black and tan that does not carry liver and tan recessive will not produce liver and tan puppies. In this litter the puppies will all be black and tan. However, some of the puppies will carry the liver and tan recessive gene.

Two red Bloodhounds mated will produce reds and black and tans. Two black and tans can never produce reds. Reds, under the right circumstances, may produce liver and tan. A liver and tan can be bred to a black and tan or to a liver and tan. This writer is very definitely against breeding liver and tan to red. Doing this dilutes the pigmentation in the reds and the result will be puppies of an undesirable light color, not in accordance with the Standard.

To summarize:

A black and tan can be bred to all three colors.

Reds should be bred only to reds or to blacks and tans.

Liver and tans should be bred only to liver and tans or to blacks and tans.

While discussing liver and tan Bloodhounds, it is of interest that Ch. Willis' Attilla the Hun, owned by Raymond and Dorothy Willis, was the first liver and tan to win BB at the ABC Specialty. He achieved this honor in 1972, owner handled, under judge Alva Rosenberg at the Monmouth Country KC show and then continued on to second in the Hound Group. As an added honor, this win was made from the classes.

The first liver and tan to win Best in Sweepstakes was Ch. Lime Tree Swithin, owned and bred by Mrs. Robert Lindsay. He was Best Puppy in Sweepstakes at the Midwest Specialty in 1972, and then he went on to WD and BW. He was sired by Ch. Lime Tree Soames out of Knightcall's Abigail. The breed judge was Stanley Hanson.

MANAGING A STUD

To the owner of the stud dog goes much of the responsibility for maintaining the quality of the breed. If your only interest is in stud fees, don't keep Bloodhounds. There are not enough Bloodhound bitches available even to a top-quality stud to justify maintaining an expensive animal. Indiscriminate breeding won't make you rich, and it can degrade the breed severely.

Having considered these genetic factors, we will assume you are a true breed lover who has an excellent stud and wants to use him on quality bitches. You should have also ascertained that he has no major hereditary faults. The first step is continuing the balanced feeding and care program you must already have established in raising a quality animal. A hound used only infrequently needs only the food required for his maintenance. He should be well fed with ample meat in his diet, and he should be exercised to keep him in peak physical condition, neither too fat nor too thin.

Hounds used as stud often should receive more care. A vigorous stud dog could easily serve two bitches a week without serious effect on his health if he is well nourished; however, studs this much in demand are few and far between. Add a little liver to his diet and increase the volume of his food slightly, adding some vitamin supplement.

The hound that is offered for public stud service should always be kept in top condition. Not only does his own health deserve this, but you can never tell when prospective clients will appear without notice to examine your dog or bring bitches to be bred. He should always look his best. His food should include a good grade of dog meal, meat, eggs, cottage cheese, milk, liver and some fat. Organ meats are also recommended. Be sure the food is never moldy, spoiled or rotten. It should be protected from fouling by mice and rats, which are carriers of leptospirosis.

Ch. Willis' Attilla the Hun, owned by Raymond (handling) and Dorothy Willis, was the first liver-and-tan to win BB at the ABC Specialty. He is shown receiving his rewards for this in May 1972 under the late Alva Rosenberg. Later the same day he was GR2 at the Monmouth County KC show of which the Specialty was a part.   *Gilbert*

Check your stud dog periodically for parasites, both internal and external, and be sure he is free of disease or skin infections. As with any dog, his claws should be kept short, with special attention to the dewclaws, if any. These may rake the bitch when he mounts her if they are too long.

HANDLING INQUIRIES

When approached by the owner of a bitch, you should be interested in seeing both the bitch and her pedigree. It is equally as possible to find an excellent animal with an undistinguished pedigree as to find an animal with a pedigree heavy with famous names but who has managed to inherit the less-favored characteristics of each ancestor. An excellent animal may come from an owner who has had no interest in dog shows and the attendant fame, and has therefore made no big name for his dogs. On the other hand, an owner of marginal-quality dogs may have attained a championship for his hound by carefully entering it only in shows with poor competition, as by entering the best of a litter against only its littermates. The value of that championship certificate must therefore be weighed against the competition over which it was won.

DUAL PATERNITY

You will want to know something of the conditions under which the bitch has been kept, to assure yourself that she could not have been accidentally (or otherwise) bred by another dog before being presented to your stud. Does the owner have a secure yard or other holding area into which another male dog could not have entered? Some dogs are very adept at fence climbing, especially with the incentive of a bitch ready and willing on the other side.

It is equally important that the bitch be protected after breeding, as even if your stud does his work it is possible for another dog to breed her and sire puppies. Some bitches will ovulate over a period of days, and a later breeding may reach fertile eggs. No stud owner who values his reputation could risk signing a litter registration in a case where some of the puppies appeared to be purebred Bloodhounds, when some obviously were not. This can be a distressing case, especially if the stud fee was to have been a puppy.

A case is known of a stud owner who traveled a considerable distance with a hound to breed a bitch. Four days after the desired breeding, another Bloodhound stud gained entrance to the bitch's pen and she was bred by this second stud. The puppies were born sixty-four days after the first breeding. Since Bloodhounds whelp a few days before the full sixty-three considered normal as often as they are late, can the first stud owner ethically sign the litter registration? We would think it doubtful. Yet, since the bitch was under the control of her owner, the stud owner should not be penalized as to payment of stud fee. The stud had done his duty.

Ch. Lime Tree Swithin, owned and bred by Nancy Lindsay, was the first liver-and-tan to win Best in Sweepstakes at the Parent Club Specialty. He is shown here winning BB at the Walkill KC under judge Jerry Watson; handler Robert Fowler.   *Gilbert*

SECURITY MEASURES FOR THE BITCH

Usually, the bitch is brought to the stud, often being shipped by air. In these cases, the responsibility for her care is upon the stud owner. He must meet the plane, care for and protect the bitch while she is with him, guarding against loss or accidental outside mating. He should therefore be equipped with a secure pen, safe from digging or climbing. If he does not have such a pen it may mean keeping the bitch in a crate in the house, and exercising her on a lead.

In cases where the stud owner is not confident that the bitch will be kept secure from accidental mating in her home, he may wish to have her sent to him early in her season, and keep her under his own control until she is past the time she will accept the stud. In these cases, he may be expected to charge a boarding bill.

CONTRACTUAL ARRANGEMENTS

Before breeding any bitch, it is essential that a stud contract be agreed upon and signed by both owners. The stud fee may be cash or a pick-of-the-litter puppy. While a puppy is more valuable than the usual stud fee, the stud owner takes the risk that the bitch may die or fail to conceive, or that the puppies may die.

There are standard form contracts which may be purchased from kennel supply stores, or you may write your own. You may wish to make additions, such as specifying that any puppy born deformed, or not meeting the breed Standard as to color and markings, be destroyed at birth. Although your only responsibility as a stud owner is to assure a breeding with a potent stud, you may wish to give a free return breeding if only one live puppy is born. Or you may choose not to take the sole puppy, if your stud fee was to have been a puppy rather than cash, and to give another breeding from which to choose your puppy. This is your choice. However, it should be part of the stud contract to prevent any misunderstandings and hard feelings later.

HANDLING THE MATING

Now you have passed these preliminaries and the bitch has arrived for breeding. This is where the work begins. If you expected to merely turn the lovers into a pen together and leave them to tie the knot by themselves, let us explain it doesn't usually happen that way—except in cases like that described earlier where the match is unplanned. Bloodhounds are notoriously difficult to breed. Frequently a male shows slight interest in romance, and there is not a great deal you can do about it. A male which has not been used for stud by the age of four years will frequently refuse to perform.

The greatest danger to the animals (and owners) is likely to come from the bitch. Even if she is normally gentle, she may react violently at this time. She may attack the stud, and could even kill him. She should be muzzled before being introduced to the stud, unless her owner is present and able to hold her head firmly. A nylon stocking makes a good item for this purpose, as it can be crossed above and below her muzzle and tied without hurting her.

The breeding should take place in a quiet area, such as a garage or barn, where there will be no distractions or interferences. The person holding the bitch should have a chair, as the breeding is a lengthly procedure—a tie normally lasts from ten to forty minutes, and the bitch may be restless and difficult to hold. When she is under control, the stud should be introduced. He should be on a choke chain and lead for later control, but may be left loose, to approach the bitch. A second person should assist by preventing the bitch from sitting down, if she is so inclined. When the stud mounts, the assistant should place a hand under the bitch's vulva and tilt it upward to ease the stud's entry. Do not touch the stud's organs, or you will probably cause him to waste his time. Try to guide the vulva and keep the bitch's tail out of the way.

Once the male has penetrated, a tie quickly follows. When the male has finished his work, help him turn and get down off the bitch, so they can stand end to end and wait out the tie. During this time the second assistant should keep a knee under the bitch to keep her from sitting down and hurting the stud. He should also hold her rear end firmly to prevent any shifting about.

If the stud seems to have difficulty entering the bitch and becomes overexcited, lead him away and walk him about a bit before trying again. We are assuming that the bitch has been examined by a vet prior to this, and that there is no impediment to breeding.

Once a tie is achieved, all you can do is wait it out, holding the dogs to prevent injury to either. By all means, do not allow the bitch to move or release her head. A case is known of a bitch who, while tied, managed to swing around and bite the stud's testicles. This can be a shattering experience to a male, and may discourage a young animal from any future stud work.

If possible, breed your novice stud to an experienced bitch who may be more cooperative. When he has succeeded in the mating, praise him and let him know you are happy with him. It will add to his willingness the next time.

While the dogs are tied you may offer them a drink, as they will probably be warm and thirsty.

After the tie is completed, elevate the bitch's rear for about five minutes and then confine her to a crate for an hour to discourage urination, which might flush out the semen.

The male should be laid down and his underside washed thoroughly with warm suds or a mild disinfectant, flushing out the sheath. This removes the odor of the bitch and discourages masturbation. The dog will then quiet down sooner when returned to his pen. The love call of an amorous Bloodhound is a haunting melody that can arouse a neighborhood. Bathing also reduces the possibility of infection being contracted from the bitch.

Do not put a stud back into a pen with other males after breeding. The others may be jealous and a fight could result.

If this procedure proves simple, you are one of the lucky ones. Consider the experience of a friend of ours. His male, at three years, was a novice. The hound became wildly enthusiastic when introduced to the female, and knew there was *something* interesting about her, but could not figure out what to do about it. He crawled under her, licked her underside, licked her face, lay down beside her and crooned, jumped over her, and in general acted very mixed-up. Finally an assistant picked up his front end and dropped him into position in the proper location. That roused him to new levels of enthusiasm, and eventually, his efforts were met with success. By this time everyone was tired, the bitch was disgusted, bored, and shifting from one foot to the other, and there was still the tie to wait out.

Pet owners inexperienced in dog breeding may occasionally catch you off base. One day some years ago a man called the office of the then only veterinarian in Grand Forks, North Dakota. He was looking for a Bloodhound owner, he explained, as he wanted to breed his Black and Tan Coonhound to a Bloodhound. The veterinarian and his assistant thought this was a huge joke, and gave him the writer's name.

The man called with his proposal for crossbreeding. Thinking he owned a bitch, and wishing to turn him off politely, he was asked, "Do you know what the stud fee is?"

"Oh, I wasn't going to charge you a stud fee," the man breezily replied. "I thought I'd just take half the litter."

SHOULD YOU BREED YOUR BITCH?

Like the stud owner, one who contemplates breeding his bitch should analyze his animal critically. Do not let yourself be trapped by sentiment into deciding that you "ought to let her" have a litter. You ought to do no such thing unless she is good enough to produce puppies which will be a credit to the breed; and unless you are prepared to take the time and face the expense of properly raising and selling them. Bloodhounds are no longer an endangered species in which every pup is needed. Once she has come out of season she will be as happy without puppies as she would be with them, and possibly happier, with your undivided attention. If her seasonal frustration disturbs you, and you do not plan on showing her, have your bitch spayed.

WHAT BREEDING ENTAILS

If you are sure your bitch justifies breeding and has no major hereditary faults, have you considered the cost and work involved in raising a litter? Even without medical problems, the cost of raising an average-sized litter can easily exceed $1,000. You may have to keep some of the puppies several months before you find the right buyers for them. Do you have the space they will require? Remember that you will be tied to the house quite closely, between their four

228

meals a day and constant cleanup work. A litter of puppies can produce enough fertilizer to create a sizable compost heap!

While Bloodhound puppies have an undeniable charm, have you ever gone through the ordeal of pushing worm pills down a dozen puppies and then later finding a pill or two on the floor of the pen? The dreadful realization strikes you that one of the little rascals has managed to spit them out, and that after all of the stomach-turning work of cleaning up after the pills take effect, one of them didn't get wormed and will reinfect the lot.

During the first few days, you should expect to spend day and night with mother and litter, to prevent the inexperienced bitch from lying on some of those valuable puppies; to be certain that all are feeding; and to be alert for emergencies that may arise with mother or babies. More than one bitch has gone into gastric torsion after whelping, and an owner away for even part of a day can return to a dead hound.

If you are certain that breeding is for you, start doing your homework early and chose the right stud for your bitch. Be sure he does not have the same faults that she has. Do not try to balance her weak points by selecting a stud with those features in exaggerated degree. Look for one that meets the ideal. Try to see puppies produced by the prospective sire, and if possible see them at different ages. Were the dams of these puppies similar in type to yours? The best way to pick a stud is on the excellence of his progeny. If you choose a stud dog which is from excellent stock, and has already proven his worth by producing excellent stock, you cannot go far wrong.

At the same time, do not forget to investigate the family of your bitch. Remember, all sires are not prepotent. Some bitches produce pups similar to themselves no matter what the stud is like. Solicit the opinion of someone who is not emotionally involved, if there is a nearby breeder whom you respect.

Once you have decided to breed your bitch, start saving newspapers for the whelping box. Unless you subscribe to a paper with the bulk of the *Los Angeles Times*, you may collect paper for six months and still find yourself running out before the puppies move to an outdoor pen.

BEST BREEDING AGE

Do not breed your Bloodhound bitch before a minimum age of eighteen months. Two years or two and a half is better, as Bloodhounds mature slowly. If you wish to show her, it is best to finish her before breeding her. It is difficult to shrink up her udder after nursing, and she will not look as attractive in the ring after being bred.

It is not recommended that you breed your bitch after age six years. Some people do this, but any older bitch should be checked by a veterinarian before breeding. Never breed a bitch if there is any suspicion that she may require a Caesarean. Even a young bitch should be checked by a veterinarian before breeding to ascertain that she has no obstructions or physical problems. Have her wormed and be sure all her shots are up-to-date before she comes into season.

BREEDING CONDITION

Never breed a bitch that is not in excellent health and proper condition. Bloodhound litters are frequently large, and put considerable demand on the bitch's system. If she has the added handicap of poor health or overweight, it will add to the whelping problems. If her diet is inadequate, the puppies will be weak and she may lack sufficient milk for them.

BREEDING ARRANGEMENTS

Make your arrangements with the stud owner in advance of the expected breeding season. He will want to know, so that he will not have other bitches scheduled for breeding at the same time, or be away on other business. Then when Sweetie comes into season you will call him and make definite plans for the day you will ship her, or will drive out with her, whichever is the case. Details on shipping by air are given at the end of this chapter.

As a precautionary measure, plan to have the bitch arrive at the kennel of the stud owner a few days before the expected breeding date. Although most Bloodhounds are of a placid nature, a trip to a strange home may upset her. Success is more likely if she has time to become accustomed to her surroundings and the breeder who will handle her.

THE MATING CYCLE

The bitch will ovulate between the tenth and seventeenth days after she begins her discharge. We usually breed on the twelfth and fourteenth days, and feel that the reason so many bitches do not conceive is because the overanxious owner is breeding too early. If the bitch is arriving from a distance and you want to be absolutely sure of the correct time, you can take the bitch to a veterinarian for a smear test, which will show if she is ovulating. Another test you can try is with a tape used by diabetics, called Tes-Tape, which can be purchased at a drugstore. Insert a piece of this into the bitch's vulva. Wait a minute, remove it, and if it turns dark green, the bitch is ready to be bred. Bitches are usually in season for three weeks, and ovulation usually takes place between the tenth and fifteenth days of the period. However, this can vary from one bitch to another, and even vary in the same bitch from season to season. The vaginal discharge tends to taper off about the time the bitch is ready to be bred.

An experienced stud dog quite often knows when the bitch is ovulating, and may smell her and walk away without breeding her, although she is willing to stand, because he could tell by the smell that she was not ovulating at that point. The old reliable indication of the bitch's readiness for breeding is her willingness to stand for the stud dog and hold her tail to one side or "flag." It has been our experience that bitches will fight off the advances of the stud earlier or later in the season.

During pregnancy the bitch should receive moderate exercise, but not be made to jump or be more active than she chooses. She should not be allowed with the other hounds after her thirtieth day of gestation, as in the normal rough play that Bloodhounds enjoy, she could be hurt. Walking her is ideal exercise.

THE WHELPING BOX

The whelping box should be prepared about a week in advance, and she should be introduced to it so that it is not strange to her. Let her spend the nights there. Remember that the whelping room should be dry and warm, and it should be a quiet place where she will not be excited or worried.

The whelping box should be four feet by four feet, with an adjoining section four feet by three feet. The sides of the box should be high enough to prevent drafts, and a railing should be built around the inside about two or three inches above the floor and out from the sides. This prevents the bitch from crushing or suffocating the puppy that might get between her and the sides of the box.

There should be a twelve-inch-high partition between the main whelping box and the smaller section, which gives the mother a means of escaping from the puppies when she wants to rest. When the puppies are older, you may remove this divider and let them have the entire box.

If you paint the whelping box, be sure you use a lead-free paint so the puppies will not be poisoned if they chew on it.

Cover the bottom of the whelping box with several layers of loose newspaper, thick enough to absorb all the moisture. Remember that the papers must be removed and replaced frequently. An old quilt or cotton rugs are good bedding for puppies, if they are washed frequently. Indoor-outdoor carpet is also a good product for this purpose, as it gives the puppies good traction and can be scrubbed down and hung in the sun to dry. This should be the type without the rubber backing.

THE ROLE OF AIR TRAVEL

A bit of information on shipping by air is appropriate here, since bitches are so often shipped to distant studs. Later on, you will probably be shipping many puppies to their new homes by air. The jet age makes long distances shorter for dogs as well as people.

In the many years that Dakota Kennels has been breeding and showing Bloodhounds, they have been fortunate in never having had a bad experience with the airlines. One or two puppies have been waylaid for a flight, but they have always arrived in good condition. It is a fact, however, that there have been unfortunate experiences in shipping animals, and airlines are now tightening their requirements for shipping live freight. One recent ruling is that they will not accept more than three puppies per crate, and they prefer a maximum of two puppies per crate. Grown dogs must be in separate crates. Prior to this ruling a case is known of a buyer who purchased two grown bitches from another breeder, and was horrified when she picked them up at the airline to find that they had been stuffed into the same crate.

Airlines have the right to reject a shipment if it does not meet their standards. They require that the crate must be durable and have adequate ventilation. The standard airline fiberglass crate is the best type, in our opinion. Its shape prevents other crates from being too close and blocking off ventilation. The heavier wooden crates add weight and shipping cost.

Avoid, if possible, shipping on holidays and weekends. The airlines operate with a reduced staff on weekends, which adds to the risk in shipping live animals. Monday is a day of heavy traffic. Tuesdays through Thursdays are the best days for shipping.

A health certificate is required whenever shipping by air. Your veterinarian will check the requirements of the state into which your puppy is going, as some require a rabies vaccination. Most states will waive this requirement for pups under four months.

We agree with the airlines in preferring that no tranquilizers be given to dogs before shipment. Unless you have had previous experience with your dog's reaction to tranquilizers, you have no way of knowing that he will not have a dangerous reaction while in flight, with no one to attend to him. Airlines also prefer that dogs not be fed immediately before shipment, as they may become airsick. This could be messy.

Your bitch or puppies can be shipped either prepaid or collect, but be sure that the person at the receiving end knows if he is to pay the charges and is prepared for this. Be sure to take out adequate insurance. The rates vary with airlines.

Get your puppies acquainted with the shipping crate before they are shipped. If they have never been in a crate before, the close quarters may be a terrifying experience. If you let them play around and in the crate a few days before shipping, and feed them some goodies there, they will accept a crate without problem in shipping.

Be sure to take newspapers with you to the airport. Put a heavy layer on the bottom of the crate, and some shredded paper on top of that. This will soak up the moisture if the puppy has an accident on the way, and will help keep him clean.

The larger airports usually require that you have the puppy (or grown dog) at the shipping office two hours ahead of flight time. Smaller airports may not require as much time. Be sure to call the air freight office a few days before you plan on shipping and schedule the shipment. There is frequently a limit to the amount of live animal freight they will accept on a flight, in order to assure adequate oxygen while traveling.

Your crate must be clearly labeled with the shipper's name, address and phone number as well as that of the consignee. Attach a note asking that the shipper be called if the animal is not picked up promptly by the consignee. On top of the crate in big letters (red helps get attention) you should have the notice: LIVE DOG. DO NOT LEAVE SITTING IN HOT SUN. Under this notice put the final destination.

Some airlines provide an additional service for a cost of about one dollar. This is called signature service, and means that any time a dog is transferred from one airline to another, an agent supervises the transfer and signs his name to indicate it. The same is done at the final destination. If you pay for this type of service, you may at any time request that a teletype be sent to the agent who will receive the dog at a transfer point, alerting him to the fact that a live dog is aboard. It is most important that you keep the air bill number, the flight number, and the estimated time of arrival. The airlines regard the air bill as the most important means of identification when tracing a shipment.

Of course you should never ship a dog unless you have called the consignee and are certain that they will meet the flight when the dog arrives. After you have shipped the dog and he is on the airplane, call the consignee and give him the air bill number, the flight number, the estimated time of arrival, and also the weight. These also help the airlines in tracing a shipment. Ask the consignee to call you immediately upon the arrival of the dog so you can be assured it has arrived safely.

If your dog is traveling with you, it will require the same preparation as far as crate, care, and health certificate are concerned. You may not have to arrive at the air terminal as early in this case, although this should be checked with the airline. The dog would travel in your plane as excess baggage, for a nominal fee—much less than when being shipped alone. However, if you change from one airline to another, you and you alone are responsible for transferring your dog at the transfer point. This means you will have to claim it at the transfer point and find a baggage man to transfer it to the next airline, which may be at the opposite end of the airport. You should therefore be sure you have enough time between planes to allow for this.

Ch. Home's Jurisprudence with her litter by Ch. Buccanneer of Idol Ours.

12

The Whelping

THE HONEYMOON is over, and there is a date circled on your calendar. You are impatiently awaiting the patter of a horde of little feet.

PREGNANCY

The canine gestation period is usually sixty-three days; however, we find that in the case of Bloodhounds sixty days is as common as sixty-three. Notify your veterinarian of the expected date as soon as you are sure the bitch is pregnant, so he will be available in case of need. Get his home number also, or a number at which he or his assistant may be reached after business hours. Then when the time draws near, *stay home*!

A case is known in which the owners took their bitch on a trip a few days before she was due to whelp, with the result that she whelped in the home of another Bloodhound owner. She could have found a worse time during the trip, and it was pure good fortune all around that there was no trouble as a result. This might well have ended up as a tragedy with the loss of bitch and litter as well. There are cases where a nervous bitch, in strange surroundings, has eaten her puppies. This is especially possible in the case of an inexperienced bitch; and once she has done this, she is likely to be a repeater.

Canine pregnancy is sometimes difficult to ascertain for several weeks after breeding, but by the sixth week true pregnancy is unmistakable. There will be swelling of the abdomen, and the nipples become puffy. However, if you are suspicious of a false pregnancy, between the thirtieth and thirty-fifth days you may take her to the veterinarian and he can palpate her. At that time he will probably give you dietary instructions.

We do not change the regular maintenance diet of a bitch until thirty days after breeding. At that time, we add the extra supplements of vitamins and minerals, and she is put on a diet with more protein, especially meat, and including liver, milk, cottage cheese, eggs, calcium phosphate and Vitamins A and D, which are found in cod liver oil. If she has not already been on two meals a day, put her on two now, and add to the amount you have been feeding. Toward the end of the gestation the puppies will be taking up much of the space in the body cavity and she will not be able to hold a full meal at a time. It is now best to divide the food into three or four smaller meals.

One of the problems of pregnancy is constipation. Keep an eye on your pregnant bitch in case she needs a little mineral oil or milk of magnesia. About three days before she is due to whelp, give her a mild laxative, such as four milk of magnesia tablets.

THE LITTER ARRIVES

It is frequently true that the bitch will refuse food the day before she whelps. She is also usually uneasy, pants heavily, and moves her bedding around, making a nest. She may have chills. If you take her rectal temperature twice a day, starting about the fifty-eighth day, you will find it dropping from a normal 101 to 102 degrees to 99 or 100. It will stay at 99 or 100 for a day and a half or two days. When it drops below 99 you can expect the bitch to whelp within twelve hours.

If the bitch does not show signs of preparing to whelp after her temperature has fallen below 99 degrees, there may be an obstruction. Take her to your veterinarian and have him check her.

Most Bloodhound bitches are easy whelpers, and too much interference may make them nervous. It is wise to have one person in the room with them in case there is some sign of trouble. However, it will be no help to the bitch if the owner is not calm and soothing.

Sometimes a young bitch delivering her first litter will be extremely frightened of her first puppy, especially if she has been a house dog. She is so used to being in the house that she has a great fear of fouling it, and the birth of the puppy goes against her housebreaking training. You must be there to act quickly in case the bitch tries to disassociate herself from this "mistake" and does not take care of the puppy. Break the sac and dry the puppy. Rub it gently with a rough towel to stimulate it, holding it head down to drain the fluid from the lungs.

Bloodhound bitches frequently are slow whelpers, and there are few things you can do to stimulate them after the first puppy arrives. Puppies may arrive in intervals of ten to forty minutes, but it is common to have them as long as two hours apart. If it is more than an hour between pups, it may be advisable to take the bitch out for a little walk. You will have to put a lead and collar on her, because she will not want to leave the puppies. However, the exercise may stimulate her and it will give her a chance to relieve herself.

236

A Lime Tree bitch with her new litter. During the whelping it is imperative that the bitch be attended so that no puppy is accidentally crushed by the dam and puppies already born can be removed when the bitch shows fresh contractions.

When the whelping is over and all the puppies are safely in the world, the dam will really relax for the first time while her new family gets that important first meal.

Be sure the puppies have at least one good meal as soon as they are dry. Most puppies don't have any difficulty in finding the nipples, but you may have one or two hardheads that can't seem to understand what it is all about. You may have to forcibly open their mouths and put them on the nipples. If you squeeze a drop or two of milk from the nipple, this gives them the idea.

After the puppies have been fed, put them into a small box with a heating pad, covered by a towel. The box should be small enough to fit into the whelping box, as if the bitch cannot see her puppies she will be very upset. If they are left with her while she is still whelping, she may step or lie on them when she has the next pup, or they may be repeatedly soaked by the rush of water from later arrivals. This will chill them and lead to hypothermia if they are not promptly dried and warmed.

It is advisable to have a scale and notebook nearby and record the weight of each puppy as it is born, any identifying markings, and also the time of arrival. In delivering a large litter you may lose track of time, and the record will enable you to know if the puppies are being born at regular intervals or if the time between pups is unreasonably long and the attention of a veterinarian is called for.

Keep the temperature in the puppy box between seventy-five and eighty-five degrees. We feel that about 50 percent of puppy losses at birth are due to hypothermia (chilling). The temperature of a newborn puppy ranges from 94 to 97 degrees the first week of life, and it maintains this temperature from radiant heat, mainly from the bitch, whose body temperature is normally between 101 and 102 degrees. Some bitches are poor mothers, and will not lie on their sides so the pups can keep in contact with them for warmth. If the newborn litter is not closely supervised and artificial heat provided when needed, many healthy puppies will be lost to hypothermia.

The following excerpt is based on material originally published by the Gaines Dog Research Center on the care of the brood bitch.

Use caution in adjusting the heating source. If puppies scream and crawl to the edges of the box, it is a good indication that the heating pad or lamp is too hot. If they are cold, they whimper and huddle together. Hungry puppies give little angry yells, and actively search for something to suck. If you pick up a healthy puppy, it will show vitality by moving and pushing against your hand, as it does in searching for its mother's nipples. A normal puppy sleeps sprawled out, often twitching in a manner that gives the impression it is dreaming. However, this activated sleep is nature's normal means of exercising the newborn puppy.

The sick puppy, on the other hand, lies limply. He will feel cold and clammy, and refuse to suck. His temperature may drop to between 78 and 83°. Sometimes this condition may be caused by infection or birth defect, but it can also be the result of poor care from an inexperienced bitch. Perhaps she has been upset by the presence of too many spectators; as in the case of an owner who thought this was a good way to teach the children the "facts of life." In any case, if the puppy is not warmed, he will die of hypothermia.

At the same time, the puppy must not be warmed too rapidly. If this happens, his system will require more oxygen than his heart, in the cold interior of his body, can pump through him. The chilled puppy will have a heartbeat of only six or seven

Sizes and designs of whelping boxes vary somewhat depending upon the breeder's requirements and available space. Any whelping, box however, should be fitted with a guard rail and be large enough to ensure the comfort of the dam and puppies.

After the entire litter is whelped, the dam must be made to exercise. Most bitches will not want to leave their puppies for this, but an outing is necessary at this time. While the bitch is away, the puppies can be weighed and examined and any irregularities duly noted.

239

beats per minute, whereas fifteen to thirty are required. This lack of sufficient oxygen will be as fatal as the chilling factor.

This fact should be strongly emphasized, as many people try to warm a cold puppy too fast. The proper way to warm a cold puppy is by rubbing against the coat to stimulate circulation and using your own body heat by putting the puppy against your chest. If artificial heat is used, be sure the puppy is turned frequently.

The second fact to remember is that a sick puppy with low body temperature should not be fed formula or milk. It cannot utilize the food, since the digestive tract is not functioning properly, and the formula remains in the stomach undigested. However, it does need quick energy and fluid, to prevent dehydration. Sugar water is the best source. A teaspoonful of sugar to an ounce of warm water, fed by drops, every half hour, will be absorbed directly through the stomach. This answers both needs.

The bitch's first milk is called *colostrum*, and it contains elements which give the puppies a degree of immunity to disease while they are nursing. The nursing seems to stimulate contractions and helps the uterus expel any placentas or even an unexpected puppy which may arrive late.

TUBE FEEDING

When all the litter is born and everyone is calmed down, we like to feed the entire litter with at least 5 cc's of some kind of simulated bitch's milk. During the rush of delivery it is sometimes difficult to distinguish which puppies were fed and which were not, so to get them off to a good start we usually tube-feed the entire litter at this time.

I would caution that no one should tube-feed a puppy unless he has had it demonstrated to him by a veterinarian. It consists of taking a narrow plastic tube, such as is used for premature babies in the hospital, and inserting it into the puppy's stomach. The tube should have a mark on the outside, and if you stretch it out beside the puppy so the end of the tube is below the rib cage, the mark should come to the puppy's nose. When you insert the tube into the puppy, and it goes up to the mark, you know it is in the stomach. If it does not go up to the mark, it may be in the lungs, and must be withdrawn immediately, as you do not want to pour the milk into the puppy's lungs and drown it.

If the tube is put into the mouth and the puppy swallows, the tube goes down without any resistance. If you meet any resistance, the tube must be withdrawn immediately. Once the tube is in the stomach up to the mark, the other end of the tube is connected to a syringe containing the formula. You slowly release the formula through the syringe and tubing into the puppy. **Do not** pull back on the plunger of the syringe. Withdraw the tube quickly but smoothly.

This is a good way of feeding small, weak puppies, but be sure you learn the technique from a veterinarian.

If the puppies are large and vigorous, you can bottle-feed them, using one of the small nipples made for premature babies. Do not enlarge the hole in the nipple too much, but be sure the puppy is getting milk without having to tire itself out.

240

THE NEW MOTHER

Once all the puppies have arrived, had a meal, and are comfortable, put them back in the whelping box with the mother. You could offer her a bit of milk at this time, and after a few more hours, see if she is ready for a small meal. You will find her reluctant to leave her puppies, and it is as well to keep her calm by feeding her in the whelping box.

The nursing bitch should have all the nourishing food she will eat. She should be fed three or four meals a day, as this will keep the milk flow steady. It is hardly possible to feed her too much at this time. In addition to protein foods, vitamin and mineral supplements should be included. Fresh water should be available at all times. Leave a dish of dry dog food near her during the night for snacks.

Do not allow any strangers into the room with the bitch and new litter, as she is very likely to be hostile at this time. In addition, visitors may carry infection and expose the puppies to disease, especially if they have animals of their own. Children with measles can give distemper to puppies, as the diseases are closely related.

MONITORING NEWBORN PUPPIES

Keep a weight record of the puppies' growth, as this is a sure way of knowing that they are getting enough to eat and growing properly. The newborn puppy should double his birth weight in the first eight to twelve days. If you are not alert to the possibility, you may not be aware that puppies may have missed the nipple and are sucking at a bit of loose skin. This is especially possible with a large litter. The puppy is getting no nourishment and may dehydrate or even starve to death if you are not aware of this possibility. In this case, it may be advisable to divide the litter so that all the puppies get a fair share, and the smaller ones will not be crowded out. Give the little ones extra time with their mother.

The rapid growth of Bloodhound puppies is illustrated by the weight gain chart below, which was kept on nine litters of puppies at Dakota Kennels.

Age	Weight Range
Birth:	11 oz. to 31 oz.
1 week:	1 lb., 5 oz. to 3 lb., 12 oz.
2 weeks:	3 lb. to 5 lb., 2 oz.
3 weeks:	4 lb., 3oz. to 6 lb., 11 oz.
4 weeks:	6 lbs. to 9 lbs., 1 oz.
5 weeks:	8 lbs. to 11 lbs., 3 oz.
6 weeks:	11 lbs. to 15 lbs., 1 oz.
2 months:	17 lbs. to 28 lbs., 3 oz.
3 months:	27-1/2 lbs. to 35 lbs.
4 months:	40 lbs. to 50 lbs.

The Explosive Growth of a Bloodhound Puppy

At nine days

At sixteen days

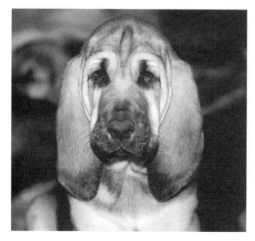

At eight weeks

At four weeks

At six weeks

At fourteen weeks

The series of puppy pictures with this chapter shows one of the puppies from the litter of Ch. Hilltop Acres Nana Van Rinkle, owned by Laura Keating, of Missoula, Montana, and sired by Ch. Lime Tree Soames. These pictures, taken at nine days, sixteen days, four weeks and six and one-half weeks, illustrate this rapid growth of Bloodhound puppies.

SUPPLEMENTARY FEEDING

If the litter is larger than eight, it is wise to supplement the feeding. There are excellent commercial, simulated bitch's milk formulas available. A commercial baby formula would work well if simulated bitch's milk were not available. The formula used at Dakota Kennels is as follows:

One can of goat's milk, two tablespoonfuls of lime water, two beaten egg yolks, one-half can of distilled water, six drops ABDEC vitamins, one tablespoonful honey. Mix well and serve at body temperature.

After the first few weeks, if you live out in the country where you can get fresh, whole, unpasteurized milk from Guernsey or Jersey cows, you can feed this with good results. These breeds produce a rich milk which is closer to bitch's milk than milk sold commercially.

LITTER SIZE

The largest litter produced at Dakota Kennels was seventeen, fifteen of which lived and were raised without trouble. The smallest litter consisted of one puppy. A litter of one can be almost as much trouble as a litter of fifteen, because there can be more problems with the bitch. She will have the normal large supply of milk and only one puppy to feed. You may have to watch her carefully and use a breast pump to remove the excess milk, or she could develop mastitis. Feel her udder frequently and be sure it remains soft and pliable. With a normal-sized litter, when an area of the udder seems too full, put a big, strong puppy on that nipple. However, if the udder becomes hard, caked and hot, this is a sign of trouble, and the bitch must get to the veterinarian at once.

It is normal for the bitch to clean up the stools of the nursing puppies, repulsive though this may be to you. She will stop when they begin eating other food.

ORPHAN PUPPIES

If you have a litter of orphan puppies, you will have to use a cotton swab dipped in oil, or something similar, and rub the puppies' abdomens after feeding to enable them to urinate. This is what the bitch accomplishes by washing them. You must take her place, and induce elimination also by stroking the rectum.

244

This assistance may be needed for a week or so. Watch the puppies carefully until you are sure they are functioning properly alone.

You may have to keep orphan puppies in individual boxes to prevent them from nursing on each other's external organs. They may also try to nurse on ears and tails, and may cause painful sores. If they are separated, careful regulation of the heat will be even more important, as they will not be able to warm each other by cuddling together.

While the puppies are very young, orphaned or not, they are best not disturbed except for essential care, so that they can sleep and grow. I like to leave a radio playing in the whelping room to accustom the puppies to noises and human sounds. Keep them off slippery surfaces, which make it difficult for them to walk, and keep their claws trimmed, so they will not scratch the bitch's udder. This constant scratching from their needlelike little claws can make the bitch want to wean them early, and it will be better for them if she nurses them for six weeks.

COLIC

Colic in a young puppy is a very pitiful and frightening thing to see; they scream and crawl in circles. Unless relief is provided, they will shortly die. Their little hearts will be unable to survive the pain and activity. We have learned that a good medication for colic in puppies is Pamine PB Drops, which is a prescription medicine for human infants. You will therefore need a prescription from your veterinarian to buy it. Give 0.2 ml by mouth three times a day. Remove the puppy from the litter and put it in a box with a heating pad, well covered. Tube-feed 10 cc of 5 percent Dextrose every half hour for two hours; then once every hour. If you don't know how to tube-feed, use an eyedropper. After twenty-four hours the puppy should be ready to return to the litter.

EYES OPEN

Puppies usually open their eyes at about nine or ten days of age. If they were whelped earlier than the full sixty-three days after the breeding, the difference should be added to the nine to ten days, and the eyes will usually open at that time.

Early eye color of the puppies is no criterion of the color they are likely to be, as most eye color is subject to change, as in humans. The eyes of infant puppies usually show a distinct bluish cast for some time. It is too early to worry about light eyes when they are first opened.

NATURAL WEANING

When the puppies are about four or five weeks old, the bitch may feed them by regurgitating food, which they will then eat. This may appear very disgusting to the novice, but it is a perfectly normal procedure, and a carryover from their wild instinct. The food is warmed and partly digested in the mother's stomach, making it easier for the puppies to eat. This practice is another reason you must be careful that the food the bitch eats is sound, clean and nutritious.

DEWCLAWS

Dewlaws on the hind legs, if any, should definitely be removed, and this is done by the third or fourth day. Whether or not you remove the dewclaws on the front legs is a matter of choice.

POSTNATAL CARE OF THE BITCH

The bitch will normally have a slight vaginal discharge for several weeks after the whelping. If the discharge is bloody, take her to the veterinarian for a checkup, as it could indicate serious internal injury.

After the litter is weaned, keep the bitch on calcium and cod liver oil for one month. This helps her maintain her coat and get back into condition faster.

Her udder should be massaged daily for a time with either white vinegar, camphorated oil, or bag balm. These will help her draw back into her normal shape; however, brood bitches rarely completely regain their maiden form. This is especially true with Bloodhounds, which have so much loose skin; and the more she has, the harder it will be to get her back in show condition. Her championship, and exposure at dog shows, will attract the puppy customers.

13

Grading the Litter

PEOPLE OFTEN SPEAK of having "an eye for a dog." This means that the person possessing the "eye" has the uncanny ability of being able to sort the good from the bad virtually every time. Nowhere is an eye for a dog of greater value than in evaluating a litter of puppies. Given the great differences between a grown animal and an infant, it takes some practice and experience in observing puppies to select those youngsters who will grow into the stars of tomorrow. It is far from easy to do and many hounds are singled out early in their lives on the strength of an educated guess. There are a number of guidelines and certain particulars every breeder should look for to get a clearer idea of the quality present in each litter. These are noted in this chapter and it is hoped that they will help those who read this to recognize the infant flyer every breeder hopes to produce with every litter he breeds.

COPING WITH DEFECTS

As each puppy is born, check it for any deformities. If a puppy is born malformed, minus a limb, or with a short limb, with cleft palate, lacking its external organs, or with markings that do not meet the breed Standard, it should be euthanized at birth. Do not wait a few days, as then it will have developed a personality and the job will be more painful for you.

Do not destroy a puppy which has a little white spot on the top of its head, or a few white hairs scattered here and there on the body. These will normally disappear by the time the puppy is four months old. However, a puppy born with white stockings, or a white blaze, or white collar should be put to sleep humanely.

White on the tip of the tail, the toes, or on chest or under chin is acceptable. There was a time when the Bloodhound was in danger of extinction, and every puppy was cherished. That danger is past, and breeders should make every effort to improve the quality of the breed. A dog or bitch that does not possess the quality we would like to see should definitely be spayed or altered. It can be an excellent mantrailer, and represent the breed with honor in that manner.

Sometimes a puppy will be born with a kink in the tail. This is not frequent, but it does happen, and breeders should watch for it. Some are of the opinion that if the kink is near the tip of the tail it should be cut off by a veterinarian. I have seen these puppies grow up, and I am of the opinion that the bit that is removed, say one-half an inch in a newborn puppy, will make quite a difference in tail length when the dog is grown.

The short tail makes the dog look unbalanced and spoils its appearance more than the kink would have. It is my suggestion that if the puppy is otherwise healthy and normal, it be raised and sold to someone who wants a Bloodhound for mantrailing or as a pet. There should be a definite understanding that it is not to be shown or used for breeding.

I have recently read, in a Dachshund magazine, that kinked tails in newborn puppies can be considerably improved if the tail is kneaded between thumb and forefinger several times a day. During the early days of life the bones are very soft, and repeated gentle manipulation can straighten out the kink to some degree; at least to the point where it is not readily noticeable.

THINGS TO LOOK FOR

Some breeders say they can grade a litter at birth. An answer to that is, "How can you tell what color eyes they will have? How can you judge the bite?" We check for abnormalities, and feel that is all one can safely judge at the time of birth, except perhaps tail set. You can take the newborn puppy by the head and tail, very gently of course, and see if the legs fall straight down as they are supposed to do. The thick, fat ear will usually be the long ear. Look for health and vigor, for the lively puppy that wiggles and pushes with its nose, and sucks eagerly.

Do not grade by birth size. The little ones will usually catch up with the big babies by the time they are three months old if given good care, and can prove to be outstanding in type. As long as they show vitality, do not cull them if they are within a normal size range.

Watch the puppies as they grow and notice which is the first one to walk, the first to climb out of the whelping box, etc. Sometimes you will get a hint that way as to vigor, aggressiveness and the inquisitive nature that makes a good show and trailing hound.

At four weeks we seriously grade the litter. It has been my experience that a puppy that is well balanced at four weeks will be a well-balanced hound when grown. One must always keep the Standard in mind when grading puppies. Have

Bloodhounds are fascinating animals, and, in many ways, breeding them is the most intriguing side of the hobby. All who contemplate becoming Bloodhound breeders should bear in mind that the cuddly handfuls above soon grow into the lordly giant shown below. To be a Bloodhound breeder is to assume a responsibility never to be taken lightly.

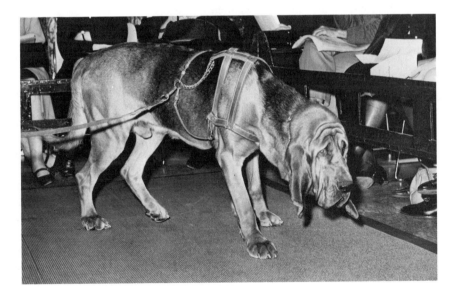

in your mind's eye the picture of the ideal Bloodhound, and look for the points that prove this puppy is unmistakably a Bloodhound. A puppy with heavy bone will sometimes lighten, but never to the extent that it will be too light. However, a puppy with light bone will never have enough substance. In other words, they do not improve; at least not in my experience. A short neck remains a short neck. A head that appears a bit heavy at four weeks will mature into a better head. Often, a head which at four weeks appears a good head, as far as backskull and width, will end up being a head that is too narrow when grown.

You can tell correct tail set very early, but whether or not a puppy will carry its tail correctly requires time and development.

Be sure to evaluate the puppy's gait, both coming and going, to ascertain that it is moving properly.

Check the bite. You can see if it is overshot or undershot, but you cannot guarantee a bite until the second teeth are in. One of the most disappointing things that can happen to any dog breeder is having one of his top specimens become undershot. Sometimes this will show up in the first three or four weeks of growth, and other times not for three or four months, or until the permanent teeth are cut. It is not necessarily those which are most seriously affected which show early.

The undershot jaw is an inherited characteristic, but at this time nobody seems to know exactly how it is inherited. It is said to run in families, and seems to be a recessive trait, yet is not consistent.

There is also the opposite condition, when the lower jaw is too short for the upper jaw, and this is the overshot jaw. The desired bite is the scissor bite, in which the lower incisors slip behind the uppers.

Ear sets are fairly easy to see. Experienced breeders who have whelped several litters can tell ear sets almost at birth; but a novice should definitely be able to tell ear set when the puppy is four weeks old. A high ear set in a puppy will always be a high ear set in the grown hound.

A bad front almost never straightens. A front that is "east and west" very often will turn out to be an acceptable front by the time the hound is eighteen months old and his chest drops. "East and west" means that the toes are turned out. If they are turned in, that is a French, or fiddle, front; then it is hopeless. If cow hocks are evident at four to five weeks, they are there to stay. A good rear end may develop a tendency toward cow hocks later in life, especially if the puppy is confined and does not get the exercise it should have.

Check the male puppies for the presence of both testicles. If one is missing, that puppy will be disqualified from the show ring, and should never be bred, as this defect is hereditary. He can, however, be used successfully for trailing or as a pet.

Toplines can be unpredictable as puppies grow. It is not uncommon for a puppy to be a little high in the rear during adolescence. However, if a puppy has a good topline at four weeks, the topline will eventually settle back.

If you pick a puppy on type and soundness, with the Standard always in

250

Six-week-old puppies by Ch. Sims' Stormin' Norman of Dakota out of Ch. The Rectory's Armageddon, bred by Judy Kruse. Picking show-potential puppies from a young litter is always an educated guess. Any evaluation of an individual litter member (top photo) and the litter as a whole must take into account that many things can happen between the whelping box and the winners' circle to affect the final picture.

mind, you should have a show puppy with definite, desirable breed characteristics. Loose shoulders might sometimes tighten. However, a long-backed puppy will grow into a long-backed adult.

Grown dogs are never as dark as puppies. The very black puppies usually retain a solid black saddle or may be predominantly black, but never as much so as when they are born. Those which have a brownish tinge at birth usually have a less distinct saddle when grown, with red liberally mixed in.

We have a little system for determining which puppies are using their noses at an early age. Even before they open their eyes, they can be heard sniffing and searching for their mother. When we change the papers in the whelping box, we make a little trail by running a hand along the paper, and watch to see which puppy first puts its head down and tries to find us.

When the puppies are older and can walk, one of us will tie a rope to the food dish and drag it across the yard, leaving it in some remote corner. Then we let the puppies out and notice which one drops its head, picks up the trail and finds the food dish first.

ESTABLISHING A REPUTATION

If you want a reputation as a good breeder, grade your litters very carefully and sell only those very top specimens as potential show dogs. It is foolish to expect that every dog in the litter will be of show quality. Moreover, it will cause resentment if you sell a dog as a show specimen for a high price, and the animal does not develop into a winner. There are so many things that can go wrong with a good puppy between the time he leaves you and enters the show ring with a new owner that one should not take chances by selling a second-class puppy as a likely show prospect.

Puppies that are not show quality can be used for mantrailing and will represent the breed very well in this field. However, if a bitch is sold as a trailing dog because she does not come up to the Standard, or has some kind of hereditary fault, she should be sold with the agreement that she will be spayed. In order for this to be legal, there must be a written contract, made out in triplicate, to be signed by both buyer and seller. Both parties will then each retain a copy with the third copy going to the American Kennel Club, so a record of the agreement will be on file at the AKC.

It is important to know that even if a dog is sold for trailing, it should be registered. Without proper registration a dog's testimony will not be valid in court in the event that it should be required.

WORKING WITH SHOW PROSPECTS

There is no person, no matter how experienced, who can always pick the best puppy from any given litter. Even the most experienced breeders can sometimes make mistakes. Once you have satisfied yourself that you have graded your litter to the best of your knowledge, and feel that certain puppies are definitely not of show quality, place them in their new homes as soon as possible, but not before eight weeks of age, when they are eating well and able to get along without their mother.

Keep the puppies which you feel are your best show prospects until they are at least twelve weeks old, or older, when you will be able to evaluate them more reliably. If a puppy is a real show prospect, it is never too old to sell. Serious show people prefer buying puppies that are six months old or over, as a puppy this age will rarely fall apart. What faults a dog has will be obvious by this age.

From the breeder's standpoint, the reason for keeping a puppy six months or more is that he will not then accidentally sell his best puppy, which he may want to keep for breeding.

SELLING PUPPIES

It is important to remember that the owner who decides to breed his bitch is responsible for the litter. He should have every interest in the future of the resultant puppies, and make the effort to place them all in desirable homes. Evaluating the prospective owner and home is as important as any step in the production of the litter. It is up to the breeder of high-quality, carefully planned litters to do a superlative job when he sells each puppy. He should be prepared to keep any or all puppies until Hell freezes over, if need be, rather than be forced by any reason to sell even one puppy to the wrong person.

Find out if both husband and wife are equally interested in the puppy. Ask where they will keep the puppy, if they want it for breeding, trailing or as a show dog. If they had a previous dog, be interested in how it died, or why it was given away. No puppy should be sold until it has had its permanent distemper, hepatitis and kennel cough (parainfluenza) innoculations. Give detailed directions as to what shots the puppy should receive after it leaves you, when it should have its next shot, or booster shot. Give new owners the worming schedule you have followed and advise them when the puppy should be wormed again. Explain the importance of keeping dogs free of parasites, and give with each puppy a feeding chart and grooming and house-training instructions. In the case of female puppies, explain the care that should be taken during the heat season.

A Bloodhound puppy should never be sold to anyone who would keep it tied, or who does not have a yard or pen of reasonable size for it, and adequate housing to protect it from the weather.

The large dog food companies publish considerable material on the subjects of care, training and feeding. These free brochures can supplement the instructions you would routinely provide. Instructions on how to enter dog shows, and a list of recommended reading could also be given with each puppy. This will go far in giving the new owner understanding and appreciation of his unique pet.

253

A twelve-week-old puppy by Ch. Lime Tree Soames out of Ch. Lu-How's Dakota War Bonnet, bred by Catherine Brey. The long ears on this youngsters are a hint of good things to come.

14

Raising a Litter

$\mathbf{H}$OW A LITTER OF puppies is cared for exacts a tremendous influence on how these young Bloodhounds will finish up as adults. The routines of feeding, cleaning, housing, veterinary attention and related matters are surely more mundane than the glamour of the show ring or the romance surrounding an accomplished mantrailer. Notwithstanding, once a litter goes on solid food those puppies are the sole responsibility of the breeder. These hounds will, on maturity, reflect, both in temperament and physical condition, the amount of work and care that has gone into them during this important, formative period of their lives.

Hopefully, what you read here will help you put more into your future litters, and in doing so, get more from your hounds as adults.

INTRODUCING SOLID FOOD

If the litter progresses normally, with no problems, at ten or fourteen days mix high-protein Pablum with calf milk replacer and feed it from a bottle. Enlarge the hole in the nipple so the mixture can pass through easily, and start the puppies on this. Puppies will get their ears caked with food and waste much of it when fed from the dish at this age. Giving them the bottle feeding lets each puppy get personal attention and socializing; and you will sooner learn to distinguish one from the other as you handle them.

After they are eating the Pablum well, we start them on raw hamburger. We mix a couple of egg yolks with the hamburger and pick off little bits the size of a small pea. I feed these to the puppies off my fingers while I am holding them. I give each puppy about a teaspoonful by the time they are two and one-half or three weeks of age. At first I feed the meat once a day. When they are

255

eating this eagerly, I soak puppy kibble in milk and mix it with the hamburger, feeding it to them in small bits from my fingers. By that time you can hardly hold them; they are eager to go right after the dish.

After they graduate to the stage where they are eating from the dish, I make an egg custard for them. If you can buy goat's milk, that is the best; otherwise use calf milk replacer. This is a powdered milk sold in agricultural supply stores. It contains antibiotics which prevent diarrhea, and we have had good results with it. This egg custard recipe is sufficient for a litter of about six puppies. It consists of two cups milk, four eggs, two tablespoons honey, one tablespoon corn oil and one teaspoon vanilla. Beat these together and bake the custard in the oven or cook it in a double boiler until it is soft. Feed this to the puppies in addition to the cereal, meat, puppy food, etc.

At this time, begin adding calcium phosphate supplement and ABDEC vitamin drops. We recommend giving the ABDEC drops individually, so that each puppy will be sure to get its share. We begin giving those at ten days or two weeks—sooner if the litter is a large one.

FEEDING WEANLINGS

When the puppies are four weeks old, put them on four meals a day. At our kennel we feed on a schedule similar to this: From four to twelve weeks, we feed at 7:00 A.M., noon, 5:00 P.M. and 10:00 P.M. From three to six months we feed at 7:00 A.M., noon and 5:00 P.M. From six months and thereafter we feed at 7:00 A.M. and 5:00 P.M.

Remember that the puppies grow rapidly, and the amount of food must be increased with demand. Puppies should not be forced to eat more than they want, but they should never be allowed to go hungry. Bloodhounds are large, active dogs, and as puppies they need ample bone-building food, such as milk, meat and fat. The fat will promote the shiny, healthy coat that is the mark of a well-cared-for puppy.

An easy way to raise the food dish for tiny puppies is to join two equal-sized cake pans bottom to bottom, and tape them together with masking tape. A set of muffin pans is good also, because puppies are less likely to walk into the food or crowd each other when they are used. When they outgrow that size dish, it is simple to recover your pans. For the next step, we use galvanized feed pans used for feeding pigs, and weld a pair of them bottom to bottom.

When puppies are about five or six weeks old, after they have finished one of their meals we give them some dry kibble for chewing practice. At about this time we also begin adding boiled eggs and cottage cheese to the diet. At least three times per week we give them tomato juice as a mixer in place of milk.

Dachshund breeders in England introduced us to the use of tomato juice in feeding dogs as an aid to developing a good coat. In the past, it was believed that dogs did not need vitamin C, which is in tomato juice, but more recent research has led to the decision that they do. Normally, the canine system synthesizes vitamin C, but occasionally it fails, and scurvy will result unless the vitamin is added.

You should also be aware that calcium phosphate must be accompanied by vitamin D, or the animal system cannot utilize the minerals. Even an excess amount of calcium will be useless without the vitamin D. This is usually provided by cod liver oil.

SPECIAL NEEDS OF GIANT PUPPIES

Rickets is a deficiency disease, caused by a group of conditions, one of which is an inadequate amount of vitamin D. In addition, the calcium and phosphorus provided must be in the ratio of 1.2 parts calcium to 1 part phosphorus, as too much phosphorus will cause hypocalcium in the dog.

Small breeds are less susceptible to clinical rickets, as the ratio of rate of growth to leg strength and bones capable of supporting the body is not as far apart as in the giant breeds, such as Great Danes and Bloodhounds. Doses as high as three hundred units vitamin D per pound may be advisable in the large breeds, particularly during the winter months.

The calcium content for giant and heavy breeds should be approximately 1 percent of the wet weight of the food, while one-half of 1 percent is normal for the lighter breeds. Your veterinarian can guide you as to the proper amount for your hound. As the dog approaches total growth, the calcium supplement should be reduced closer to a maintenance requirement of one-half of 1 percent of diet.

There are some veterinarians who may tell new owners that the puppy does not need cod liver oil and calcium because it is getting milk. It is a definite error where our breed is concerned, as due to the rapid growth, the puppies are likely to get rickets without these needed supplements.

A puppy can go down on his pasterns, and then back up again, for various reasons. He will go down when he is teething, or if he gets wormy. If you have a puppy who was up on his pasterns and you notice that they have suddenly become weak, have a stool sample checked for worms by the veterinarian. If worms are present, take care of that problem immediately. I would recommend that the veterinarian give the puppy an injection of vitamin D, and then keep him on a high level of vitamin D for a few weeks. As a rule, this will bring him back up on his pasterns.

Puppies under stress can also go down on their pasterns. Shipping them away from home can cause them to arrive down on their pasterns. However, they will soon be back up if their diet is correct.

If newborn puppies have diarrhea you can obtain a product from your veterinarian which cures it. It is important that diarrhea be stopped quickly, as it can lead to dehydration and death in young puppies.

WORMS

Worms can infest puppies prenatally. Even though the bitch has been wormed before breeding, there may be worm eggs retained, and these can infest the unborn puppies. It is therefore important that the puppies be wormed

257

periodically, and that a veterinarian ascertain which worms are present so that the correct medication may be prescribed.

Puppies can be wormed at three weeks with no harmful effects, but this should definitely be done only under a veterinarian's guidance. At Dakota Kennels we worm at five weeks, seven weeks, and nine weeks. After that, we check them routinely every two months until they are a year old, and thereafter, three times a year. Twice a year blood samples are taken to check for heartworm.

When the veterinarian supervises the worming of puppies he should also check their eyes to be sure they do not have entropion. This problem is covered in chapter 9.

VACCINATIONS

We recommend the following program of vaccinations. At seven weeks our puppies are vaccinated with a straight distemper vaccine. At nine weeks, they are vaccinated with a distemper-hepatitis vaccine. At twelve weeks they are vaccinated with what is called the DHL, which is distemper-hepatitis-leptospirosis vaccine. However, check with your own veterinarian, who may have a different program he prefers, and which may be influenced by local conditions.

A new vaccine which seems very promising is called DHLLP, and is a combination vaccine for protection against canine parainfluenza, distemper and hepatitis. It has been developed by Pitman-Moore, and according to the company, the vaccine makes solid protection against kennel cough available for the first time. This is especially valuable for dogs that are boarded out, or taken to dog shows, as kennel cough is a considerable problem under these circumstances. Although much is known about the disease, the control of kennel cough has been incomplete. Major causes of the upper respiratory disease are canine distemper, canine infectious hepatitis, and canine parainfluenza, as well as bacterial agents. Distemper and hepatitis are controllable, and bacteria can be fought with antibiotics. Parainfluenza remains the main obstacle in the control of kennel cough, but it now can also be controlled.

There is also a new rabies vaccine that can be used before age four months. However, we have not yet seen enough testing or use to recommend it.

If you are traveling with your dog, or shipping a dog to an area where hookworm is prevalent, check with your veterinarian for a medication to provide your dog adequate protection.

TEETH

The puppy's first set of teeth starts appearing at four or five weeks of age, and will be replaced by permanent teeth at four or five months of age for the incisors, with the molars coming through a month or two later. Check on the teething puppy, and be sure that the first teeth fall out normally before the second teeth arrive. Occasionally they may not, and then must be pulled so that the second teeth will come in straight.

A six-week-old puppy by Ch. Lime Tree Soames out of Ch. Lime Tree Libby of Dakota, bred by Kelly Brey and Nancy Lindsay. This puppy came from a litter of 17, 15 of which survived.

Eight-week-old puppies by Ch. Bugle Bay's Amos of Dakota out of Canadian Ch. Little Eva of Dakota, bred by Ernie and Camille Danylchuk.

The veterinarian should also check the dog's teeth and if necessary remove tartar. If a young puppy has an illness for which it is given an antibiotic, this will often discolor or pit the enamel. If this occurs when it has its baby teeth, there is no cause for concern; however, if it has its permanent teeth they may be permanently discolored by the use of certain antibiotics.

KEEPING ALERT

Watch for umbilical hernias. A lump over the navel might be a sign that the navel has failed to heal properly. If the deformity is slight, danger is unlikely. However, if the opening is large enough for a loop of the intestine to protrude, this must be surgically repaired by a veterinarian. If neglected, a strangulation of the gut could result, and cause death.

One of the less-common ailments from which a puppy may suffer, even before the eyes open, is an eye infection which causes swelling and a small pocket of pus. This should be attended to by a veterinarian, who can lift the corner of the eyelid and drain and medicate the area.

Beware of infected navels in the young puppies. The problem could be caused by a rough or hard whelping box surface rubbing and irritating the navels before they have healed. We find that the best prevention is soaking the navel in iodine as soon as the puppy is born and cleaned by the mother, and by keeping the bedding soft.

A clean whelping box and sleeping quarters will reduce the possibility that fleas or ticks may infest the puppies. Of course, the mother should be clean before the whelping so she will not introduce parasites to the nursery.

A problem puppies sometimes have is a skin condition which I call "cradle cap," as it reminds me of the similar problem human babies may have. If it occurs, it usually starts around two and one-half to three weeks of age, and involves a flaking off of the skin in great quantities. I have tried several products, and finally in desperation I called a local pediatrician. He suggested bathing the puppy with a shampoo called Sebulex, which can be purchased at a drugstore. After the puppy has been bathed with this shampoo, dry him well and use a fine-tooth comb to comb out the dead skin. Two or three times during the day soak the affected portion of the puppy's body with baby oil, and again use the fine-tooth comb. Bathe him with the Sebulex every fourth day until the problem is past. Be sure the bath water is comfortable, and that the bath is given in a warm, draft-free area, so the puppy is not chilled.

Hard pad is another infectious ailment of young puppies. They will run a high fever and have intestinal problems. The footpads are very tender. Here again, the puppy should see a veterinarian immediately.

While growing puppies need ample exercise, as long as the litter is together they will exercise each other by playing. Give them enough room, and enjoy the fun.

260